THE M. & E. HANDBOOK SERIES

Auditing

Leslie R. Howard
FCA, FCCA, FHKSA, AMBIM

*Head of Department of Accountancy Studies,
Hong Kong Polytechnic*

SIXTH EDITION

MACDONALD AND EVANS

Macdonald & Evans Ltd.
Estover, Plymouth PL6 7PZ

First published 1966
Reprinted 1967
Second edition 1968
Reprinted 1969
Third edition 1970
Reprinted 1971
Reprinted 1972
Reprinted 1973
Fourth edition 1974
Reprinted 1975
Fifth edition 1976
Sixth edition 1978
Reprinted with amendments 1979

© Macdonald & Evans Ltd. 1978

7121 0169 1

Printed in Great Britain by
Richard Clay (The Chaucer Press) Ltd,
Bungay, Suffolk

M. & E. HANDBOOKS

M. & E. HANDBOOKS are recommended reading for examination syllabuses all over the world. Because each Handbook covers its subject clearly and concisely books in the series form a vital part of many college, university, school and home study courses.

Handbooks contain detailed information stripped of unnecessary padding, making each title a comprehensive self-tuition course. They are amplified with numerous self-testing questions in the form of Progress Tests at the end of each chapter, each text-referenced for easy checking. Every Handbook closes with an appendix which advises on examination technique. For all these reasons, Handbooks are ideal for pre-examination revision.

The handy pocket-book size and competitive price make Handbooks the perfect choice for anyone who wants to grasp the essentials of a subject quickly and easily.

Preface to Sixth Edition

Once again the production of another edition of this book has
been necessitated by new statutory regulation and professional
recommendation. The raising of standards in the business world
and the increasing complexity of operations demand an ever-
increasing depth of knowledge and exercise of professional skill
on the part of the auditor. In this edition, opportunity has been
taken to include the Companies Act 1976 requirements together
with the relevant Statements of Standard Accounting Practice
and the relevant International Accounting Standards.

Although this volume is taken to final examination standard,
foundation students with no previous knowledge of auditing
should find the succinct presentation helpful in both understanding and memorising the subject.

Acknowledgments are due to the various accountancy bodies
for permission to use their examination questions. In addition,
acknowledgment must be accorded the Institutes of Chartered
Accountants and the Association of Certified Accountants for
the extensive use of quotations from their Statements of Standard
Accounting Practice and other publications; where these have
not actually been quoted, the techniques outlined have been
closely followed in the text, since they constitute authoritative
recommendations to the Accountancy profession. The following
publications are particularly relevant:

Section		Page
E	*Professional Conduct*	
E.2	Changes in professional appointment (1968)	15
I	*International Accounting Standards*	
I.A.S.1	Disclosure of accounting policies (1975)	4–6, 269
I.A.S.2	Valuation and presentation of inventories (1975)	181, 186, 188, 190, 192
M	*Statements of Standard Accounting Practice*	
M.2	Disclosure of accounting policies (1971)	3, 4–6

M.7   Accounting for changes in the purchasing power
        of money   166
M.9   Stocks and work-in-progress (1975)   181–92
M.10   Statements of sources and application of funds
        (1977)   270
M.12   Accounting for depreciation (1977)   156
M.15   Accounting for deferred taxation (1978)   144

N   *Recommendations on Accounting Principles*
N.13   Accountants' reports for prospectuses; fixed
        assets and depreciation (1949)   236
N.16   Accountants' reports for prospectuses; adjust-
        ments and other matters (1953)   236, 238

S   *Financial Statements and Reports*
S.6   Terms used in published accounts of limited
        companies (1962)   141
S.15   Accountants' reports on profit forecasts (1969) 242
S.17   Stock Exchange (1962)   238
S.18   Absence of detailed stock records (1972)   236, 239
S.20   Valuation of company property assets (1974) 168–71
S.22   Inflation accounting interim recommendation
        (1977)   167

U   *Statements on Auditing*
U.1   General principles of auditing (1961)   27, 109
U.3   Audits of building societies (now issued separ-
        ately)   218
U.4   Internal control (1964)   42, 43
U.7   Verification of debtor balances (1967)   39, 129
U.9   Attendance at stock-taking (1968)   39, 177
U.10   Auditors' reports: forms and qualifications
        (1968)   261, 266, 268
U.12   Auditors' working papers (1969)   17
U.13   Auditors' reports under *Friendly and Industrial
        Provident Societies Act*, 1968 (1969)   255
U.14   Internal control in a computer-based accounting
        system (1969)   97, 98
U.15   The audit of computer-based accounting systems
        (1969)   97, 105
U.16   The ascertainment of . . . contingent liabilities
        arising from pending legal matters (1970)   148

U.17   The effect of standard accounting practice on
       auditors' reports (1970)   266, 271
U.18   Audit problems of the smaller company (1972)   39
U.21   Group accounts—reliance on other auditors
       (1976)   262
U.22   Bank reports for audit purposes (1976)   138
U.23   Auditors' reports on funds statements (1977)   270
U.24   Goods sold—reservation of title (1977)   192
U.26   Auditors' reports—Friendly Societies (1978)   256

V   *Legal and Regulatory Background to Accountants'*
       Work
V.5   Books and papers (ownership and lien) (1953)   258
V.8   Accountants' liability to third parties—the
       Hedley Byrne decision (1965)   277, 279
V.10   Interpretation of material in relation to accounts
       (1968)   271
V.12   Unlawful acts or defaults by clients of members
       (1968)   281
V.15   Solicitors' accounts (1975)   226
V.16   Engagement letters (1969)   249
V.18   Professional liability of accountant and auditor
       (1972)   279
V.24   Accounting goods sold—reservation of title
       (1976)   192

1978   L.R.H.

Contents

	Preface to Sixth Edition	**v**
	Table of Cases	**xi**
I	*The Nature of Auditing*	**1**
	Nature of auditing; Classification of audits	
II	*General Procedure of Work*	**15**
	Professional ethics; New audits; Audit working papers; Audit programmes; Summary of audit work procedures; Advantages and disadvantages of audit programmes	
III	*Internal Control*	**26**
	Introduction; Practical application; Audit problems of the smaller company; Relationship between the independent and the internal auditor	
IV	*Systems Auditing*	**46**
	Cash receipts; Cash payments; Petty cash; Purchases; Sales	
V	*Mechanised Accounting*	**83**
	Mechanised accounting; Specific audit difficulties; Punched card accounting	
VI	*Electronic Data Processing*	**91**
	Procedural controls; Computer system controls; Internal control in a computer-based accounting system (U.14); The audit of computer-based accounting systems (U.15); Specimen questions for evaluating the system of control in a computer-based accounting system	
VII	*Verification of Balance Sheet Items*	**122**
	Initial procedure; Verification of assets; Proprietors' funds and liabilities	
VIII	*Depreciation and Appreciation*	**154**
	Depreciation; Appreciation; Accounting for depreciation; Legal aspects of depreciation; Business policy and depreciation	

IX   *Valuation of Assets*   166
       Valuation; Types of asset

X   *Verification and Valuation of Stock and Work-in-Progress*   176
       Verification; Valuation

XI   *Retention and Distribution of Profits*   201
       Nature of profits; Distribution of profits

XII   *Specialised Audits*   217

XIII   *Investigations*   231
       Investigations and reports; Accountants' reports on profit forecasts

XIV   *The Auditor*   249
       Terms of office; Rights and responsibilities

       Appendix   Examination technique   286

       Index   289

Table of Cases

(Where the facts are noted, the page number is in italics)

Aluminium Industrie Vaassen *v.* Romalpa (1976)   *192*

Ammonia Soda Co. Ltd. *v.* Chamberlain (1918)   *210*

Armitage *v.* Brewer and Knott (1932)   *274*

Arthur E. Green & Company *v.* The Central Advance and
    Discount Corporation Ltd. (1920)   *204, 274*

Bolton *v.* Natal Land and Colonisation Co. Ltd. (1892)   *161*

Bond *v.* The Barrow Haematite Steel Co. Ltd (1902).   *163,* 209

Borden (U.K.) Ltd. *v.* Scottish Timber Products (1978)   *192*

Brown *v.* Gaumont British Picture Corporation Ltd. (1937)   *162*

Burland *v.* Earle (1902)   *209*

Candler *v.* Crane, Christmas & Co. (1951)   277

City Equitable Fire Insurance Co. Ltd., *Re* (1925)   *276*

Colmer *v.* Merrett, Son and Street (1914)   232

Dimbula Valley (Ceylon) Tea Co. Ltd. *v.* Laurie (1961)   207

D. M. Carr and Company Ltd. (1961)   259

Fisher *v.* Black and White Publishing Co. (1901)   *209*

Foster *v.* The New Trinidad Lake Asphalt Co. Ltd. (1901)   *206*

Fox & Son *v.* Morris Grant & Co. (1918)   *273*

Hedley Byrne & Co. Ltd. *v.* Heller & Partners Ltd. (1963)   277

Herschel *v.* Mrupi (1954) (S.A. 464)   278

Hill *ex parte* Southall, *Re* (1848)   258

Hoole *v.* Great Western Railway Company (1868)   212

Irish Woollen Company *v.* Tyson and Others (1900)   *273*

Kingston Cotton Mill Company, *Re* (1896)   *176,* 275

Lagunas Nitrate Co. *v.* Schroeder (1901)   213

Lee *v.* Neuchatel Asphalte Co. Ltd. (1889)   *161,* 162, 209

Leicestershire County Council *v.* Michael Faraday and
    Partners Ltd. (1941)   258

London and General Bank, *Re* (1895)   204, 211, *275*

London Oil Storage Co. Ltd. *v.* Seear, Hasluck & Co. (1904)
    121, *273*

Lubbock v. British Bank of South America Ltd. (1892)   *205*

Monsanto *v.* Bond Worth (1979)   *192*

Moxham *v.* Grant (1910)   211

Oakbank Oil Co. *v.* Crum (1883) 212
R. *v.* Wake and Stone (1954) *232*
Rance's Case (1871) 213
Romalpa case (*see* Aluminium Industrie, etc.) *192*
Short and Compton *v.* Brackett (1904) *232*
Smith *v.* Sheard (1906) *273*
Spanish Prospecting Co. Ltd., *Re* (1911) 201
Stapley *v.* Read Bros. Ltd. (1924) 123, 174, *210*
Ultramares Corporation *v.* Touche (255 N.Y. 170) 278
Verner *v.* General and Commercial Investment Trust (1894)
160, 163, 203, 206, 209
Westburn Sugar Refineries Ltd. *v.* I.R.C. (1960) 270
Westminster Road Construction and Engineering Co. Ltd.,
Re (1932) *276*
Wilde & Others *v.* Carpe & Dalgleish (1897) *273*
Wilmer *v.* McNamara & Co. Ltd. (1895) *162*, 204, 209

CHAPTER I

The Nature of Auditing

NATURE OF AUDITING

1. Introduction. Originally, an auditor was one to whom the receipts and payments of an establishment were read (the Latin verb *audire* means to hear); this practice was known to have existed in ancient civilisations such as Egypt.

The increased complexity of modern commerce calls for a high degree of skill and discernment, and has greatly expanded the scope of the auditor's operations, but the basic need to examine completed transactions still exists. With this background in mind, we can turn to a general definition of the word *audit*.

2. Definition of an audit. An audit may be described as an examination by an auditor of the evidence from which the final revenue accounts and balance sheet of an organisation have been prepared, in order to ascertain that they present a true and fair view of the summarised transactions for the period under review and of the financial state of the organisation at the end date, thus enabling the auditor to report thereon.

Examining the definition a little more closely it will be observed that the auditor examines the evidence, i.e. mainly the books, accounts and vouchers of the establishment. But, in certain circumstances it may be necessary for the auditor to go even further in his examination, e.g. to examine actual assets held.

Such definitions often refer to the ascertainment of the true and fair view of the *profit or loss* for the period, but it is felt that the foregoing wording is more inclusive since many organisations, such as those of non-trading bodies, do not use the term profit or loss but rather an excess of income over expenditure (or vice-versa). Further, not only are the end figures of a revenue account important in themselves, but the constituent parts of the revenue account must also give a true and fair view of the transactions they represent.

It is important to remember that the examination must be such as to enable the auditor to report thereon.

1

3. Concomitant features. It is commonly, and mistakenly, thought that the purpose of an audit is to detect errors and fraud. This might be the case when an investigation of a set of accounts and supporting documents is conducted, but this is not the main purpose of an audit.

An audit may reveal the presence of errors and fraud, but this is a subordinate feature, arising only in the course of the normal auditing work and of relevance only as an advantage arising. The moral check created by the carrying out of the audit also does much to prevent the incidence of error or fraud, so these two vital features—detection and prevention of errors and fraud—emerge as *subsidiary* to the main purpose of the audit.

4. Audit and accountancy work compared. The assumption has so far been made that the accounts and balance sheets are submitted to the auditor, but in practice the auditor frequently prepares the accounts and balance sheets himself.

A clear distinction must be drawn, however, between the work of an auditor as such and the work he does as an accountant. To return to the original definition, the auditor's task is to "audit" the completed work, and although in preparing the accounts he may carry out certain auditing work, this preparatory work is only carried out in his capacity as an accountant.

Frequently in the course of his work the auditor may become aware of weaknesses and inefficiency in the working of the system, and he may bring such matters to the notice of the client or his staff. The auditor is again acting in his capacity as an accountant (since as an auditor it is not his duty to advocate certain methods of working). Nevertheless, with his skill and experience, the auditor will be most helpful to those by whom he is engaged but any accountancy work he does must always be considered apart from the work of the audit.

This distinction is important, since various liabilities and duties are inherent in his work and these may in certain circumstances be called into question, with far-reaching consequences.

5. The audit and standard accounting practice

(a) *The U.K. Standards.* In seeking to ensure that the balance sheet and accounts of an organisation reveal a true and fair view of its transactions and of its position in monetary terms, the auditor has to see that the various regulatory factors, whether statutory or otherwise, are complied with.

Legal directives must obviously take precedence, but for work to be carried out effectively, credence must also be given to further recognised requirements. The Institute of Chartered Accountants in England and Wales have issued a number of statements on auditing which serve as guidance and as indicators of the best practice to follow. These are persuasive in nature and departures from them do not necessarily require disclosure as do departures from "accounting standards".

Statements of Standard Accounting Practice (S.S.A.P.s) describe methods of accounting approved by the councils of the accounting bodies. The councils expect members to comply with these "accounting standards" when they assume responsibilities in respect of financial accounts (signified by the association of their names with such accounts in the capacity of directors or as other officers or as auditing or reporting accountants). The onus will be on members not only to ensure disclosure of significant departures but also, to the extent that their concurrence is stated or implied, to justify them. Each council, through its professional standards committee, may inquire into apparent failures by members to observe or to disclose such departures.

While the subjects dealt with in the S.S.A.P.s are mostly of a specialised nature, Statement M.2 may be summarised here, as it contains the accepted principles governing the preparation and presentation of accounts and balance sheets for organisations generally.

A distinction has to be made between:

    (*i*) fundamental accounting concepts;
    (*ii*) accounting bases;
    (*iii*) accounting policies.

    (*i*) Fundamental accounting concepts are the broad basic assumptions which underlie the periodic financial accounts of business enterprises. Those of particular importance are:

    (1) the going concern concept;
    (2) the accruals concept;
    (3) the consistency concept;
    (4) the prudence concept.

There are particular problems in the application of the fundamental concepts.

The main difficulty arises from the fact that many transactions have financial effects spread over a number of years. For example, goods or services for which revenue is received may still involve some later expenditure. In such cases, a decision is required as to how much revenue should be carried forward. Such decisions require consideration of future events of uncertain financial effect, and this necessitates the exercise of commercial judgment.

(*ii*) Accounting bases are the methods which have been developed to express or apply fundamental accounting concepts to financial transactions and items. These are by their nature more diverse and numerous than fundamental concepts, since they have evolved in response to the needs of numerous types of business. Accounting bases are used to provide fair and objective solutions, but judgment is still required as to which should be adopted when there are different bases. The most suitable in the particular circumstances should always be used. This does not vitiate their usefulness, however, as their real significance lies in the way that they provide limits to the areas of judgment and guard against arbitrary, excessive or unjustifiable adjustments where there is no yardstick available. Significant matters for which different accounting bases are recognised, and which may have a material effect on reported results and financial position include:

(1) depreciation of fixed assets;
(2) treatment and amortisation of intangibles such as research and development expenditure, patents and trademarks;
(3) stocks and work-in-progress;
(4) long-term contracts;
(5) deferred taxation;
(6) hire-purchase or instalment transactions, etc.

(*iii*) Accounting policies are the specific accounting bases judged by business enterprises to be most appropriate to their circumstances and adopted by them for the purpose of preparing their financial accounts.

Where any departure from the basic concepts occurs, or where the accounting policies followed are judged material or critical, then explanatory notes should be appended to the accounts, giving explanations as clearly, fairly and briefly as possible.

The effects of the Statements of Standard Accounting Practice on auditors' reports is dealt with later (*see* pp. 266–8).

(*a*) *The International Accounting Standard.* International Accounting Standard 1 is very similar to S.S.A.P. M.2 outlined above. It lists a number of items where differing accounting policies exist (such as consolidation policy, conversion of foreign currencies) and states the need for uniformity of presentation. It says:

> Financial statements should include clear and concise disclosure of all significant accounting policies which have been used.
>
> The disclosure of the significant accounting policies used should be an integral part of the financial statements. The policies should be disclosed in one place.
>
> Wrong or inappropriate treatment of items in balance sheets, income statements or profit and loss accounts, or other statements is not rectified either by disclosure of accounting policies used or by notes or explanatory material.

The foregoing statement is of great importance to the auditor. In effect, it does not excuse any treatment in balance sheets and accounts which is not in accord with the expected accountancy standards. This is understandable for, as mentioned in another part of the submission, such documents are read by all types of interested parties who may not always be aware of implications. To give a simple example—it would be quite wrong to value stock at selling price and then to disclose this as though disclosure was in effect sufficient notice to all concerned.

If any matter is inappropriately or wrongly dealt with in accordance with the accepted standards and then disclosed in notes or otherwise and the auditor cannot persuade the directors or those concerned to rectify the state of affairs, then the auditor would have to qualify his report accordingly:

> Financial statements should show corresponding figures for the preceding period.
>
> A change in an accounting policy that has a material effect in the current period or may have a material effect in subsequent periods should be disclosed together with the reasons. The effect of the change should, if material, be disclosed and quantified.

There is a slight difference in the analysis of the content of the Standard, but this is not to vary the overall agreement. The going concern, consistency and accrual, are fundamental accounting assumptions. "Prudence, substance over form and materiality should govern the selection and application of accounting policies."

The similarity of I.A.S.1 and S.S.A.P. M.2 are apparent save that the "substance over form" expression is used which is explained as "Transactions and other events should be accounted for and presented in accordance with their substance and financial reality and not merely with their legal form".

6. Complexity of an audit. The complexity of manufacturing and commercial transactions and the methods by which they are recorded for accounting and other purposes has turned a simple "hearing" by the auditor of miscellaneous receipts and payments into an intricate operation requiring skill and experience commensurate with the work involved.

As yet many audits can be conducted by those with no specified qualification, but where the interests of the public at large are affected, statutory requirements have been laid down in respect of those who may undertake such work. These legal requirements are discussed in more detail later (*see* XIV) but at this stage it is emphasised that although auditing may be carried out in most cases by any person requested to do so, such duties may only be carried out efficiently if the professional skill and experience of those qualified to do so is exercised.

CLASSIFICATION OF AUDITS

The various types of audit which may be undertaken can be placed in the first instance in two main categories:

(*a*) According to the *nature of the work* undertaken.
(*b*) According to the *method of approach* to the work.

7. Classification by nature of work undertaken. Under this class can be grouped the following basic types of audit:

(*a*) Private audits.
(*b*) Statutory audits.
(*c*) Internal audits.

8. Private audits. In such cases, the auditor will conduct an *agreed limit of work*. This does not mean that the whole of his work is specifically stated before commencement, but some broad agreement as to what work is required will have been laid down. This may be in the form of an understanding to do all the work the auditor considers necessary for the issue of a report, the terms of which are indicated.

He may, for example, report that he has received all the information and explanations he required, and that he is satisfied that the accounts and balance sheet in question give a true and fair view of the financial affairs and position of the organisation. A report such as this would involve conducting a *full audit*.

On the other hand, it may be specified in the instructions to the auditor that he is required to give a report stating his satisfaction only that the accounts and balance sheet are in accordance with the work he has undertaken. His report would then be in accordance with the information and explanations given to him.

The specification of the extent of the work to be carried out can take different forms. The auditor may be appointed by a letter giving details of requirements, but (where an organisation such as a club or charity is concerned), he may be employed to complete the audit in accordance with the *rules and regulations* of the organisation, as laid out in its constitution.

In any case, the auditor should always be most particular to obtain a statement in writing as to the nature and scope of the work he is to undertake. This point is dealt with more fully on pp. 49 and 249 under Engagement Letters.

9. Statutory audits. Where statutory audits are to be conducted, the legal requirements will provide the necessary information as to the nature of the report required, and here the auditor will carry out the work in whatever manner he considers necessary and no restriction may be put upon him. The important factor to consider in this case is that the auditor's appointment is carried out in accordance with the legal stipulations, and he should be careful to examine the minutes of the meeting or any other legal document whereby he is appointed.

10. Internal audits. These differ fundamentally from the types of audit already mentioned, in that the foregoing audits are undertaken by an independent auditor who conducts his work apart from the organisation whose books he is auditing. For this reason, he is often referred to as an *external* auditor.

The internal auditor, on the other hand, is an employee of the business engaged in work on behalf of the organisation, although the nature of his work requires that he shall be given an element of independence while engaged in it.

As the duties of the internal auditor are closely bound up with the internal check and control of a business, this type of audit is dealt with more fully in Chapter III, where internal control is discussed.

11. Classification by method of approach. The auditor's method of approach to his work determines into which of the following, often overlapping, classifications an audit can be placed:

    (*a*) Final or completed audit.

    (*b*) Interim audit.

    (*c*) Continuous audit.

    (*d*) Procedural audit.

    (*e*) Balance sheet audit.

12. Final or completed audit. This implies that the audit is carried through to completion in *one continuous session*. Although it may be commenced before the end of the accounting period, it is completed at least partly after the end of the financial period.

    (*a*) *Advantages:*

    (*i*) Work can be carried through to conclusion, so avoiding the necessity of having to return on separate occasions to partially completed work, requiring notes to be made each time indicating the stage reached. The possibility of figures being altered after work has been done is also avoided.

    (*ii*) A simplified timetable can be worked out for staff.

    (*b*) *Disadvantages:*

    (*i*) Where work is of an extended nature, delays may occur after the end of the financial period, so retarding the completion of the audit. This is an important factor as it is often desired to call the Annual General Meeting and to publish the accounts as soon as possible after the year end.

    (*ii*) Where, as is often the case, financial periods of several clients end on the same date, difficulties may be experienced in deploying audit staff adequately.

13. Interim audit. This is when an audit is conducted *to a particular date within the accounting period*. The auditor may attend to audit the figures for a month or for a quarter, as the work may require. It would differ distinctly from the final audit in the extent of the work carried out; verification of assets, for example, would be left until the final audit.

    (*a*) *Advantages:*

    (*i*) This type of audit may fulfil a need where the publication of interim figures is necessary.

    (*ii*) Such interim work can speed the completion of the final audit at the end of the financial period.

    (*iii*) Error and fraud may be discovered more quickly during the accounting period.

(*iv*) The attendance of staff at intervals imposes a sound moral check as well as doing much to ensure that work is kept up to date.

(*b*) *Disadvantages:*

Figures may be altered after having been audited, so necessitating additional work to guard against this.

14. Continuous audit. This method is frequently, but not necessarily, in operation in large organisations. The work is conducted throughout the course of the financial year but *is not taken to a specific accounting period*, as is an interim audit. It might be that during the course of the continuous work interim figures are being audited, but the significant factor here is that the auditor will be engaged continuously on the audit throughout the financial period. Staff may be in residence throughout the period or may come and go at irregular intervals, but particularised set periods of operation would not apply.

(*a*) *Advantages:*

(*i*) The advantage of interim audits (*see* **13**(*a*) (*i*), (*ii*) and (*iii*) above) also apply here.

(*ii*) The moral check mentioned above applies even more, as continuous audit work need not be carried out to any specific date.

(*iii*) Audit staff may be used more effectively since they may be sent at intervals when other work is slack.

(*iv*) With the additional time made available, work may be carried out more thoroughly and in greater detail.

(*b*) *Disadvantages:*

(*i*) Figures may be altered either fraudulently or misguidedly after audit. This constitutes a real danger and action has to be taken to guard against it.

(*ii*) It may be inconvenient for a client's staff to be interrupted in the course of their work by auditors requiring their books and documents.

(*iii*) A tendency may evolve for a client's staff to rely upon the auditors to help them out of difficulties in the course of their work, e.g. to discover errors in figures found when balancing accounts. This may be helpful to the staff but may necessitate further working time on audits, which may not be easily justified by the size of the audit.

(*iv*) Additional work may be required on such audits by continually having to take up again work not fully completed.

(*v*) To lessen the effect of (*iv*) above, extensive note-taking may be necessary to maintain an even flow of work, as well as ensuring that no alterations are put through the books after they have been audited.

15. Procedural audit. A procedural audit is an examination and review of the internal procedures and records of an organisation, in order to ascertain their reliability as a basis for the compilation of the final accounts and balance sheet.

The greater importance now attached to investigating the effectiveness of the internal control of a business has caused a natural development of the procedural audit. It is not, in effect, a peculiar type of audit, but will most usually form part of the whole audit. Particular attention is focused, however, on such matters as:

(*a*) Assessing the adequacy of the internal control system.

(*b*) Ensuring that procedures laid down by management are being followed.

(*c*) Ascertaining whether any changes have been made in the internal control system of which the auditors have not been notified.

(*d*) Establishing whether the records are sufficiently reliable for the preparation of the final accounts.

From (*d*) above it can be seen that such procedural audits are used for the purpose of ascertaining the efficiency of the accounting system and all the procedures emanating therefrom, such as stock ordering and control, and making any recommendations for its improvement. But here again it must be stressed that this aspect of the work has to be viewed apart from the actual audit as such recommendations do not form part of the "ascertainment and report thereon" as mentioned in the definition of an audit on p. 1.

Depth tests may be applied, whereby certain transactions are traced from their origin to their completion to ensure compliance with procedures established to maintain adequate internal control (*see* Chapter III for more detailed explanations).

16. The management audit. The management audit may be described as the investigation of a business in all its managerial aspects from the highest governing executive downwards and the making of a report as to its effectiveness or otherwise from the point of view of the profitability and efficient running of the business.

It differs from consultancy, which is an overall investigation to improve the efficiency of a business; the management audit is concerned with management at all levels and can be very effective without entailing the time and expense necessary in a major consultancy exercise. The management audit concentrates upon the main sources of decision-making in a firm, which can achieve effective or devastating results for profitability.

Such an audit will only take place where management is of a progressive nature, as it necessarily reveals the effects of both good and disastrous decision-making. But on the other hand it can reveal strengths and weaknesses which, when acted upon or dealt with, may have immediate and possibly far-reaching effects on company profitability.

17. Balance sheet audit. This is of more recent origin than the normal type of audit, and has proved more popular in the U.S.A. than in this country. It may be, however, that with the consolidation of industry into larger economic units such audits may become more widely used.

It is convenient here to give an explanation of the operation of a balance sheet audit, although it is appreciated that the student may prefer to return to this after studying the details of work outlined in ensuing chapters.

Unlike the work entailed in the more usual type of audit, it is necessary here to commence from the balance sheet, working back to the books of prime entry and their documentary evidence. It is essential to ensure, however, that there is a reliable system of internal check and control in operation; assuming this to be the case, the following broad scheme of operation might be suitable:

(*a*) Examine the minute books of the organisation, taking notes on any matters of importance affecting the accounts and balance sheet items.

(*b*) Compare the revenue account for the year of audit with that of the previous year, ascertaining the reasons for any material differences.

(*c*) Compare the increase or decrease of variable expenses in conjunction with the variation in turnover. Unit quantities are important with regard to turnover, and adjustment and allowance should be made for price or other variations.

(*d*) Carefully investigate any changes in gross profit rates; in conjunction with this, examine stock values. The separation of various sales lines for investigation purposes should be made.

(*e*) Any items of a non-recurring nature should be examined, such as losses, or profits incurred on fixed assets. Depreciation charges should be carefully checked in conjunction with the assets concerned. The effect of these and variations in expenses mentioned above should render any change in net profit readily explainable.

(*f*) The effect of the profit or loss for the period in varying the balance sheet should be explained. Schedules, such as sources and disposition of funds statements, may be usefully applied.

(*g*) The variation in fixed asset holdings should be examined by means of schedules showing movements since the last balance sheet date.

(*h*) Examine the variation in current assets as compared with the previous year. Accounting ratios may be most useful, together with credit control schedules.

(*i*) The lists of pre-payments and accruals should be scrutinised, any material alterations being investigated.

(*j*) Examine all remaining balance sheet items, such as share capital, taxation, etc., ascertaining that these are in order in line with prevailing audit requirements, e.g. taxation being fully provided for on current profits.

(*k*) All assets held and liabilities owed should be verified.

(*l*) Ascertain whether any capital commitments exist, and that any items on which subsequent losses might arise have been provided for.

Since the foregoing (and often, at the auditor's discretion, even more detailed work) may be required by a balance sheet audit, it may be queried what advantage arises from not performing the more normal full audit. In the balance sheet audit a good deal of such work as vouching and casting, which is normally considered necessary, may be eliminated. It is essential, therefore, in the case of the balance sheet audit, that the internal check and control systems should be sound, and that the auditor carrying out the audit should be highly skilled, as much depends on his detecting any underlying error by his ability accurately to interpret accounts. Consequently, such an audit would be most efficacious in the case of a large organisation employing qualified accounting staff and preferably having an internal audit department.

PROGRESS TEST 1

1. Give a definition of an audit.   (1, 2)

2. For what main purpose is the auditor's examination carried out?   (2, 3)

3. Does the auditor's examination extend only to the books, accounts and vouchers?   (2)

4. What are the concomitant features of an audit?   (3)

5. Is it the auditor's duty to prepare the accounts and balance sheet?   (4)

6. If the answer to 5 above is in the negative, why do auditors frequently do this?   (4)

7. If the auditor finds weaknesses and inefficiencies in the system, what should he do?   (4)

8. Frequently audits are carried out by those who are not qualified accountants. Are there any reasons why this should not be so?   (5)

9. Into what main classifications do audits fall?   (7–11)

10. Name the various types of audits conducted.   (7–11)

11. By what means are the limits of the auditor's work specified?   (8–12)

12. By what means should the auditor ensure that the extent of his work is specified?   (8)

13. Where the auditor's work is carried out under statute, who may dictate the extent of his examinations?   (9)

14. When appointed under statute, what should the auditor do on taking up his appointment?   (9)

15. What is the fundamental difference between an internal and external audit?   (10)

16. What is management audit?   (16)

17. In what way does a balance sheet audit differ from a normal audit?   (17)

18. State the advantages and disadvantages of:

(a) final audits;

(b) interim audits;

(c) continuous audits;

(d) procedural audits.   (12–15)

SPECIMEN QUESTIONS

1. What are the main purposes of an audit and how may these be achieved?   *A.C.A.* (*Inter.*)

2. Explain the advantages and disadvantages of a continuous audit and indicate the steps which can be taken to minimise the disadvantages.   *I.C.A. (E.W.)*

3. Describe the disadvantages of an interim audit and state the steps you would take to minimise them.   *A.C.A. (Inter.)*

4. What is meant by a balance sheet audit? Give a suggested programme to be followed in such an audit.   *A.C.A.*

5. You are required to consider the case of a business whose trading is subject to seasonal variation, and to state the best time in which to set the close of its accounting period, having regard to:

(*a*) The preparation of annual accounts, and

(*b*) the audit of those accounts.

Give reasons for your answer.   *A.C.A.*

6. (*a*) What is a "procedural audit" and what are its objectives?

(*b*) What do you understand by the term "procedural audit test"? Describe such a test covering purchasing procedure. *A.C.A.*

CHAPTER II

General Procedure of Work

PROFESSIONAL ETHICS

1. Taking up appointment. On taking up any new audit the requirements as to professional etiquette and proper terms of appointment should first be attended to. (Regarding contractual terms of appointment, *see* pp. 40, 249–50.)

Even before receiving official recognition, it was considered a matter of professional etiquette to communicate with the retiring auditor on taking up a new appointment, in order to enquire whether any objection might be raised. This has now been recognised as a requisite part of professional etiquette by the established accountancy bodies and incorporated into their regulations. This is also now a statutory requirement under the Friendly and Industrial and Provident Societies Act 1968.

2. Regulations of accountancy bodies. The regulations laid down both by the Institute of Chartered Accountants in England and Wales and by the Association of Certified Accountants state that their members should not accept a nomination to replace an auditor without first communicating with the previous or existing auditor (such a communication being preferably in writing) to enquire whether the accountant concerned wishes to state any reason why the nomination should not be accepted. *The rule applies whether the accountant to whom the enquiry is addressed is a member of the same professional body or not.* Where permission is not granted by the client or organisation concerned for the existing auditor to discuss the company's affairs with the proposed auditor then the nomination should not be accepted.

The members of a business have the indisputable right to change their auditors, but both retiring and proposed auditor will wish to protect their own rights. The I.C.A. regulations which cover this subject are contained in Section E.2. Briefly summarised, these state that the existing auditor should request authorisation in writing from the company to discuss the company's affairs with the proposed auditor. If the existing auditor receives this authority, then he may do so without fear of an action for breach of contract or defamation if he states what he honestly believes to be true. Without such authorisation his communication would be protected by qualified privilege, which means that he would not be liable to pay damages for defamatory statements, even if they turn out to be untrue, if they were made without malice; and provided he stated only what he sincerely believed to be true, the chances of his being held malicious are remote. Moreover, although without authorisation he might technically be in breach of contract, the likelihood of an action being brought against him is small, and any damages awarded likely to be nominal. The proposed new auditor should decline to accept nomination if he is informed that the existing auditor has not been given permission to discuss the company's affairs.

NEW AUDITS

The following are the main points to which the auditor should give attention when taking up a new audit.

3. Extent of work and engagement letters. The exact scope and limit of the auditor's duties should be ascertained. In the case of a statutory audit these will be specified, but in other cases the auditor should ensure that he has been instructed in writing, with the limit of his duties clearly stated (*see* pp. 249–50).

4. Additional accountancy work. Any special requests for work outside that which the auditor considers necessary for the purposes of his audit should be brought to the attention of his client, pointing out the auditor's right to charge an additional fee for such work.

5. Regulations of the organisation. The auditor should carefully examine these, making notes of all matters of particular importance.

6. Officials and records. Lists should be obtained of:

(*a*) responsible officials and the nature of their office;
(*b*) all books, with names and designation of those maintaining them.

7. Adequacy of system. This should be examined in conjunction with internal control questionnaires and standard audit programmes, an internal control letter (formerly termed letter of weaknesses) to be sent if necessary (*see* pp. 27, 40). A tour of the business should be made so that the auditor can acquaint himself intimately with its nature and working.

8. Preparation of audit programme. *See* p. 19.

9. Background information. Previous accounts, balance sheets and any relevant analyses should be examined.

AUDIT WORKING PAPERS

Whilst not specifying any particular form, the Council in Recommendation U.12 points out that the working papers should be such as will enable the auditors to achieve their object of forming an opinion on the accounts on which they report. For this purpose, they should facilitate control of the current year's audit, provide evidence of the work done, provide schedules to support accounts and information on the business including its recent history. The following brief details have been extracted from U.12.

10. Current file. Primarily being concerned with the accounts being audited, it should normally contain the following:

(*a*) A copy of accounts or statements on which the auditors are reporting, authenticated by directors' signatures or otherwise.

(*b*) Index (cross-referenced), internal control questionnaires and standard audit programmes duly referenced to one another, plus any flow charts.

(*c*) A schedule for each item in the balance sheet and statutory profit and loss account, preferably including comparative figures, showing its make-up and how existence, ownership and value or liability have been verified. These schedules should be cross-referenced to documents arising from external verification such as bank letters and the results of circularisation of debtors and attendance at physical stock-taking.

(*d*) A check-list concerning compliance with statutory disclosure provisions.

(*e*) A record showing queries raised during the audit and their disposal, with notes where appropriate for attention the following year. Queries not cleared at the time should be entered on to a further schedule for the attention of the person reviewing the audit and for reference to the client if necessary. Material queries, which cannot be settled satisfactorily by immediate reference to the client, may require a qualification of the auditor's report and should be fully documented and supported by a note of all discussions with the client and any explanations given.

(*f*) A schedule of important statistics of working ratios, comparative figures being included where appropriate.

(*g*) Extracts of relevant minutes of directors' or shareholders' meetings cross-referenced to working schedules.

(*h*) Letters of representation, i.e. written confirmation by the client of information and opinions expressed in respect of matters such as stock values and amounts of current and contingent liabilities.

Matters which, while not of permanent importance, will require attention during the subsequent year's audit should be listed, with references to the relevant working papers, and this note should be transferred to the next current file when opened.

11. Permanent file. Matters of continuing importance affecting the company or the audit should be kept in a separate file, suitably indexed, and these should normally include the following:

(*a*) Memorandum and Articles of Association and other appropriate statutory or legal regulations.

(*b*) Copies of other documents and minutes of continuing importance.

(*c*) A short description of the type of business carried on and the places of business.

(*d*) Lists of accounting records and responsible officials and plan of organisation.

(*e*) Statements showing a note of any accounting matters of importance such as a history of reserves and bases of accounting adopted, e.g. for the valuation of stock and work-in-progress, depreciation and the carrying forward and writing off of expenditure ultimately chargeable to revenue.

(*f*) The client's internal accounting instructions and internal audit instructions, including where appropriate stock-taking instructions.

Steps should be taken to ensure that the permanent file is brought up to date at the appropriate times.

In the case of a non-statutory audit the permanent file should also contain the client's instructions as to the scope of the work to be performed.

AUDIT PROGRAMMES

12. Doubts as to utility. Some doubt used to be cast on the efficacy of audit programmes, mainly because as they constitute a programme of work to be completed on an audit, the work might be conducted rigidly within its terms, stifling initiative and facilitating possible fraud; any interested member of the client's staff, even if not actually seeing the programme, could soon become acquainted with the manner in which the audit work would be carried out.

However, it is now generally agreed that to conduct an audit without a guide to the work involved necessitates repetitive enquiries, wasting valuable time and causing annoyance to the client's staff. It might also be possible to overlook part of the audit (other advantages and disadvantages are summarised below (*see* **24** and **25**)).

13. Compilation. The programme may be compiled as initial enquiries are made at the commencement of a new audit.

It may take different forms, but would usually begin by outlining the basic work of the audit, care being taken to see that similar work viewed from two different aspects is not repeated. For example, the necessity of checking the ledger postings against the sales day book should not appear both under the section of work regarding the sales day book postings to the sales ledger and under that regarding the sales ledger itself.

SUMMARY OF AUDIT WORK PROCEDURES

14. Introduction. Having mentioned above the work to be undertaken at the commencement of an audit with regard to Memorandum and Articles, internal control, etc., the outline of an audit is now given, which is generally applicable. At this stage this may serve not only as an example of the work to be done, but also as a brief overall review of the procedures involved in an audit. (Points concerning varying types of audit are given in Chapter XII.)

15. Main cash book.

(*a*) Obtain bank certificates direct from bank (*see* p. 138).

(*b*) Check bank statements with cash book and paying-in slips, noting dates of lodgements; check direct lodgements with advice notes.

(*c*) Examine periodic reconciliations and check in detail the reconciliation at the closing date.

(*d*) Check transfers to petty cash book.

(*e*) Check postings to nominal ledger.

(*f*) Vouch a number of payments which constitute postings to nominal ledger, especially those of a personal nature, e.g. expense payments to members of the organisation.

16. Petty cash book.

(*a*) Ascertain that it is initialled periodically by a responsible official, and note size of float; ensure imprest amount not exceeded.

(*b*) Test a number of vouchers. See that payments in respect of various items appear reasonable.

(*c*) Check cash in hand plus vouchers which may not have been entered and ensure all balances, where more than one, are produced simultaneously. Have any large IOUs, or old ones, authenticated.

(*d*) Check postings to nominal ledger.

17. Wages and salaries.

(*a*) Vouch net payments in cash book with wages and salaries summaries. Vouch deductions of P.A.Y.E., National Insurance, etc., to nominal ledger, and check to wages control account (if kept).

(*b*) Test payments with time cards, etc., and rates with authorisation lists.

(*c*) Check variations in salaries with increase lists.

(*d*) Test with P.A.Y.E. deduction cards if maintained; if not, then with final summaries for submission to Inland Revenue.

(*e*) Test additions and cross-casts on sheets.

(*f*) Check that total payments to directors, etc., are in accordance with contracts and minutes passed.

(*g*) Ascertain that all summaries are initialled by a responsible official.

18. Purchases.

(*a*) Examine in depth the prevailing system, using a sample number of transactions from:

(*i*) original orders;

(*ii*) goods received book;

(*iii*) entries in stock record;

(*iv*) invoices and statements received, noting whether the stages of invoice checking work are duly initialled. Check analysis.

(*b*) Examine invoices in period following audit to ensure invoices not put through after date.

(*c*) Note any purchases made not in nature of trade and any on behalf of staff, ensuring that these are properly charged.

(*d*) Check postings to nominal ledger.

(*e*) Vouch capital expenditure and check postings to nominal ledger accounts.

19. Sales.

(*a*) Examine in depth the prevailing system by using a sample of a number of sales transactions from:

(*i*) customers' orders;

(*ii*) copies of invoices (check with goods outwards book);

(*iii*) deductions from stock;

(*iv*) entries in debtors' accounts.

(*b*) Check goods outwards book at end of period and ascertain whether sales invoices have been rendered for goods dispatched.

(*c*) Test goods outwards book with stock records to ensure goods sold have not been shown as stock where not dispatched.

(*d*) Check system and ascertain all credit notes properly authorised.

(*e*) Check day book postings to nominal ledger.

(*f*) Where fixed assets have been sold, vouch these, ensuring proper authorisation and treatment in accounts.

20. Stocks and work-in-progress.

(*a*) Observe if possible actual stock-taking and ensure internal check maintained.

(*b*) Check final sheets with rough stock sheets enquiring into any material differences.

(*c*) Test-check sheets with stock records maintained in departments.

(*d*) Check a number of values set on stock, check casts.

(*e*) Enquire into stock written off or written down.

(*f*) Compare with previous year's figures.

(*g*) Compare stock figures with stock control account, if kept.

(*h*) Check overall position as to gross profit and rate of turnover.

(*i*) Obtain stock certificate.

21. Bought and sales ledgers.

(*a*) Check control accounts from books of prime entry.

(*b*) Test postings.

(*c*) Examine accounts, noting methods of settlement, discounts, transfers and test additions.

(*d*) Check balances in and down to next period and with list of balances. Take note of exceptional items—debit balances on adequate bad debts provision.

(*e*) Enquire into bad debts written off.

22. Nominal ledger.

(*a*) Vouch direct journal entries and transfers between accounts.

(*b*) Check additions.

(*c*) Check with trial balance.

(*d*) Check with pre-payments and accruals schedule.

(*e*) Check depreciation charges.

(*f*) Examine taxation account, checking items with computations in conjunction with audit notes and correspondence with Inland Revenue, etc.

23. Final accounts and balance sheet.

(*a*) Check figures from trial balance and schedules.

(*b*) Compare with previous year's figures, using percentages for comparative purposes where useful; investigate any inexplicable fluctuations.

(*c*) Compare with any internal accounts prepared, such as those used for costing purposes.

(*d*) If cost accounts are maintained on a separate basis, reconcile with these.

(*e*) Check statutory accounts and consult audit records for any items to be shown as special notes.

(*f*) Obtain directors' signatures and append audit report.

ADVANTAGES AND DISADVANTAGES OF AUDIT PROGRAMMES

24. Advantages.

(*a*) A permanent record of the work is constantly available. This facilitates:

   (*i*) the allocation of work between clerks;

(*ii*) the resumption of work by those taking up the audit after its commencement.

(*b*) The chance of work being overlooked is obviated.

(*c*) Unnecessary enquiries on each attendance as to routine work are avoided so saving the time of both clients' and auditor's staff.

(*d*) Programmes may easily be kept up to date by variation as required.

(*e*) In the event of any subsequent enquiry, the actual audit staff engaged on the work may be ascertained.

(*f*) As definite instructions are laid down, junior clerks may need less supervision.

(*g*) A clear perspective of the work involved is made available.

25. Disadvantages.

(*a*) Work may tend to become mechanical, variations in the working system of the organisation being overlooked.

(*b*) If work is carried out according to a pre-determined plan, fraud may be facilitated.

(*c*) Work may be hurried in order to complete a required schedule, whereas greater concentration on one aspect even if this involves omission of another might be of advantage on occasions.

The disadvantages which could arise from the use of audit programmes may be overcome by encouraging initiative amongst all levels of staff. The recommendation of changes in the audit programme should also be encouraged.

26. Discretion in use of programmes.
As the disadvantage mentioned in 25(*c*) may quite possibly arise, staff should be given to understand that the audit programme should not be completed merely by the inclusion of signatures in all available spaces, but that if for some reason work has been varied by the omission of some aspects, the person in charge should make a qualifying note to this effect.

PROGRESS TEST 2

1. What should an auditor do on first being offered a new audit in the case of a continuing business? **(1)**

2. For what reasons should an auditor communicate with the previous auditor before taking up his appointment? **(1, 2)**

3. In what ways should an auditor ascertain the extent of the work he is to do? (3, 4)

4. May any restrictions be put upon the auditor where he is appointed under statute? (3–6)

5. To what documents should the auditor pay particular attention on first being appointed? (6)

6. Are *internal* control questionnaires of any importance to the statutory auditor? (12)

7. What matters are normally contained in the audit working papers? (10–11)

8. Why are doubts cast upon the usefulness of audit programmes? (12)

9. Give the basic outline of an audit programme applicable in most businesses. (14–23)

10. State the advantages and disadvantages of audit programmes. (24–25)

11. Should audit staff be given any discretion as to the completion of the audit programme? (26)

SPECIMEN QUESTIONS

1. You have been approached by the partners of Rowan and Co., who carry on a merchanting business, to audit the accounts of their business in place of Exewy & Co., Chartered Accountants, who, you are informed, have resigned.

You are required to state:

(a) The action you would take before accepting the appointment, giving your reasons; and

(b) On the assumption that you accept the appointment, the information which you would require before commencing the detailed audit work for the first year. *I.C.A.* (*E.W.*)

2. The partners in Black & Co. inform you that their present auditor, Mr J. White, an unqualified practitioner, will not be continuing as auditor as he is retiring from practice on December 31st, 1966. They ask you to undertake the audit of their firm's accounts as from January 1st, 1967.

You are required to state:

(a) What action, if any, you would take (giving your reasons) before agreeing to undertake the audit.

(b) Assuming you have accepted the appointment, what information you would require from Black & Co. to enable you to draft a suitable audit programme.   *I.C.A.* (*E.W.*) (*Inter.*)

3. Discuss the advantages and disadvantages of a standard audit programme.   *A.C.A.* (*Inter.*)

4. You have been appointed auditor to a partnership of three doctors. What steps would you take before accepting the appointment and what information would you require before commencing your detailed duties?   *A.C.A.*

5. "An audit programme is of importance to all personnel engaged on an audit. The partner, manager, senior and audit clerks, can all derive great benefit from it."

Comment on this statement, showing how a carefully prepared programme is important at each level of responsibility.   *A.C.A.*

6. What are the objects of preparing audit working papers, and what categories of information should these provide if they are to fulfil their purpose?   *I.C.A.* (*E.W.*)

7. What information would you expect to see on a permanent audit file of a limited company?   *A.C.A.*

CHAPTER III

Internal Control

INTRODUCTION

1. Purpose of internal control. Increasing attention has been paid to the methods of internal control in recent years. Not only the complexity of modern business techniques but also the increased size of business units have encouraged the adoption of methods which, whilst increasing the efficiency of the business, also act as safeguards against error or fraud. Furthermore, the regulation of business activities under an efficient system of internal control may obviate the necessity of protracted detailed work by external auditors, with beneficial results for all parties concerned.

The Institute of Chartered Accountants' publication Statement on Auditing covering the subject of internal control provides a valuable guide on this matter, and gives a basic outline of the techniques involved; quotations in this chapter are all from these statements.

2. Definition of internal control. Internal control is defined as "not only internal check and internal audit but the whole system of controls, financial and otherwise, established by the management in order to carry on the business of the company in an orderly manner, safeguard its assets and secure as far as possible the accuracy and reliability of its records".

The inclusive nature of internal control is immediately apparent, as it embraces both internal check and the internal audit, if there is a department or section engaged on this.

3. Internal check. This forms a valuable part of the internal control and consists of "the allocation of authority and work in such a manner as to afford checks on the routine transactions of day-to-day work by means of the work of one person being proved independently by another, or the work of one person being complementary to that of another", so affording a means whereby fraud is prevented, or its early detection is facilitated.

4. Internal audit. This is described as "a review of operations

26

and records, sometimes continuous, undertaken within a business by specially assigned staff". Where there is an internal audit department, this may form a valuable part of the whole system of internal control, and according to its efficacy or otherwise, may influence considerably the conduct of the audit (*see* p. 41).

5. Internal control and the auditor. Where internal control is properly operated it may influence considerably the conduct of the audit. It will be necessary in the first instance for the auditor to satisfy himself as to its working, and in the case of a new audit this will take place on the first occasion. If he is not satisfied as to the efficacy of the internal control and its concomitant internal check, he may be forced to do a greater amount of detailed work than would otherwise be the case.

On the other hand, the overall system may be working satisfactorily but certain sections of the work may be inadequate, in which case he should inform the client in writing requesting the installation of certain methods whereby the weaknesses may be corrected. This would also apply if the system were unsatisfactory as a whole, and he should be careful to point out the dangers of letting the prevailing state of affairs continue. Such notification should be of help to the client as well as safeguarding the auditor in the event of any errors of fraud arising. The letter, formerly termed "letter of weaknesses", has been renamed "Internal control letter". (*See also* p. 40.)

To quote the Institute of Chartered Accountants' Recommendation U.1, *General Principles of Auditing:*

> In exceptional cases, auditors may find that the records and the system of internal control are so seriously inadequate that no useful purpose could be served by embarking upon extensive detailed checking, because even the most exhaustive tests would not enable them to form an opinion on the balance sheet and profit and loss account. In that event their appropriate course will be to report to that effect to the shareholders and to inform the directors of the respects in which the records and system are deficient.

The difficulties experienced in auditing the accounts of smaller companies has warranted the publication of I.C.A. Recommendation U.18 (*see* p. 39 *et seq.*)

Should the internal control system be adequate, then the detailed work of the audit may be restricted and sectional auditing in depth may be applied.

6. Audit tests and evaluation. To satisfy himself that the internal control system is adequate, the auditor will need to acquaint himself with not only the financial controls but also "the whole system of controls, financial and otherwise" (U.4.). An over-all knowledge of the business must be obtained, including the nature and history of the company, trading areas, staff organisation and control, and the exercise of authority throughout the business. Evaluation tests of the system will be conducted, using such documents as internal control questionnaires, organisational and flow charts and evaluation forms, the last named being for the over-all assessment of key points in the system and on which are stated the strengths and weaknesses revealed. These tests will include the following:

(a) *Walk through tests.* To ensure the system is complied with, a certain number of items of each transaction are checked through the whole system.

(b) *Compliance tests.* Here a larger number of items are checked at "key points" where deviations could be serious (e.g. a deviation in the internal control system of cash receipts).

(c) *Transaction tests.* These are concerned with individual transactions and include compliance and substantive tests, with examination of documentation and arithmetical accuracy.

(d) *Substantive tests.* These are not evaluation tests, but are mentioned here for convenience. They are, in effect, verification tests and are carried out to substantiate the existence, ownership and value of assets and liabilities of a business and to prove the accuracy of profit and loss items. Here monetary values are verified. Where deemed necessary, additional evidence may be obtained in the forms of market reports or financial analyses of the final accounts. This financial aspect of testing items is relevant throughout the whole area of auditing and is dealt with when considering standard audit programmes.

7. Auditing in depth. In order that the auditor may test the efficient working of the internal control system it will be necessary to put into operation the tests mentioned in **6**. For this purpose, the auditor will have to acquaint himself thoroughly with:

(a) the nature of the business and its activities;

(b) the system of book-keeping and accounting;

(c) the duties and responsibilities of the management and staff;

(d) the prevailing system of internal check;

(e) the internal audit, if this is in operation.

How the auditor may obtain the information he requires will no doubt differ from business to business. In some concerns he may be able to obtain network analysis diagrams, flow charts, duties and responsibilities of staff set out in writing, but in other cases he may have to compile his own records from enquiries made. The Institute of Chartered Accountants has divided such work into three stages—*ascertainment*, *testing* and *assessment*—which summarises the work required and the order in which to carry it out.

8. Application of auditing in depth. Having become acquainted with the matters mentioned above, auditing in depth may be applied, whereby examinations are made by probing into the system. Such an examination in depth involves:

> ... *tracing a transaction through its various stages from origin to conclusion*, examining at each stage to an appropriate extent the vouchers, records and authorities relating to that stage and observing the incidence of internal check and delegated authority. For example, verification of a payment to a creditor for goods supplied could be made by examination of a paid cheque which had been drawn in favour of the creditor and crossed "Account payee only".

> Complete verification of this transaction "in depth" might involve the examination of the transaction at all stages including the following documents or records:

> (a) The invoice and statement from the supplier.
> (b) Evidence that the goods had been recorded in the stock records.
> (c) The goods received note and inspection certificate.
> (d) A copy of the original order and the authority therefor.

9. Internal control and management. This term implies that the responsibility for the application of internal control must rest with those in authority within the business itself. The auditor may help, advise and report, but has no power to demand that an adequate system of internal control should exist. The final responsibility remains with those in authority.

In any efficiently controlled organisation there must be clear lines of demarcation between the responsibilities and duties of the staff, and these can only be operated in conjunction with properly compiled records of the various activities of the business and by the circulation of written information as to the duties of the staff.

10. Divisions of internal control. The three recognised divisions of the elements of internal control are:

(*a*) the plan of organisation (with particular reference to the allocation of staff duties);

(*b*) authorisation, recording and custody procedures (including internal check);

(*c*) managerial supervision and reviews (including internal audit).

11. Plan of organisation. The necessity of an adequate plan of organisation has already been mentioned. Such a plan should cover the activities of both management and staff at all levels, stating clearly their duties, responsibilities and their power to authorise various activities of the business. This latter point is of importance since subordinate duties may on occasions have to be varied, which may leave the way open to abuse by those with authority over other members of staff who are not in a position to question directions they receive.

12. Authorisation, recording and custody procedures. Where authorisation, recording and custody procedures are concerned the financial and accounting controls should be such as to facilitate efficient working and at the same time obviate any chance of fraud or error arising.

Here the practical division of duties should be such as to ensure that the internal check system is operating at all stages. Internal check has already been defined as "the checks on day-to-day transactions which operate continuously as part of the routine system whereby the work of one person is proved independently or is complementary to the work of another, the object being the prevention or early detection of errors or fraud".

This internal check involves the need for the work of at least two persons to be conducted, as far as possible, independently. This in itself will involve the division of responsibility in the various procedures whereby transactions are authorised, performed and recorded, and on completion are verified and reconciled independently with pre-ascertained totals or by examination.

13. Managerial supervision and reviews. By *managerial supervision and reviews* is implied that management should constantly review and give consideration to the financial position and financial procedures within the organisation. This may include the use of an internal audit department, but not necessarily so. Budgeting control and standing costing systems greatly assist the working of internal control whereby variances are revealed and investigated. Special reviews of departmental systems may also take place from time to time apart from normal internal audit procedures.

14. Internal audit. Internal audit, as stated above, has been termed "a review of operations and records, sometimes continuous, undertaken within a business by specially assigned staff" and where this exists internal control is greatly facilitated, and may do much to ensure that the accounting systems are efficient and working in accordance with planned procedures.

Before turning to some practical aspects of internal control it is relevant to point out the danger of being so concerned with the system that the end product is overlooked. No two businesses are exactly the same, a set of procedures for one business may be quite unsuitable for another; it requires thought, skill and experience in actual working before suitable methods may be formulated, but in so doing the ultimate gain must be considered.

> For example, one large group of departmental stores, having considered the losses which could arise on stocks, ceased to employ their internal auditors on routine stock checks as the expense involved in payment of salaries for such work considerably outweighed the possible stock losses which might arise.

This is an exceptional case, but it is useful in pointing out the necessity of making the internal control system suit the business rather than organising the business to suit the system.

We can do no better here than to consider closely, but rather more briefly, the procedures outlined by the Institute of Chartered Accountants in their notes on this subject of internal control.

PRACTICAL APPLICATION

15. Classification of sections. The sections involved in the operation of an internal control system can be classified as follows:

(*a*) Overall financial control (*see* **16**).

(*b*) Receipt and payment of cash, including balances held (*see* **17–22** below).

(*c*) Remuneration of employees (*see* **23**).

(*d*) Trading transactions (*see* **24** and **25**).

(*e*) Stock control (*see* **26**).

(*f*) Fixed assets and investments (*see* **27** and **28**).

16. Overall financial control. The proper allocation of work and responsibilities including internal check has been dealt with, but for this to work effectively there must be the following:

(*a*) An efficient accounting system in operation.

(*b*) Adequate supervision with a clear and up-to-date supply of information to management. This would normally involve the preparation of interim statements with, if possible, a system of budgetary control whereby variances from standards are revealed, and reports are made from time to time on various sections of the system.

(*c*) Maintenance of adequate recording and duplicating systems.

(*d*) Efficient staff control, with written directions as to responsibilities and duties of both management and staff.

In this respect care should be exercised to maintain the human touch. For staff control to degenerate into a machine-like system can greatly damage harmonious and willing staff relationships, which can defeat the ultimate object for which the control system is installed.

17. Receipts and payment of cash, including balances held. The systems prevailing with regard to the receipt and payment of cash are covered in the relevant sections of Chapter IV, but certain particular precautions must be taken (*see* **18–22**).

18. Cash receipts.

(*a*) The internal check system once installed must be maintained. This may involve checks at irregular intervals by responsible members of the staff or the internal audit department if there is one. Likewise, arrangements must be made to meet exceptional circumstances, such as staff illness or holidays.

(*b*) The receipt of cash, including the opening of post, must be made under the supervision of a responsible official. An immediate recording of all cash receipts should be made for subsequent checking purposes at a later stage. All cheques, money orders and postal orders should be cancelled on receipt, by means of a stamp with a crossing of "Not negotiable—account payee only".

(*c*) Specific instructions must be given with regard to receipt of cash by cashiers, travellers or otherwise, and the manner in which they are to be evidenced must be stated. For example, receipts should be issued for all cash (as opposed to cheques received) and sealed till rolls should be in operation for cash sales.

19. Control of funds.

(a) Specific instructions must be given to members of staff for the handling of all cash receipts and payments as well as with regard to the recording and checking thereof.

(b) All moneys received must be recorded, cross-checked and banked frequently, preferably daily.

(c) Where cash registers or cash offices are used, definitive instructions must be laid down as to collection intervals and authorised personnel.

(d) Duties as to preparation of bank paying-in slips and actual banking should be stated. Preferably this should be done by two different persons.

(e) Paying-in slips should not be prepared by those receiving and recording cash, and such slips should be checked regularly against the documents recording receipts of cash.

(f) Cash for disbursement purposes should never be deducted from cash received.

20. Balances held.

(a) Specific rulings must be made with regard to the number of cash floats to be held and their amount, including tills and cash desks, as well as petty cash balances for disbursement purposes.

(b) Persons allowed access to balances as mentioned in (a) must be stated and limits imposed as to amount in respect of petty cash disbursements. Rules as to amount and duration of IOUs should be stated, as in certain cases the granting of sums on IOUs may be justified. All petty cash floats should be maintained on the imprest system.

(c) Rules should exist to ensure that cash floats are checked by responsible staff at frequent intervals; rules should also be laid down concerning the safekeeping of moneys retained on the premises out of business hours.

(d) Stated procedures should exist for the handling of funds of employees, such as unclaimed wages, holiday funds, etc.

(e) Bank reconciliations should be required at stated intervals, if possible by a person whose work is independent of the receiving and disbursement of cash. If an internal audit department exists the regular checking of such reconciliations should be required. Whoever is deputed to check the reconciliations should be instructed to examine such exceptional matters as unpresented cheques outstanding for an undue length of time, or any stop-payment notices.

21. Cheque payments. The following are the main headings which should receive attention:

(*a*) Safe keeping, control and supply of cheques.

(*b*) Who may prepare cheques and traders' credit lists.

(*c*) Supporting documents for cheque payments and safeguards, such as signatures for various stages of work, so ensuring no payment of same bill twice.

(*d*) Authorities to sign and limitations as to amount, and rules to obviate the signing of blank cheques in advance or in favour of persons signing.

(*e*) Cheques to be restrictively crossed.

(*f*) Rules to ensure cheques signed in time to obtain benefit of discounts receivable.

22. Division of duties. The size of staff employed may restrict the allocation of duties in such a manner as may be desirable for absolute safety, but as far as possible the following rules should apply:

(*a*) The cashier should not write up accounts in respect of receipts and should not be responsible for the safe-keeping of securities or title deeds of the business.

(*b*) Staff preparing cheques or traders' credit lists should not be cheque signatories, or vice-versa.

23. Remuneration of employees.

(*a*) *Allocation of duties.* The internal check system should be operative at all stages in employee remuneration. The work of making up wages sheets should be sub-divided to ensure that work is both checked and complementary to that of the previous stage. Such duties must be clearly defined and the following matters properly allocated:

(*i*) Authority to engage and discharge employees and fix or change rates of pay.

(*ii*) The recording of all notifications of the foregoing to be dealt with only on receipt in writing, duly initialled.

(*iii*) The method by which employee deductions are dealt with.

(*iv*) Proper time recording (or work recording in the case of piece-work), the records of which should be counter-signed by the foreman.

(*v*) The payment of holiday pay or payments in advance; here, authorisation is important, as is designation of who shall deal with queries arising.

(b) *Payment of employees.*

(i) Proper arrangements should be made for the drawing and encashment of the wages cheque.

(ii) The staff making up wage packets should be different from those preparing the wages sheets, and the right amount of notes and change should be drawn in accordance with the wages sheet.

(iii) The arrangements for payment of wages should include the supervision of a responsible official and payment should be made by a person other than any of those preparing the wages sheet and pay packets. Specific arrangements should be made for dealing with unclaimed wages.

(iv) Special checks should be made at irregular intervals of balances held in wages departments, such as cash floats.

(v) In general, reconciliations should be made explaining the difference between total wages and deductions from one period to the next. Total columns and P.A.Y.E. deductions should be checked with the returns of the Inland Revenue as well as with the P60 forms to be issued to employees.

24. Trading transactions: purchases. The factors to be covered are as follows:

(a) *Authorisation.* Procedures must be laid down to cover the requisition and authorisation of purchase orders. Certain firms should be listed with whom orders are to be placed, having been specified by those with authority to do so. Order forms should be kept in safe custody.

(b) *Receipt of goods.* The flow of goods received from their receipt, inspection, acceptance and transfer to departments, and authority of those concerned should be laid down. The checking of purchase orders against goods received must be arranged.

(c) *Accounting.* Proper allocation of duties must cover:

(i) checking invoices received;

(ii) maintaining a day book system (whether slip system or otherwise) regarding purchases and purchase-returns;

(iii) the writing-up of the ledger accounts and checking of suppliers' statements;

(iv) payment authorisation. Before this is given, the procedures stated (*see* pp. 63–4) must be followed to ensure goods have been properly ordered, duly received and advantage taken of any discounts allowable.

25. Trading transactions: sales. The internal control should cover the following:

(*a*) *Authorisation and recording.*

(*i*) Arrangements to ensure that sales are made at correct prices and under agreed terms of discount or otherwise, and where part-exchanges are allowed correct allowance must be checked.

(*ii*) Authority to accept orders, grant credit terms, and to pass on orders for production or supply.

(*iii*) Proper allocation of duties and authority with regard to issue of invoices or credit notes, the completion of these as to quantities, prices and totals, and their retention, before use, in safe custody.

(*iv*) Procedure to be laid down regarding goods sent on approval, free, or on other terms.

(*b*) *Dispatch of goods.*

(*i*) Authority for dispatch of goods and evidence thereof to be fixed.

(*ii*) Arrangements to be made for examination and recording of goods dispatched by staff other than those concerned with stocks maintenance or invoicing duties.

(*iii*) Procedure laid down for the regular comparison of records of goods dispatched with original orders, dispatch notes and invoices.

(*c*) *Accounting.*

(*i*) If staff numbers make it possible, no sales ledger staff should be concerned with cash records or stock and should not be responsible for sales invoicing or sales staff duties.

(*ii*) If possible separate staff should be engaged on the duties of recording sales and sales returns, of maintenance of customers' accounts, and of preparation of statements to customers. Care should be taken that, when prepared, statements should not be subject to alteration before dispatch to customers.

(*iii*) Procedures to ensure that sales returns, price adjustments and special allowances are operated under an efficient system of internal check.

(*iv*) Where goods are dispatched in an accounting period but not invoiced then, adequate procedures should be in force to ensure that they are invoiced in the next period, and also that the goods held are not shown in stocks of the company if the sale is included in the earlier period.

(v) The proper allocation of authority with regard to arrangements for special terms and discounts (and how these shall be evidenced), the writing-off of bad debts and personnel to deal with customers' enquiries.

(vi) Procedure for the receipt of and dealing with overdue accounts.

(vii) The operation of control accounts on debtors' ledgers, including their regular preparation and review by an independent responsible official when completed.

26. Stock control. Stocks are not only particularly vulnerable to misappropriation, but have also been used as a cover for the payment out of sums of money other than on the stocks purported to be purchased. The procedures involved in internal check may in some cases be quite numerous, especially where various types of stock are held (whether of finished goods, work-in-progress or raw materials).

Each business will vary in its arrangements, and in installing these the use of internal control questionnaires can be most helpful. The following are some of the main items to be considered:

(a) *Receipt of goods.* The procedures to be followed in dealing with goods inward (including the receipt, checking, passing to departments and recording).

(b) *Allocation of responsibility.* The proper allocation of responsibility for the safeguarding and maintenance in good condition of stocks, including stock records authorisation for issues, and regular reconciliation of store records with those of the accounts department. To preserve internal check those engaged on stock-keeping should have no access to stock records in the accounts department.

(c) *Outside stocks.* Procedures with regard to stocks held outside the business and likewise goods held on behalf of others, as to authorisation and evidence required for issues to be made. Stock held at outside warehouses should be most strictly controlled and inspected as the notional holding of such stocks has been the source of serious irregularities.

(d) *Stock-taking procedures.* These are important with respect to independent checks, reconciliation of records, pricing of goods, the intervals at which stocks are taken, including irregular checks from time to time. The "cut-off" procedures to be operated (*see* p. 177).

(e) *Writing off stocks.* The systems to be applied in valuation of stocks and the review of slow-moving or obsolete lines. The issue and receipt of returnable packages, the control of scrap and the authority required for writing-off and disposal of old lines.

27. Fixed assets. The following are some of the main points to be dealt with:

(a) The designation of authority to sanction capital expenditure and in what way this should be evidenced.

(b) The designation of authority to sanction the sale, exchange or disposal of assets, how this is to be evidenced and the internal check regarding this, since it should not be under the authority of one person only.

(c) The maintenance of proper information about all fixed assets acquired by means of accounting records, plant registers, etc., and the arrangements for the physical inspection of such assets. Where assets are transferred to sites, branches, or within a group, the maintenance of adequate records and their checking from time to time independently to ensure that such records are up to date.

(d) The fixing of rates of depreciation or arrangement for revaluation, the authorisation of the staff concerned and the evidence to be supplied.

28. Investments. The internal control concerning these is especially important as they may afford the possibility of misappropriation, more especially by staff in higher-paid grades.

Such arrangements should include the following:

(a) Authority to purchase or sell investments and the evidencing of such authorisation, preferably by staff working apart from cash or documents of title.

(b) The proper recording of all transactions, including the maintenance of records of investments held, the latter to be checked with the accounting records and the actual documents of title (or certificates where held outside), from time to time.

(c) Adequate arrangements to ensure that advantage is taken of rights issues, the due receipt of bonus issues and receipt of relevant share certificates and interest and dividends arising.

(d) The safeguarding of documents of title, with not less than two persons evidencing the safe deposit of such documents, and authorising either access to them or their withdrawal.

AUDIT PROBLEMS OF THE
SMALLER COMPANY

29. Size of organisation. Statement on Auditing U.18 is included in this chapter on internal control, for it is at this vital point that the main problems arise for the auditor.

Difficulties are experienced in the application of auditing principles and procedures because of certain features often present in many companies employing a small number of administrative staff and controlled and managed by a single proprietor or at most by a small number of proprietors. These problems mainly derive from:

(a) substantial domination of the accounting and financial management functions by one person;

(b) limitations in the effectiveness, from the audit point of view, of the system of internal control, rendered inevitable by the small number of employees.

Either or both of these can be present to a significant extent in many small companies. While internal control, including internal check, may be effective in the small company for its primary purpose as a check for management use, the organisation will usually mean that it will be defective as a check on management itself.

30. Conduct of the audit. These limitations in the effectiveness of the internal control from the audit point of view may so reduce its value that the auditors will need to consider extending their audit procedures. This will require them to increase the amount of testing of transactions and to intensify the procedures for the verification of liabilities and assets, including, for example, attendance at stock-taking (Statement U.9) and confirmation of debtor balances by direct communication (Statement U.7).

Despite an extension of detailed audit procedures, it will become necessary to rely to a more significant extent than with larger companies on the representations of management, frequently not directly confirmed by outside evidence, or by opinions of, or records maintained by, other personnel of the company. In these circumstances, the auditors must consider whether their examination of the records of the company, the evidence available to them and their knowledge of all the circumstances affecting the company, are consistent with and support the representations of, management, and provide sufficient evidence on which to assess the reliability of the records. They will have regard to matters such as significant ratios (e.g. rate of gross profit), their knowledge of the scale and scope of the company's operations, the type of business in which the company is engaged and the materiality of the items under examination. While this is a matter for the cautious exercise of the auditors' judgment, it does not necessarily follow that representations of management for which direct confirmatory evidence is not available may not be relied on by the auditors. They must consider whether the surrounding evidence as a whole is consistent with, and sufficient in their judgment to support, these representations.

The auditors' use of the representations of management will not of itself require them to qualify their report, provided such representations are examined critically against all the available evidence. The auditors must judge whether the evidence is consistent with, and is sufficient to support, those representations to their satisfaction in deciding whether or not to give an unqualified report.

31. Procedural points. Some procedural points are mentioned in an appendix to the Statement. These cover the following:

(a) *Accountancy work.* Where accountancy work is also undertaken, it is desirable to separate the accountancy and audit work in order to ensure the objectivity and independence of the audit. Where it is impracticable to separate the two functions, an audit programme should nevertheless be maintained and this should include an audit review on completion.

(b) *Letters of Engagement.* It is advisable for the auditors to submit to their client, and to receive, an acknowledgement of the precise scope of their responsibilities in respect both of the audit and of any additional work to be undertaken.

At the time of engagement, the auditors should explain to the directors management's responsibilities for the preparation of the accounts and for establishing a system of internal control appropriate to the needs of the business (*see* p. 249).

(c) *Internal control letters.* At an early stage in the audit, the auditors should bring to the directors' attention their findings on the system of internal control and possible improvements. In the situation where a director is responsible for most of the records and there is no check on his work, and this is reasonable in the circumstances of the company, a sentence should be included in the internal control letter or in the engagement letter acknowledging the impracticability of a (complete) system of internal control in the particular case, drawing attention to the directors' personal control of the records and stressing the importance which attaches to the effective exercise of this control if records of the company's transactions, from which reliable accounts can be prepared, are to be available.

Where shortcomings in internal control arise because of the small number of employees, the internal control letter, whilst acknowledging this, should if appropriate include suggestions for improvement. In such circumstances, these would frequently take the form of suggestions for strengthening the directors' supervision and control (e.g. by opening the incoming post, recording all remittances received and crossing cheques to the company's bankers, and by inspecting and signing wages sheets).

(*d*) *Letters of representation.* After discussion with the directors at the conclusion of the audit and before signing the auditors' report, a letter of representation on the company's letter heading addressed to the auditors should be obtained. The purpose of such letters is to place on record representations of management on significant matters affecting the accounts, such as the ownership and basis of stating the amounts of assets, liabilities and contingent liabilities. In addition, they act as a reminder to management of their responsibilities. Such letters do not, however, relieve the auditors of any of their responsibilities.

RELATIONSHIP BETWEEN THE INDEPENDENT AND THE INTERNAL AUDITOR

32. Common interest.

On accounting matters the internal auditor and the independent auditor operate largely in the same field and they have a common interest in ascertaining that there is:

(*a*) An effective system of internal check to prevent or detect errors and fraud and that it is operating satisfactorily.

(*b*) An adequate accounting system to provide the information necessary for preparing true and fair financial statements.

33. Fundamental difference of work.

Although the two forms of audit have a common interest in the important matters mentioned in the preceding paragraph, there are some fundamental differences:

(a) *Scope.* The extent of the work undertaken by the internal auditor is determined by the management whereas that of the independent auditor arises from the responsibilities placed on him by statute.

(b) *Approach.* The internal auditor's approach is with a view to ensuring that the accounting system is efficient so that the accounting information presented to management throughout the period is accurate and discloses material facts. The independent auditor's approach, however, is governed by his duty to satisfy himself that the accounts to be presented to the shareholders show a true and fair view of the profit or loss for the financial period and of the state of the company's affairs at the end of that period.

(c) *Responsibility.* The internal auditor's responsibility is to the management whereas the independent auditor is responsible directly to the shareholders. It follows that the internal auditor, being a servant of the company, does not have the independence of status which the independent auditor possesses.

34. Similarity of method.

Notwithstanding these important differences, the work of both the internal auditor and the independent auditor, on accounting matters, is carried out largely by similar means, such as:

(a) Examination of the system of internal check, for both soundness in principle and effectiveness in operation.

(b) Examination and checking of accounting records and statements.

(c) Verification of assets and liabilities.

(d) Observation, inquiry, the making of statistical comparisons and such other measures as may be judged necessary.

The foregoing quotations from Statement on Auditing U.4 (Appendix 2) serves to show that the work of the internal auditor and the statutory auditor may be beneficial in obviating unnecessary duplication of work.

35. Co-operation between statutory and internal auditors. The wide experience of the independent auditor may be of assistance to the internal auditor while on the other hand the latter's intimate acquaintance with the business concerned may be of help to the independent auditor.

Co-operation in planning of the respective audits may save unnecessary work, although the independent auditor must always satisfy himself as to the work carried out by the internal auditor.

36. Procedural co-operation. More specifically, such co-operation may exist in the following matters:

(*a*) The independent auditor may be able to rely to a large extent on the internal auditor regarding the continuous operation of the internal check system and in the reliability he may place on the accounting records.

(*b*) Agreement as to various aspects of the work being carried out only by the internal auditor or together with the independent auditor, such as cash counts and visits to branches.

(*c*) Where the internal auditor so co-operates the independent auditor may accept work done in respect of such matters as the confirmation of customers' accounts, the verification of assets and the audit working schedules prepared by the internal auditor.

Finally, to quote Statement on Auditing U.4:

> The internal auditor's responsibility is to the management and he is in no sense a servant of the independent auditor. It follows therefore that the extent to which the internal auditor can so arrange his work as to be of specific assistance to the independent auditor will depend upon decisions of the management on the scope of the internal audit and the number of staff employed thereon. Consultation between the two auditors, and where necessary with the management, should however ensure that so far as is practicable the fullest possible assistance is available to the independent auditor.

PROGRESS TEST 3

1. Give a definition of internal control.   (2)

2. Define internal check and internal audit.   (3, 4)

3. Has the internal control system any influence on the conduct of the external audit?   (5)

4. What should the auditor do if he is not satisfied with the efficiency of the internal control system?   (5)

5. What tests should be applied to internal control?   (6)

6. With what must the auditor acquaint himself in order to test the efficient working of the internal control system?   (7)

7. Give an illustration of how auditing in depth is carried out.   (8)

8. Is it the auditor's responsibility to ensure that there is an efficient system of internal control?   (7, 8)

9. State the main divisions of internal control. (10)

10. Classify the sections involved in the operation of an internal control system.   (15)

11. State the matters which are necessary for efficient overall financial control. **(16)**

12. What are the essential features of the efficient control of funds? **(19–21)**

13. State the matters which comprise an efficient system of internal control regarding employee remuneration. **(23)**

14. In dealing with purchases, what matters should be specified to preserve a proper system of internal check? **(24)**

15. What are the main divisions of the internal control system affecting sales? **(25)**

16. State the essential features of internal control regarding stocks held. **(26–28)**

17. What matters are of common interest to the internal and external auditor? **(32)**

18. What are the fundamental differences in the work of the internal and external auditor? **(33)**

19. In what ways may co-operation exist between internal and external auditors? **(35, 36)**

SPECIMEN QUESTIONS

1. Outline the purposes and major characteristics of a sound system of internal control.

As auditor how would you determine the effectiveness of such a system? *I.C.A.*

2. What is meant by internal auditing, internal check and internal control? How may the internal auditor and the statutory auditor co-operate and what are the fundamental differences between them? *A.C.A.*

3. Indicate the main considerations which determine the amount of detailed checking to be carried out by the auditor of a limited company. *I.C.A. (E.W.) (Inter.)*

4. On being appointed auditor of a firm for the first year, you find that there is no effective supervision of the cashier and that the cash receipts are not lodged in the bank in total, but are used to make cash payments for purchases and expenses. What are the objections to such methods of dealing with cash and what recommendations would you make to the firm? *A.C.A. (Inter.)*

5. Discuss the main principles of internal check and its advantages to the auditor. Draw up a system of internal check for the sales side of a wholesale supplier. *A.C.A. (Inter.)*

6. Indicate ways in which the work on the audit of a sub-

stantial limited company can be facilitated by the company's own internal organisation and the help of the company's officers. *I.C.A.* (*E.W.*)

7. In addition to the audit required by Statute, many large companies have an internal audit carried out by staff appointed for this purpose.

Discuss, briefly, the fundamental differences between the two forms of audit and the extent to which the statutory and internal auditors can co-operate to their mutual benefit. *A.C.A., I.C.A.* (*E.W.*)

8. What is meant by internal audit and what are the fundamental differences between it and the statutory audit? *A.C.A.*

9. Lapwills Ltd., of which you are the auditor, has decided to dispense with the use of personal ledgers in its accounting system for purchases.

Indicate the matters to which you would direct particular attention in relation to internal control. *I.C.A.* (*E.W.*)

10. "On accounting matters the internal auditor and the independent auditor operate largely in the same field."

"The presence of an efficient internal audit department considerably reduces the responsibilities af the statutory auditor."

Discuss these two statements. *A.C.A.*

11. (*a*) What is the essential difference between what is often termed a procedural audit programme and what is known as a vouching audit programme? In what circumstances should each be used?

(*b*) Set out concisely the principal matters that an auditor needs to consider, whichever programme is used, when deciding on the extent of the audit tests to be made. *I.C.A.* (*E.W.*)

NOTE. Procedural audit programme—test of procedures, internal control, etc., vouching, audit programme—where business too small for effective internal control.

12. What are the principal factors to be considered by an auditor in connection with his review of a system of internal control relating to purchases, insofar as the authorisation and the recording of transactions are concerned? *I.C.A.* (*E.W.*)

CHAPTER IV

Systems Auditing

In dealing with the detailed work procedures to be carried out by the auditor, it should be mentioned first that *in all cases* he should satisfy himself as to the *satisfactory operation or otherwise of the system of internal control, including the internal check system and internal audit* (*if the latter exists*). These have been dealt with in the previous chapter and will only be mentioned here in passing, but their importance as to the amount of work and methods of procedure is of great significance in all matters affecting the detailed work carried out.

In order to afford a simple guide as to the amount of work likely to be undertaken, the following classification is often used in respect of each type of audit:

A class. Organisation with efficient system of internal control, qualified staff and internal audit department.

B class. Efficiently run organisation but with no internal audit department and not so many qualified staff as in *A* above.

C class. A large, or more often, a medium-sized company with an internal control system, not of same standard as in the previous classes and subject to certain weaknesses.

D class. Medium-sized and small companies with little internal control and ineffective allocation of authority.

E class. Small companies with no internal control, and authority mostly residing in one person.

We commence with the audit of the monetary transactions of a business.

CASH RECEIPTS

1. Auditing difficulties and internal check.

(*a*) *Indirect evidence*. In vouching cash receipts, the auditor is faced with peculiar difficulties in ascertaining the true position. If certain transactions are kept out of the double entry system entirely, it is difficult for the auditor to detect this and often evidence can be obtained only of an indirect nature.

It is essential, therefore, that the auditor should first ascertain that a system of internal check is operating efficiently and he should be careful to obtain a list of books maintained with regard to all transactions.

(*b*) *Rough cash book*. In the previous chapter, the maintenance of a rough cash book in respect of daily cash receipts was mentioned. Such a book should be checked exhaustively by the auditor with the main cash book kept by the cashier, ensuring that each day's takings agree with the daily receipts shown in the main cash book, as, in the event of teeming and lading (*see* 3(*b*)), or if the cashier is misappropriating funds, these two books would not agree on one or more occasions. Likewise, the paying-in book should be checked to the main cash book to ensure that cash entered as received is duly banked.

2. Cash sales.

(*a*) *Necessity of internal check*. The auditor should satisfy himself as to the system of internal check in operation, as cash sales afford easy opportunity for misappropriation of funds.

Where cash registers are used, the daily till rolls should be checked with the total day's takings shown in the cash book.

(*b*) *Checking receipt counterfoils*. Where receipts are handwritten in conjunction with the use of tills, the counterfoils should be checked with the daily summaries of sales staff, and these daily summaries should be checked with the cash takings shown in the cashier's analysis thereof. The daily totals of the receiving cashier's cash books should be cross-checked with the main cash book, agreement being reached in conjunction with credit sales bankings of the amounts banked according to the paying-in book counterfoils.

3. Credit sales.

(*a*) *Non-use of receipts*. As under the Cheques Act 1957, receipts are not usually issued in respect of cheque payments, the auditor cannot normally verify the receipt of cheques in respect of credit sales, although by consulting the sales ledger accounts he may obtain information of assistance in this respect. Furthermore, it is possible to detect any misappropriation of funds where teeming and lading takes place by examination of the rough cash book maintained on postal opening in conjunction with the main cash book.

(*b*) *Teeming and lading.* This is the term used to express the method of misappropriation of cash received by falsifying records of subsequent transactions. (In Scotland, the expression "carry over frauds" is used.)

If, for example, a cheque for £100 is received in full settlement of a debt by A, this may be misappropriated. A's debt, therefore, is still shown as outstanding. At a later date, a cheque for £100 is received from X. In order to not leave A's accounts in debit for too long a period, which might cause the other staff concerned to send a reminder to A, the more recent cheque from X is entered as received from A and is posted to A's account. X's account is now shown as unpaid, and the foregoing procedure may be repeated. The most simple method has been illustrated in order to make clear the procedure. It may be complicated by the splitting of amounts over various accounts, and more than one misappropriation may be in the course of being covered at the same time.

(*c*) *Prevention of teeming and lading.* To ensure that such fraud is not practised, the following procedures should be carried out:

(*i*) Examine the make-up of the sales ledger balances, making special inquiry into accounts which appear to be falling into arrear, particular attention being given to accounts where credits have been entered for payments on account where previously the debtor has settled his accounts regularly.

(*ii*) Obtain the original paying-in slips from the bank and compare the details thereon with the entries in the cash book, to see if any remittances have been split, part having been credited to one account and part to another.

(*iii*) If receipts for remittances are issued, check the counterfoils with the entries in the cash book, noting differences in the amounts and dates of entry.

(*iv*) Send statements of account, prepared under the vision of the auditor's staff, to all debtors, asking for confirmation of the amounts shown to be outstanding to be sent direct to the auditor.

4. Vouching receipts.

(*a*) *Checking receipt counterfoils.* In some businesses or organisations, such as charities, receipts are still issued for moneys received, whether by cheque or otherwise. In this case the auditor should vouch a number of these with the main cash book. It is realised that it is not difficult for a receipt to be issued for an amount and a different amount to be entered through a carbon on to the receipt counterfoil, nevertheless, should the copy differ from the amount in the cash book, the auditor might be considered to have failed in his duty had he not checked any such counterfoil receipts. The dates as well as amounts should be checked and the top copy of all cancelled receipts should be required to be attached to the counterfoils.

(b) *Collection of moneys by travellers*. Where travellers have authority to collect payments, their counterfoil receipts should be checked with the counterfoil paying-in books, where they bank away from the main office, as well as with the subsequent entries in the main cash book. Their returns should be checked with the main cash book where moneys are handed in at the main office.

(c) *Discounts allowable*. Where discount is allowed, the possibility of entering discount against debtors' accounts instead of cash received must be considered. Therefore, the internal check regarding this should be ascertained, showing who agrees these with debtors, and a list of such discounts allowable should be obtained where there is no one overall policy regarding such discount. The rates of allowance should be tested with a number of accounts. The total of discounts allowed should be checked to the relevant account after casting the columns in the cash book.

5. Rents receivable. Briefly, the auditor should:

(a) inspect agreements and counterparts of leases, note terms as to rents receivable and repairs to be carried out;

(b) ascertain that all rents have been received, carefully checking all deductions from amounts receivable;

(c) vouch rent books. A number of tenants' rent books should be vouched and tests made of total collections made with amounts handed in by collectors on particular dates;

(d) investigate all payments in arrears for any undue length of time and enquire into un-let properties to see whether amounts are being paid but are not being paid into the business;

(e) where agents collect rents, examine their accounts and vouch with amounts received.

6. Investment income. Separate accounts should be kept for each investment held, with particulars as to dates on which regular income is due. The auditor should:

(a) note that all dividends and interest due are received;

(b) in respect of fixed interest or dividend stocks, check the amount received with the nominal value of the stock and the rate receivable;

(c) where no fixed rate is receivable, examine counterfoil dividend warrants;

(d) note that when stocks are sold *ex div*, the dividends are duly received, and likewise where stocks are purchased, *cum div*.

7. Sales of investments. The brokers' sold notes should be vouched with the amounts received. (*See* I.C.Q. and S.A.P. for investments and income (p. 136–7).)

8. Interest received.

(a) *Interest on bank deposits.* Where interest is received on bank deposits:

(i) vouch with bank statement;

(ii) check the amount in accordance with the agreement, although fluctuating rates may complicate this.

(b) *Interest on loans.*

(i) When the loan is *unsecured*, the agreement should be inspected for particulars of amounts receivable.

(ii) In the case of a loan *secured by a mortgage*, the deed should be inspected for particulars of amounts receivable.

INTERNAL CONTROL QUESTIONNAIRE

CHEQUES AND CASH RECEIPTS

1. Is mail opened by at least two persons under the supervision of a responsible official?

2. Are cheques, postal orders, and money orders crossed when mail is opened?

3. Can unopened letters, other than private mail, go direct to any member of staff?

4. Is a list of receipts prepared when the mail is opened?

5. Is this list checked by someone other than the cashier?

6. Is a reconciliation prepared daily between the total cheques and cash received and total credited to debtors?

7. Are receipt books used by the cashier for all cash received in the form of notes and coin?

8. Are such receipts numbered?

9. Is a record kept of serial numbers of such receipts?

10. Are unused books kept securely and recorded on issue?

11. Can receipts be issued by the cashier for special purposes?

12. Is there a control to prevent fictitious discounts being allowed to customers?

13. Are all cash and cheques received banked daily?

14. Are there proper safeguards with regard to taking monies to and from the bank?

15. Are the paying-in slips prepared by the cashier? If not, by whom?

16. Are duplicate paying-in slips received stamped by the bank?

17. Are bank debit advices notified to anyone other than the cashier?

18. Are bank reconciliations prepared regularly?

19. Has the cashier any connection with debtors' control or writing off bad debts?

20. Has the cashier any connection with the keeping of the nominal ledger?

21. Has the cashier any connection with the purchases day book or creditors' ledger?

22. Does the cashier make journal entries or originate any entries otherwise than through his own book?

23. Are rent, dividends, interest received, etc., controlled so that if not received on due dates it would be observed?

24. Does the cashier count and balance his cash daily?

25. Are the staff permitted to cash personal cheques?

26. If so, are the cheques made payable to "Cash"?

STANDARD AUDIT PROGRAMME

CASH RECEIPTS

(A) *Cash received via post*

1. Ascertain that procedures are laid down for post opening and are complied with.

2. Check items in rough cash book to main cash book and ascertain that staff have initialled when they have compared these.

3. Verify with remittance advices, etc., so as to ensure correct amounts entered.

4. Check entries with counterfoil receipts where issued, ensuring that counterfoils are complete numerically, with spoiled or cancelled receipts attached.

5. Check that copy paying-in slips are stamped and initialled

by the bank with the cash books, identifying a number of individual items in the rough cash book and the paying-in slips. Investigate thoroughly any alteration in the paying-in slips.

(*B*) *Cash sales*

6. Check items from original sources, e.g. till rolls, cash desks, into cash book (recent periods), noting that reconciliations are prepared daily.

7. Test a number of copy cash receipts with summaries.

8. Verify that copy cash receipts are numerically complete and that any spoiled or cancelled receipts are attached to copies.

9. Ascertain that receipts are controlled on issue and that those used in the period have been currently supplied.

10. Check that staff have initialled on comparison of till roll and cash sales summaries with cash book and paying-in slips.

(*C*) *Miscellaneous income*
(Cash received by travellers and salesmen.)

11. Note serial continuity numbers on copy receipts and agree these with receipts books issued.

12. Test-check casts on travellers' receipt books of amounts paid in.

13. Check items from original cash received documents prepared by travellers to cash book.

14. Rents received, etc.: check income with original documents as to amount receivable and when due.

15. Investment income. (This is dealt with under Investments, p. 49.)

16. Check postings to nominal ledger.

CASH PAYMENTS

9. Main cash.

(*a*) *Cheques Act 1957*. Since the Cheques Act 1957 has been in force, it is not usually the practice of businesses to give receipts in respect of amounts received. The auditor has often, therefore, to rely on a returned cancelled cheque as evidence of payment, for (in accordance with the Act) paid unendorsed cheques may be accepted as evidence that the payee named therein has received the amount stated on the cheque. Two points to notice are:

(*i*) the cheque must be unendorsed, i.e. a cheque payable to A must not be endorsed over or transferred to B by A;

(*ii*) it is not regarded as evidence of payment in respect of any particular matter, i.e. it only states that the sum shown has been paid over and not the consideration for which it was given.

(*b*) *Returned cheques as evidence of payment.* If cheque payments are made with the crossing "account payee only", they cannot be endorsed to third parties, and the auditor can accept them as evidence of payment to the party concerned, and where further evidence is available as to why the payment is made, such as he will obtain in vouching the bought day book and in dealing with the bought ledger accounts, then the returned cheques are sufficient for his purposes. Where, however, cheques are not restrictively crossed "account payee only", then the auditor may request the production of an actual receipt where he considers this necessary, e.g. in the acquisition of assets. When accepting unendorsed paid cheques, these should be checked with names and dates shown in the cash book (*see also* p. 48).

(*c*) *Omission of bought ledger.* Numerous businesses, to obviate the work in writing up bought ledger accounts, now retain invoices received during each month until a specified date and then make out cheques in settlement of all invoices received. In such cases the auditor should request that the returned cheques should be attached to the invoices and statements concerned; in this way he may obtain:

    (*i*) *evidence of the payment;*
    (*ii*) *evidence of the consideration* for which payment is made.

In respect of trading purchases, the auditor will, in vouching the day book, ascertain the consideration for which such payments are made; the same will also apply with regard to the system mentioned above, but where payments of a different nature are made, such as in respect of assets acquired, the auditor must satisfy himself that the consideration was in respect of the requirements of the business, with proper authorisation and initialling by those responsible.

INTERNAL CONTROL QUESTIONNAIRE
CHEQUES

(*A*) *Issue*
    1. Who has the authority to sign cheques and are there any limits to their authority?

2. Are all cheques drawn "to order" and marked "a/c payee only—not negotiable"?

3. Is a mechanical cheque signer used, if so, what system prevails to prevent its unauthorised use?

4. Are cheques and traders' credit lists prepared on production of authorised vouchers or cheque requisitions, and are these vouchers produced to the signatories?

5. Who carries out the checking process, and are all such vouchers cancelled?

6. Are all cheques drawn, despatched immediately? If not, who has control over these and how are they dealt with?

7. Is there a fixed date in each month when payments are made?

8. Are payments on account made, and if so, who authorises these?

9. What control is maintained over the issue of cheques?

10. How are cancelled cheques controlled?

11. Are subsidiary bank accounts fed only from the main account and not by miscellaneous items?

(B) *Recording*

12. Who keeps cash payments records?

13. Who has authority to open bank accounts?

14. On whose authority can bank loans or overdrafts be arranged?

15. How are transfers between banks controlled?

16. Has the paying cashier any control over sales, purchases, or nominal ledgers, sales invoices or credit notes, or other funds?

17. What system is in operation to ensure that full advantage is taken of interest receivable?

18. How frequently are bank reconciliations prepared?

19. Who prepares the reconciliations?

20. Do receiving and paying cashiers have access to bank statements?

21. Are the bank reconciliations checked and initialled, and if so, by whom?

STANDARD AUDIT PROGRAMME

CHEQUE PAYMENTS

(A) *Generally*

1. Verify items—including those in payment of purchases invoices selected for testing the internal control system—a number covering the most recent period.

2. Note properly authorised signatories on cheques tested.

(*B*) *Payments for goods and services*

3. Obtain invoices and bills rendered and ascertain that these have been properly checked and authorised, ensuring that all such documents have been properly cancelled.

4. In respect of traders' credits, trace items selected for testing to copies of lists of suppliers stamped by bank, and verify amounts of cheques made in settlement of totals on lists.

5. Verify that all discounts have been taken advantage of.

6. Examine suppliers' statements with bought ledger accounts.

7. Verify all payments in respect of wages, salaries, petty cash with their relative records, such as wages sheets, etc.

8. Ascertain that cheque numbers agree with control records of books issued. Enquire as to any missing numbers, ensuring that spoilt or cancelled cheques are properly cancelled.

9. Check transfers to petty cash or other books maintained.

10. Test-check additions and test-check balances brought forward.

11. Check postings to nominal ledger, including control accounts.

(*C*) *Bank reconciliation*

12. Check all payments and receipts with bank pass sheets near end of period and for selected periods covered by reconciliations during the period under review.

13. Ascertain that all items in the reconciliation of the previous period are cleared in accordance with the reconciliation.

14. Verify all contra items in both cash book and pass sheets.

15. If possible, check through items in reconciliation through to next period.

16. Verify that reconciliations are made at regular intervals throughout the period.

17. Obtain bank certificate direct from bank (clients' permission necessary for this) requesting bank to give details of all accounts held by them.

10. Employees' remuneration.

(*a*) *Internal check.* The internal check system is vital regarding employee remuneration (*see* p. 34).

(*b*) *Auditor's duties.* The procedures are as follows:

(*i*) Ascertain that the wage sheets have been initialled by those compiling them and by comptometer operators for checking of additions. The whole to be signed by a responsible official.

(*ii*) Test-check rates of pay of new staff and alterations in rates with the written authorisations.

(*iii*) Check items with the P.A.Y.E. cards.

(*iv*) Check deductions with records applicable to individual employees, e.g. holiday funds, savings fund, etc.

(*v*) Test-check additions on wages sheets and check the totals to the relevant accounts and the total with the control account, if kept. The total amount should be checked with the amount drawn from the bank.

(*vi*) Check the method of dealing with uncollected wages, whether immediate recording is made of them, and examine the records maintained in respect of these.

(*vii*) The auditor should also attend the actual payment of workmen from time to time.

11. Time-rate workers. The auditor's duties are to make the following queries:

(*a*) The clock cards of a selected number of employees should be called for and checked.

(*b*) The rates of pay should be checked and, in conjunction with the hours worked, the gross wages should be agreed. (Overtime working should also be checked.)

12. Piece-work employees.

(*a*) *Production tickets.* These should be examined in respect of a selected number of workers, noting that any deductions in respect of defective working have been made.

(*b*) *Piece-work rates.* These should be obtained and in conjunction with the production tickets, the gross pay should be checked, subject to any minimum rates of pay which may supersede the piece-work earnings.

INTERNAL CONTROL QUESTIONNAIRE

WAGES AND SALARIES

(*A*) *Generally*

1. Who has authority:

    (*a*) to engage,

    (*b*) to dismiss employees?

2. Are history cards maintained of all employees, containing the employee's signature?

3. Who authorises (*a*) overtime and (*b*) general and individual increases in pay?

4. Is such authority always evidenced in writing?

5. Is the person with such authority separate from the salaries personnel?

(*B*) *Recording*

6. What records are maintained in respect of:

    (*a*) time work,
    (*b*) piece-work?

7. How are piece-work quantities checked and how is partly finished work dealt with at the end of each week?

8. If job cards or piece-work cards are produced, who authenticates these?

9. Are those authenticating records on the shop floor independent of the wages department?

(*C*) *Payroll*

10. Who prepares the payroll?

11. Is the work so allocated that no one aspect of the compilation of the payroll is carried out completely by one member of staff?

12. Is the payroll checked periodically with the history records as to names and details of payment?

13. Is this carried out by a person independent of those preparing the payroll?

14. Are all calculations and additions checked independently?

15. Are all sections of the work duly initialled by those carrying them out?

16. Is the payroll authorised by a responsible official when completed and before the cheque is drawn?

(*D*) *Payment of wages*

17. Is the cheque drawn for the gross or net amount of the wages?

18. If the gross wages are drawn, how is the cash in respect of deductions dealt with?

19. Is the exact amount of notes and coins drawn from the bank?

20. Are those who distribute wages independent of those who prepare the payroll?

21. Is authority in writing required before a representative of an employee is paid?

22. What arrangements are in force to deal with any disagreement as to the amount paid over?

(E) Unclaimed wages

23. When are unclaimed wages recorded?

24. Who retains unclaimed wages?

25. How long are they retained before being paid into the bank?

26. Who authorises the payment of unclaimed wages?

27. Is written authority required before payment to a representative of an employee *(see* 21 above)?

28. Do both payer and payee sign before payment is made?

(F) P.A.Y.E. and National Insurance

29. Are Inland Revenue standard cards completed, or is another system operated authorised by the Inland Revenue?

30. Is a control operated in respect of gross earnings, income tax, and pension funds in conjunction with employees' P45 forms?

31. How often are payments made in respect of P.A.Y.E. and National Insurance contributions?

(G) Pensions

32. Are all pensions approved by the board?

33. By what methods are payments made and are receipts obtained?

34. Are any written authorisations in use in respect of receipt of pensions for others. If so, what action is taken to ensure the existence of the pensioner?

STANDARD AUDIT PROGRAMME

WAGES AND SALARIES

(A) Generally. Test a selected number of employees from both wages and salaries sections as to:

1. Engagement and termination of employment, verifying that written authorities in both cases have been countersigned.

2. Verify salaries and wages are according to agreements and check that any changes have been properly authorised.

3. Where wages are paid on time basis, check with clock cards or time sheets.

4. Where wages are paid on production, check with piecework or job slips and note work is properly countersigned.

5. Verify that overtime working is properly authorised.

6. Verify authorities for deductions completed by employees and check deductions with summarising records.

7. Check gross wages on to P.A.Y.E. cards. In certain cases these may be dispensed with—only final figures being supplied to the Inland Revenue from salary sheets—in this case check on to the sheets.

8. Check wages and salary sheets as to calculations, additions and cross-casts to net pay.

9. Verify that salary sheets are initialled by those dealing with the various stages of preparation and checking and that the whole is signed by a designated responsible official.

10. Check totals to control accounts.

(B) *Unclaimed wages*

11. Test the entries in the unclaimed wages book with entries on the wage sheets.

12. Test a number of items to ensure that payments have been authorised and receipts obtained from employees, or if paid to representatives of employees, that proper authority was given to receive payment.

13. Ensure that both payer and payee sign the book.

14. Examine a number of signatures for receipt of payment with original signatures on commencement of employment and enquire into any names appearing frequently on the records.

15. Ascertain that balances of unclaimed wages are banked regularly in accordance with the directive.

(C) *Salary and wage deductions*

16. Ascertain that such deductions are paid over to the funds concerned and that P.A.Y.E. payments are paid over to the Inland Revenue. (This check is greatly facilitated if the gross wages and employers, national insurance and the deductions are recorded on a control account basis.)

17. Ascertain that agreement is made from time to time between gross wages and deductions for income tax and national insurance with employees' records.

PETTY CASH

13. Importance of petty cash. The term *petty cash* suggests that it is of minor importance viewed from the point of view of the complete audit. Such an idea, however, is quite erroneous. Often quite large balances are maintained, especially where the petty cash system may be used for the purpose of paying out weekly wages in cash for certain departments in a business.

14. Internal check and petty cash.

(*a*) *System involved.* Before proceeding to the actual audit of the petty cash book and its relative balance of cash in hand, the auditor should ascertain that an adequate system of internal check is in operation covering such matters as the following:

(*i*) The duties of the petty cashier being both properly designated and defined.

(*ii*) Ensuring that the person in control should, if at all possible, be someone other than the main cashier and that he should be a responsible person. The latter point signifies that the responsibility of dealing with loose cash should not be allocated to someone in such a position that it is likely to constitute a temptation. Being considered of an unimportant nature, petty cash duties are sometimes allocated to young members of staff who, not always due to dishonesty but sometimes owing to lack of experience, are inclined to become confused in their task and the temptation then arises to put through fictitious entries to make the figures agree.

(*iii*) The only receipts entered into the petty cash book should be in respect of cheques cashed for petty cash purposes.

(*iv*) The method applied should be that of the imprest system, with the amount of the float being specified.

(*v*) Sums should be paid out only on production of a petty cash voucher duly initialled and limits up to which certain members of staff may obtain payment without further authorisation should be laid down.

(*vi*) Where the granting of sums on IOUs is allowed, rules governing this should be specific and also the length of time for which such IOUs may be left outstanding should be fixed. IOUs should only be granted in respect of advances for expenses to be incurred on the firm's business.

(*vii*) A responsible official should be required to check and initial the petty cash book and vouchers at irregular intervals, the length of time within which such checks should be made being stated.

(*b*) *Adequacy of system.* Before proceeding to the audit of the petty cash book, the efficacy of the prevailing internal check system should be investigated. If this appears to be satisfactory, then much detailed checking work may be avoided. If, however, the auditor is not satisfied with the system being operated, then it may be necessary to vouch a large number of items (although discretion would still be exercised as to trifling amounts). In such circumstances the auditor should report the position to his client, making recommendations as he thinks necessary and pointing out his inability to assess the true position due to the unsatisfactory state of affairs.

Where the internal check system is sound it should only be necessary to check items at random or to *block vouch* certain specified months throughout the year.

(c) *Vouching.* When vouching, it will be necessary to examine supporting vouchers where required, e.g. receipts for office purchases of any material amount, and also to note that identifiable initials are appended as required. Vouchers should be examined up to the date of the checking of the petty cash in hand.

Where transfers are made to further subsidiary books, such as additional petty cash books or postage books, these should all be checked and the books examined and balances counted as necessary. Balances of stamps in hand should not be overlooked as in some types of business these may be quite large.

15. Petty cash control account. In some cases a petty cash control account is maintained in the impersonal ledger, the details of the petty cash book being posted therefrom to the various accounts, otherwise the totals of analysis columns are posted from the petty cash book direct to the various accounts. After casting the petty cash book, total columns and checking cross-casts, the various postings should be checked into the relative accounts. The amount shown as the petty cash balance in hand in the book should be agreed with the amount shown in the impersonal ledger control account where such an account is maintained, as well as with the figure shown on the trial balance.

The verification of the balances of petty cash and the bank balances are dealt with in Chapter VII.

INTERNAL CONTROL QUESTIONNAIRE

PETTY CASH AND POSTAGE

A list should be prepared in the first instance in respect of all floats stating:

    (a) petty cashier,
    (b) amount of float,

(c) purpose for its maintenance,

(d) method of reimbursement.

1. Does petty cashier control other funds, in particular receipt of cash?

2. Has the petty cashier sole access?

3. Are vouchers issued on all payments and signed by recipient?

4. Is a limit fixed on the amount of disbursements, if so, what is the limit?

5. What system is operated in respect of IOUs?

6. What limits as to amount and duration of time are fixed on IOUs?

7. Are employees allowed to cash cheques, and if so, is any limit imposed?

8. Is the petty cash book regularly examined by a responsible official and initialled? Is such an examination carried out on the event of each reimbursement?

9. If such examinations take place, by whom are these done?

10. Is the float reasonable bearing in mind the purposes for which it is maintained?

11. Is a proper double entry system operated with an imprest amount as the balance?

12. Is the float reasonable in view of the use involved? (In the case of airmail and parcel post the float may be comparatively large.)

13. Is the postage book examined and the balance checked periodically by an independent member of staff?

14. Who authorised the reimbursement of the float?

15. What system of control is in operation regarding the franking machine?

STANDARD AUDIT PROGRAMMES

I. PETTY CASH AND POSTAGE

1. Vouch the petty cash expenditure including items of recent date (i.e. after end of period), ensuring that external payments are supported wherever possible by external receipts.

2. Ensure that all petty cash payments have been properly authorised, and cancelled, and are within the prescribed limits.

3. Ensure that the books have been properly initialled in respect of periodic examination and balance checks.

4. Check transfers to any subsidiary petty cash books and to

postage book, ensuring that balances held are reasonable having regard to the purpose for which they are held.

5. Examine postage books to see that amounts of expenditure are of reasonable amounts.

6. Check costs and balances carried down of petty cash book.

7. Check postings to nominal ledger.

II. CASH AND PETTY CASH ACCOUNTS

1. Make surprise counts in respect of cash and petty cash and postage balances held. Such balances may include luncheon vouchers and balances on staff funds. Where more than one balance is held, all should be produced at the same time.

2. Ascertain that all cheques held have been crossed in favour of the client "a/c payee only—not negotiable".

3. Check totals of cash counted with balances on books—which should be properly written up to date. The "Cash" cheques drawn for petty cash or other funds should be checked through to date (i.e. after the period under audit).

4. Ascertain that cheques held and counted are subsequently met.

5. Note IOUs and enquire where any appear excessive or are outstanding an undue period of time.

6. Verify stock of unused receipts, check with control records and printers' invoices.

PURCHASES

16. Purchases.

(a) *Slip system and bought day books.* It has been mentioned when dealing with cheque payments that bought day books are frequently dispensed with, settlement being made direct from invoices and suppliers' statements received. Nevertheless, the information for which the day books are maintained is still necessary, namely, the total purchases made, and where necessary, their proper analysis.

Where the original form of day book is maintained, the total column should be cast and individual sub-totals checked to the main total for the period under review. Similarly, cross-casts of analysis columns should be checked.

If slip systems are in operation, then the required information as to total purchases should be checked in the main cash book which will be necessarily analysed as to payments in respect of trading transactions. In this case the invoices will be vouched in conjunction with the cash book records.

(b) *The settlement of invoices.* This usually takes place after the month end, so care should be taken to ensure that all invoices awaiting payment are included in the outstanding liabilities. A list of such unsettled invoices should be requested by the auditor. The goods received books or copy goods inwards notes for the period prior to the end of the financial period should be checked to ensure invoices have been received and are properly included in the list of unsettled items, if not already paid.

(c) *Vouching invoices.* Vouching invoices involves checking them in order to establish their authenticity for inclusion in the records of the business. This involves checking:

(*i*) that each invoice was properly addressed to the client;

(*ii*) the date of the invoice;

(*iii*) that each invoice was in respect of goods normally dealt in by the client—if this is not so, then special attention must be paid to its authenticity;

(*iv*) the accuracy of the document as to extensions and total;

(*v*) that those responsible for the work of checking the invoice in its various aspects and passing it for payment have duly appended their initials;

(*vi*) that the goods or services have actually been received by the business;

(*vii*) that the order was properly placed in the first instance;

(*viii*) that items in respect of capital expenditure or expense items are properly segregated from trading purchases.

(d) *Goods received book.* The goods received book is an important link, enabling the auditor to ensure that goods have been received for which invoices have been rendered and a number of items should be checked into the goods received book. In some cases, copy goods received notes may be attached to the invoices, so facilitating checking.

(*i*) *Inclusion of invoices.* It is of the utmost importance to ensure that goods included in stock figures at the end of the financial period should be shown as having been purchased, since the inclusion of such goods would inflate stock values so erroneously creating a greater profit, or reducing a loss. Care should be exercised, therefore, to ascertain that goods shown as received in the goods inward book towards the end of the period are checked with the purchases day book. Invoices received after the closing date should also be examined as these may reveal a delivery date prior to the close of the period. If a sound system is not in operation in respect of goods received, suppliers' delivery notes should be examined, or stock records, as to date of inclusion in stock.

(*ii*) *Unsatisfactory records.* The additional work involved for the auditor may still not lead to an entirely satisfactory conclusion and his dissatisfaction with the state of affairs should be pointed out to the client, stating his non-acceptance of responsibility with respect to the stock figures concerned.

(*e*) *Forward purchases.* In some cases businesses may enter into contracts for the purchase of goods at a later date at a fixed price. Such deals are termed "forward purchases". If the contracts are abnormally large and it is anticipated that loss may arise which would materially affect the company's position after the balance sheet date, then provision should be made against such losses. If this is not done, then the auditor should qualify his report accordingly.

17. Purchases returns.

(*a*) *Ensure credit received.* Where goods purchased may be returned to suppliers, it is essential that a proper system should be in force for ensuring that due credit is received. Without such a system the credit receivable may afford an easy source for misappropriation of funds.

(*b*) *The internal check system.* Such a system should cover such matters as notification by the returning section to the accounts department in duplicate, the second copy being returned to the department of origin duly initialled. If the original invoice for the goods has not been settled, the returns outwards note should be attached and the amount deducted. If the invoice has been settled, then a credit note is obtained from the supplier to which the returns outwards note is referenced, while the credit note should be entered in the purchases returns book and attached to the invoices awaiting settlement to ensure deduction from the subsequent amount due.

(*c*) *Audit procedure.* The auditor should check the returns outwards book maintained by the dispatch department with the purchases returns book, and the credit notes should be vouched with the purchases returns book and those attached to the invoices awaiting settlement to ensure deduction from the subsequent settlement.

18. The bought ledger. Before dealing with the final aspect of the purchasing side of the business, it should be repeated that a considerable amount of work may be obviated if the system of internal check regarding the compilation of the bought ledger is sound.

(*a*) *Postings.* They may be checked into the ledger from the purchases and purchases returns day books, but this should only be necessary on a test basis, and provided the internal check system is considered satisfactory, it may be omitted, assuming that a control account is maintained. Opening balances should be checked in from the list compiled in the previous period and casts within the ledger may be checked, but in any case the balances should be examined and the total creditors' figure checked with the control account.

(*b*) *Suppliers' statements.* These should also be examined in conjunction with suppliers' statements received after date as well as cash payments made after date. The checking of the suppliers' statements constitutes a further safeguard with regard to the proper inclusion of invoices for goods received and shown as stock, as mentioned previously. If debit balances are shown on any accounts, these should be enquired into as they may signify payments in respect of invoices withheld for the same reason.

(*c*) *Transfers.* If these are from the bought ledger to the sales ledger, or vice-versa, where amounts are set off, they should be carefully examined and the documents arising regarding them should be vouched.

INTERNAL CONTROL QUESTIONNAIRES

I. PURCHASES AND PURCHASES RETURNS

(*A*) *Ordering*

    1. Is there a separate buying department?

    2. Are all purchases orders executed in writing?

    3. Who authorises requisitions to the purchasing department?

    4. Are official orders issued and copies:

        (*a*) sent to goods inwards bay,

        (*b*) retained in accounts department?

5. Are such orders serially numbered and are there safeguards against misuse?

6. Is an agreed list of suppliers with discount details retained?

7. Who authorises orders and what are their authority limits?

(*B*) *Receipt of goods*

8. On receipt of goods:

    (*a*) Are arrangements made for inspection?

    (*b*) Is a goods inwards book made up from goods inwards notes properly referred to purchase order?

    (*c*) Is a copy of goods inwards note sent to:

        (*i*) Buying Department,
        (*ii*) Accounts Department?

(*C*) *Return of goods*

9. What documents are prepared on return of goods?

10. What arrangements are made to ensure:

    (*a*) Accounts and Buying Departments are notified?

    (*b*) Credit notes are received?

    (*c*) Whose duty is it to ensure that due credit is received?

(*D*) *Passing invoices for payment*

11. On receipt are invoices compared with:

    (*a*) original orders,
    (*b*) copies of goods inwards notes?

12. Are invoices properly authorised for payment as to:

    (*a*) price,
    (*b*) quantity,
    (*c*) extensions and total?

13. Who finally authorised payment?

14. Are arrangements made for copy invoices to be stamped "Copy" on receipt?

15. Are invoices passed for payment duly stamped to prevent double payments?

II. PURCHASES LEDGER

1. What system is maintained, e.g.:

    (*a*) handwritten,
    (*b*) mechanised,
    (*c*) slip system?

2. How is it ensured that employees' purchases are charged to them?

3. What system is in operation as to inter-branch or inter-company purchases?

4. Is a purchases ledger control account maintained?

5. How often is the control account prepared?

6. Are suppliers' statements compared with accounts, and how frequently is this done?

7. Is the ledger independently examined from time to time by someone other than the ledger clerk?

STANDARD AUDIT PROGRAMMES

I. PURCHASES AND PURCHASES RETURNS

1. Verify that invoices are supported by copy requisitions, copy orders and copy goods received notes.

2. Test to ensure that authorities for requisitions, orders, and passing for payment, are within agreed limits.

3. Verify that credit notes have proper supporting documents, e.g. copy goods returned notes.

4. Check extensions and additions of invoices.

5. Ascertain that purchases other than for resale are properly allocated to nominal accounts.

6. Test the numerical sequence of goods received and returned, and enquire as to missing numbers.

7. Inspect goods received or returned notes not matched to invoices or credit notes and enquire as to any outstanding for an undue length of time.

8. Check casts and cross-casts of purchases day book, and ensure that pre-lists are prepared for control accounts prior to passing to ledger clerks or cashiers department for payment.

9. Check postings to nominal ledger.

10. Check control accounts.

II. TRADE CREDITORS

1. Select a number of accounts and check these on the list of creditors, ensuring that all *comparatively* large accounts are checked, ensure that balances are composed of identifiable amounts, and if not so, compare with suppliers' statements.

2. Test-check a number of the accounts with suppliers' statements.

3. Test additions of the accounts and check out balances to list.

4. Check addition of list of balances and total with control account, ensuring that control accounts are regularly maintained.

III. ACCRUALS

1. Obtain list of amounts due and payable and check this with nominal ledger. Each account in the ledger should be scrutinised and any items not shown on the list which should be brought into account should be inquired into.

2. Where necessary, invoices, statements, or other documentation should be examined as to amounts due and not settled.

3. Invoices and payments received and made after date should be examined to ensure all liabilities are brought into the correct period.

4. Compare list of outstanding liabilities with list on previous year's audit file, enquiring into any relevant differences.

SALES

19. Cash sales. For the method employed in dealing with cash sales, *see* p. 47.

20. Credit sales.

(a) *Vouch invoices.* Where sales day books are maintained, a number of copy sales invoices should be checked with the entries and the casts of the book may be tested, the total of the sales being checked to the sales account. The usefulness of checking a large number of copy invoices is doubtful since carbon copies are in any case not completely reliable evidence of the original.

(b) *Slip systems.* Often, as in the case of bought day books, a slip system may be used whereby copy sales invoices are filed in numerical order and machine lists are prepared. Here again, a number of copy invoices may be checked with the lists and the totals should be checked to the sales account.

(c) *Audit in depth.* Various systems may prevail, the auditor should therefore test the system from its origin, the original order received, to its conclusion, the dispatch of the sales invoice to the customer. Normally a number of copies are made of the invoice and distributed to the various departments concerned, e.g. the store, the dispatch department (two copies, one for retention, one to be used as a delivery note) and the accounts department.

(d) *Omission of sales ledger.* Where the type of business

transacted allows, the copy invoices may be filed in separate folders for customers. When payment is received the invoices are removed and filed. Likewise, where credit notes are issued these are put into the customer's folder. Such a system obviates the use of a sales ledger but is only practical where customers pay regularly and mostly in full. In such a case the auditor must ascertain that an efficient control account system is in operation as there is the obvious possibility of the removal or loss of copy invoices. (The control accounts are made up from the total of sales invoices and credit notes and of the cash received, the remaining total balance representing the total of the unsettled accounts still in the folders.)

(e) *Sales control account*. The method to be employed by the auditor will vary according to the system, but in all cases he should pay particular attention to the control accounts maintained—if by any chance they are not kept, he would be wise to compile his own. Where sales ledgers are maintained, he should check a number of day book postings to the ledger, in addition to the work outlined above.

(f) *Value Added Tax*. Where VAT is charged, it should be ensured that this is properly segregated.

(g) "*Abnormal*" *sales*. If sales other than those of a normal trading nature are made, such as sales of plant, etc., these should be checked to ensure that they are not included in the sales figures but are dealt with through the relative asset accounts.

(h) *Auditing procedures*. To ensure that the *cut-off* procedures are properly operated at the end of the period a number of invoices should be checked with the goods outwards book to ensure that the goods shown as sales have actually been dispatched. If they have not been sent out then they may still be regarded as sales, but it must be ascertained that they are not included in the stock held at the end of the period, so inflating any profit figure. This matter is also dealt with in Chapter X, regarding stock.

21. Exclusion of goods not actually sold. It is essential to ensure that goods shown as sales in accounts have actually been sold for although the relative purchases may be shown against them, the gross profit will automatically be included in the accounts. The inclusion of items in respect of sales transactions not finally completed should, therefore, be avoided. Such transactions frequently fall under the following headings:

(*a*) *Goods on sale or return.* Where separate records are maintained in respect of goods sent out on the understanding that they may be returned if not wanted, no difficulty should arise regarding their being excluded from normal sales, but if such goods are debited in the ledger accounts of prospective purchasers and are credited on return, it will be necessary to check the records of goods dispatched and returned with individual accounts.

It will also be necessary to request that details of goods held by customers be compiled, which should be reconcilable with the records mentioned above. The sum involved must then be excluded from the sales account and trade debtors' figures and the goods concerned valued at cost or as otherwise advisable.

(*b*) *Goods on consignment.*

(*i*) *Change of location only.* Where goods are sent on consignment for sale, the transaction only constitutes their transfer from one place to another, no sale being concluded until the agent has disposed of them.

Such goods should therefore be included as stock and not sales, properly valued, but with the addition in this case of the expenses involved in dispatching them to the agent, and with any expenses incurred by the agent.

(*ii*) *Elimination from accounts.* If such goods on consignment are debited to the agent concerned, whether at cost or otherwise, then it should be ascertained that a corresponding entry is made to eliminate the debit and that no figure is included with that of the normal sales. If a consignment account is kept and the goods at cost shown as a deduction from the normal purchases, then the figure on the consignment account plus charges involved in the transaction may be shown as a stock of goods on consignment figure.

(*iii*) *Goods received for sale.* Where such goods are received by the client, as consignee, for sale, then these should not appear within the double entry system, any charges incurred in respect thereof being debited to the consignor's account.

22. Hire purchase sales. There are various methods of dealing with hire purchase sales which are covered in accountancy textbooks. The main concern of the auditor should be to ensure that only profit on that part of the contract already carried out should be included in current profits.

(*a*) *Provision against unrealised profit.* If full credit is taken in the year of sale for the cash price of the contract, the auditor should ascertain that a provision against unrealised profit is created in respect of profit taken on instalments not due. Where cash received during the period is brought into the accounts, the outstanding amount in respect of the contract should be reduced by the profit element in order to supply the figure for the value of the stock out on hire to be brought into the accounts. In any case, only such interest as refers to the period being dealt with should be taken as profit earned.

(*b*) *Examination of controls with accounts.* A number of the hire purchase contracts should be checked with the details shown on the hire purchasers' accounts in the ledger. The balances on the accounts should be examined and a note taken of those in arrear, care being taken to ensure that any in arrear, where goods have been repossessed, are taken out of the schedule of hire purchase debtors and transferred out as bad debts, after crediting the value of the amount received or receivable on disposal of the goods.

23. Forward sales. In certain trades, contracts are entered into for delivery of goods at a future date at an agreed price. Although a valid contract exists, nevertheless it is advisable for the auditor to ensure that no profit is taken into account before the delivery date, especially in view of the fact that often large sums are involved in such forward commitments. Where part of such goods have already been delivered, however, a proportionate sum may be brought in.

24. Returnable packages. The method prevailing with regard to returnable packages should be examined. Various systems are operated but whichever is used it should be sufficiently effective to reveal the stocks held both by the company and in the customers' hands. Where a lesser figure is allowed on return than originally charged, there can be no objection to taking the difference as a profit when containers are dispatched. Care must be taken to see that the full amount allowable on return for containers in customers' hands is provided against where the full amount has been debited to the debtors' accounts.

25. The sales ledger. As with the bought ledger mentioned above, the work of the auditor will be influenced considerably by the effectiveness of the internal check system prevailing.

(a) *Verification of balances*. After checking in the opening balance from the previous period, it should not be necessary to check many postings from the day books and cash book to the ledger, but the casts should be tested and very particularly the makeup of the balances outstanding should be examined, note being taken of increasing balances where amounts are paid at intervals on account. Likewise, the age of the balances should be noted. Each balance should be ticked down to the new period and checked with the list of debtors to be agreed with the control account. Notes against accounts may be made regarding any queries as to length of time outstanding and any balances which may be considered to be bad debts or against which a provision should be made. (*See also* p. 129 as to Verification.)

(b) *Journal postings*. Any special posting from the journal should be checked, likewise any transfers between the bought and sales ledgers, and the documents arising in respect thereof should be vouched.

INTERNAL CONTROL QUESTIONNAIRES

I. SALES AND SALES DEBTORS

(A) Goods dispatched

1. At what stage does accounting control first arise? (Normally this would be on receipt of order, but it may vary according to the business concerned.)

2. What record is compiled on receipt of order?

3. Are all orders approved before being passed for execution by a person independent of the sales department?

4. Are records compiled under 2 above duly referenced on completion of order and are checks made regularly to ensure completion of orders, and are any outstanding orders investigated after a certain period of time?

5. Are there a number of dispatch centres and are procedures similar in all cases?

6. What records are compiled in respect of goods dispatched? Are the records numerically controlled?

7. Are dispatch staff entirely independent of sales department staff?

8. How are dispatch notes referenced to relevant sales invoices and who is responsible for this? Are such documents initialled by the person responsible?

9. What procedure is in operation to ensure that all dispatch notes are duly covered by sales invoices?

(B) *Sales returns*

10. What records are compiled on return of goods from customers or claims in respect of short delivery or incorrectly priced goods?

11. Are records as in 10 above prepared by persons independent of the sales ledger and cashiers' departments?

12. Are such records filed consecutively, and are such documents matched with credit notes?

13. Is the person responsible for carrying this out independent as in 11 above, and also independent of the dispatch and control of goods?

14. Is investigation made as to any numbered documents unmatched?

II. SALES INVOICES AND CREDIT NOTES

(A) *Invoices—generally*

1. How are sales prices:

    (a) ascertained,
    (b) authorised?

2. Who authorises trade discounts and what are their limits of authority?

3. How is such authority evidenced?

4. From what sources is information supplied for the preparation of sales invoices?

5. Are those preparing sales invoices independent of staff dealing with:

    (a) acceptance of orders,
    (b) dispatch of goods,
    (c) cash receipts?

6. Are all invoices pre-numbered and controlled?

7. How many copies of sales invoices are prepared and to whom are they distributed?

8. Is the use of copy invoices for original sales obviated by the use of suitably marked copies?

9. How are invoices cancelled, altered, or marked "NO CHARGE", dealt with? Who authorises these?

10. In the case of cancelled invoices what action is taken to ensure that the goods are retained in the business?

11. Are sales invoices referenced to sales orders or estimates and the goods dispatched book?

12. Are sales invoices checked as to:

(a) price,
(b) calculations and additions,

by someone other than the person(s) preparing them?

13. Are reconciliations made between sales invoices and issues from stock, and if so, how often, and by whom are these made?

14. Is any statistical data in respect of sales checked with actual sales? Whose duty is it to do this?

(B) *Invoices—sales of a special nature*

15. What system prevails in respect of goods sent on consignment?

16. What system is in operation in respect of inter-company sales (if any)? Who authorises the rates of uplift on such sales?

17. What systems are in operation in respect of:

(a) staff sales,
(b) sales of scrap?

18. If VAT is charged on sales, is this properly segregated, and are adequate records maintained?

(C) *Credit notes*

19. What sources supply the information for the preparation of the credit notes?

20. Are credit notes prepared by someone other than staff engaged on:

(a) receipt of cash,
(b) maintaining the sales ledger,
(c) maintaining goods returned records?

21. Are all credit notes referenced with goods returned records?

22. Are extensions and totals checked, and are all credit notes authorised? Both these functions should be carried out by a person independent of those preparing the credit notes and goods returned records.

23. Is authorisation carried out by a responsible official, and is the official independent of such work as:

(a) sales ledger preparation,
(b) receipt of cash?

24. What system prevails to ensure adjustment of any sales commission disallowed on return of goods?

III. SALES LEDGERS

1. Are sales ledger staff independent of those recording the receipt of cash?

2. Does the system provide for an independent preparation of information, e.g. pre-listing, before information is passed to sales ledger personnel for processing?

3. Are control accounts maintained in respect of each sales ledger, and how often are such control accounts prepared?

4. Are the control accounts prepared by personnel independent of those maintaining the ledgers?

5. How often are statements sent to customers? Are these sent to all customers including those with credit or nil balances?

6. Are such statements prepared by staff other than those maintaining the ledgers?

7. Who authorises terms of trade and discount allowance, and how is this evidenced?

8. At what intervals are ledger balances examined for action to be taken regarding balances outstanding longer than the normal period?

9. Is special attention paid to accounts where amounts are paid on account?

10. Is such an examination carried out by staff other than those engaged on:

    (a) maintaining the sales ledger,
    (b) receipt of cash?

11. What procedure is operated for the collection of outstanding debts?

12. Are queries relating to outstanding accounts dealt with by staff other than those maintaining the ledgers?

13. What rules apply to the removal of ledger sheets?

IV. BAD DEBTS

1. What evidence is supplied to justify the writing-off of bad debts?

2. Is the approval of a responsible official required before any debt may be written off?

3. Is the responsible official independent of those maintaining the ledgers and those dealing with the receipt of cash?

4. What system is in operation to ensure that any subsequent payments received are properly received by the business?

5. How is any bad debts provision compiled?

STANDARD AUDIT PROGRAMMES

I. SALES AND SALES RETURNS

(A) Sales

1. Test a number of recent transactions relating to sales shown on records completing sales, such as copy goods dispatched notes or completion orders.

2. In conjunction with the transactions investigated, verify these with originating documents, such as customers' orders, contracts or correspondence, ensuring that orders are approved.

3. Continuing with the transactions investigated, obtain the relevant copy sales invoices and check prices charged with independent evidence, such as price lists, tenders, etc.

4. Test-check calculations and additions on copy sales invoices. (This is in the nature of a safeguard for the auditor, as such copies may be falsified.)

5. Test a number of items with stock records to ensure deduction from stock, particularly items near end of period.

6. Check sales analysis.

7. Test-check postings to sales ledger.

(B) Sales returns

8. Verify a selected number of items with the evidence giving rise to their issue.

9. Check with goods dispatched records and ensure full numerical sequence maintained.

10. Verify that all credit notes have been properly authorised by an official engaged other than in maintaining the sales ledger or dealing with cash receipts.

11. Check extensions, additions, and prices. In the latter case, with original invoices, enquire into any difference. Check analysis of credit notes.

12. Where goods have been returned, check these with stock records.

13. Check postings to sales ledger.

II. TRADE DEBTORS

1. Examine a number of accounts chosen from various sections of the ledger, in consecutive order, and check these on to list of debtors.

2. Examine evidence of any inter-ledger accounts or inter-sales and purchase ledger transfers.

3. Note age of accounts and check these with analysis of age of accounts if kept, and ascertain the likelihood of settlement in cases of doubt.

4. Note any accounts showing payments on account and investigate these as to any teeming and lading or as to credit-worthiness of the debtor. (This will necessitate tracing back to original paying-in slips—*see* p. 48.)

5. Examine discounts and allowances and enquire into any items which appear exceptional or excessive.

6. Obtain a list of bad debts written off and scrutinise a number of these, also examine payments in respect of credit balances. Ensure that all have been properly authorised.

7. Ensure that the system is adequate and functioning properly in respect of sending monthly statements and pursuing overdue accounts.

8. Compare the debtors to credit sales ratio with previous periods and enquire as to reason for any material difference.

9. Test-check additions in the sales ledger and check down balances and on to list of debtors.

10. Check totals of balances (debit and credit) to control account. Ascertain that control accounts are regularly maintained.

11. Obtain confirmation of debtors' balances. (*See* p. 129.)

26. The journal. There is a tendency to avoid the use of a journal containing details of extraneous items and no objection can be raised to this where the documents arising in respect of various adjustments are referenced to the various ledgers concerned.

For certain matters, however, the auditor should request that a journal, or its equivalent, with supporting vouchers, should be used, transfers direct between various accounts being deprecated as transfers may easily be made between revenue and capital accounts. Adjustments on accounts should be dealt with *via* the journal, in particular regarding allowances made. Such allowances granted to customers or others must be examined carefully by the auditor, since if a sum of money should be misappropriated, the matter might easily be concealed by the credit to the account of an allowance or discount.

Any allowances shown in accounts should therefore be properly dealt with through the journal or other book kept for the purpose, supported by records properly authenticated.

27. The nominal ledger.

(a) *Sub-division*. The nominal ledger may be further sub-divided by the keeping of a private ledger, where accounts may be maintained of a nature not to be made readily available to members of staff.

(b) *Examination of accounts*. The items comprising the postings to this ledger will have been vouched at their origin, but in certain cases the information contained within accounts will necessitate further investigation. For example, the postings in respect of directors' salaries will have been vouched in the cash book, but whether the amounts paid are in accordance with directors' agreements will need authentication by consulting the audit notebook, where details of such agreements should be shown.

In addition to checking the postings and casting the various accounts, the auditor should examine their contents. Any transfers between accounts here should be journalised with authenticating documents.

(c) *Pre-payments and accruals*. When examining the accounts, adjustments required due to pre-payments and accruals will be apparent, and it will be necessary to check these. This aspect of the work is dealt with in Chapter VII concerning the verification of balance sheet items. (For S.A.P. *see* p. 68.)

28. Statistical sampling in auditing.

Statistical sampling is not used for the great majority of audits. Its usefulness, however, is apparent on certain sections of work where the size of the audit justifies its application in saving both time and expense, and also makes possible the proper use of statistical methods.

Such sections of work would include the testing of purchases invoices or the checking of quantities and values of stock items, as it is essential that items dealt with should have an equal chance of selection and be of an homogeneous nature.

Those who require a fuller treatment of this subject will find it dealt with in Taylor & Perry's *Principles of Auditing*, Leslie R. Howard, nineteenth edition, Macdonald and Evans Ltd.

PROGRESS TEST 4

1. When dealing with detailed aspects of the audit, what is the first matter to which the auditor should pay attention? (1)

2. Why is there unusual difficulty in the auditing of cash receipts? (1)

3. Why is it essential that a rough cash book should be maintained? (1)

4. Is there any usefulness in checking counterfoils of receipts issued? (2)

5. What is implied by the expression "teeming and lading"? (3)

6. How may teeming and lading be prevented? (3)

7. Why is discount allowed of particular interest to the auditor? (4)

8. State the audit procedures involved in rents receivable and investment income. (5, 6)

9. Of what importance is the Cheques Act 1957, to the auditor? (9)

10. In what way is the auditor's work influenced by the omission of bought ledgers? (9)

11. Enumerate the procedures required in auditing the work involved in employee remuneration. (10–12)

12. What specific points should the auditor pay attention to when auditing the wages paid to (a) time-rate workers (b) piece-work employees? (11, 12)

13. What matters of internal check should operate regarding petty cash? (14)

14. "Petty cash is not of great importance and therefore little attention should be paid to it when auditing." Criticise this statement. (14, 15)

15. In what ways is the auditor's work influenced by the use of slip systems instead of bought day books? (16)

16. To what points should the auditor pay attention when vouching invoices? (16)

17. Why is the goods received book of particular importance to the auditor? (16)

18. Why should the auditor be particularly concerned with purchase returns? (17)

19. When sales day books are omitted, in what way does this influence the work of the auditor? (20)

20. What are "cut-off" procedures? (20)

21. Why are "cut-off" procedures of vital concern to the auditor? **(20)**

22. What goods should the auditor pay special attention to, so as to ensure that they are excluded from stock? **(21)**

23. What should the auditor insist upon with regard to inter-account transfers? **(25)**

SPECIMEN QUESTIONS

1. Explain what is meant by a "carry over" fraud.
How would you, as auditor, endeavour to detect such a fraud?
What internal check procedures would you advocate in order to minimise the risk of this type of fraud?

2. (a) Summarise briefly the provisions of the Cheques Act 1957. *I.C.A.*

(b) Indicate the extent to which routine auditing procedure was affected by this legislation. *A.C.A.*

3. How would you verify the following items appearing in the cash book of a limited company:

(a) Agents' and travellers' commissions.
(b) Customs duties paid.
(c) Directors' expense allowances.
(d) Rent received? *I.C.A. (E.W.)*

4. Detail the points which you consider would render a voucher inadequate for the purposes of the audit of a limited company's accounts. Give two examples of inadequate vouchers and detail the procedure you would adopt to verify the items in the accounts to which these vouchers relate. *A.C.A. (Inter.)*

5. State the advantages and disadvantages of "test-checking" and describe what factors must be taken into consideration by an auditor when deciding upon the extent of the "test-check" to be made. *A.C.A. (Inter.)*

6. Having been appointed auditor of East Coast Engineers Ltd., a company employing large numbers of men both on time rates and on piece-work, state the procedure you would adopt in test-checking the calculation and payment of wages. It may be presumed that an adequate system of internal check is in force. *I.C.A.*

7. A manufacturing company, of which you are the auditor, employs some 250 persons. The factory workers are paid weekly. About forty are paid on an hourly basis and the remainder at

piece-work rates. Management and office staffs are paid monthly.

State the steps you would take to check the payroll and the wages records.   *I.C.A. (E.W.)*

8. You wish to provide your audit staff with practical guidance as to the matters that they should include in their enquiry into, and observations of, the arrangements made by clients with regard to the safe custody, control and recording of cash received.

Draw up a form of questionnaire suitable for this purpose. *I.C.A. (E.W.)*

9. In the course of your audit of the accounts of a limited company you find that:

(*a*) Forward contracts are made for the supply of particular materials.

(*b*) The purchases ledger contains a number of debit balances. State concisely what inquiries you would make in each case. *I.C.A. (E.W.)*

CHAPTER V

Mechanised Accounting

MECHANISED ACCOUNTING

Although mechanised systems have basically similar methods of use, nevertheless there are slight variations in their operation and design; it is essential, therefore, for the auditor to acquaint himself personally with the system which he is to audit.

1. Installation of system. If he is consulted on the installation of the system at the outset, valuable co-operation may exist between the auditor and client: the system may be applied not only for the efficient running of the business but also to assist the auditor in carrying out his duties, so eliminating work in unnecessary checking. For example, often an additional carbon copy can be taken of various aspects of the work, such as pre-lists of ledger postings, which may be used for audit purposes.

2. Vital need of internal check. The danger in the installation of mechanised systems is to be so concerned with its efficient and economical working that the matter of an internal check is over-looked. The auditor should therefore pay particular attention to this aspect of the internal control system, and if satisfied in this respect, and with regard to the arithmetical accuracy of the records (which may be proved by means of control records), then he may concern himself more particularly with vouching from prime documents direct to ledgers.

Control systems must constitute a form of internal check and not merely rely upon a control account to prove the mechanical accuracy of the machine. Work should be suitably sub-divided amongst staff, the most common illustration being that of the pre-listing and totalling of invoices by one operator and the posting of these by another.

3. All-purpose machines. Using an all-purpose machine for illustrative purposes, the pre-listing and totalling of sales invoices should be carried out by one operator, possibly on a separate adding/listing machine, these then being passed to the machine operator who in one operation prepares the ledger account and statement at the same time as compiling the figures for the control account. A method of *double pick-up* is operated whereby the recording of the opening balance is checked, affording a safeguard against the bringing forward of an incorrect balance and by throwing out a nil figure at the end if correct. The figure for the total amount of postings, which is stored in the machine, should agree with the original pre-list, the total figure being used for inclusion in the sales account in the normal ledger.

From this it may seem that the arithmetical accuracy of the figures should not be in doubt. The auditor should therefore be more closely concerned with the items making up the pre-lists. Similar processes apply with regard to the posting of purchases invoices and the recording of cash items.

4. Sub-division of work. A particular type of error likely to arise is that of the mis-posting of items. Because of the use of code numbers this is more likely to arise than under manual methods, and from the auditor's point of view, is more difficult to detect, for despite the seriousness of the error, the details may be put through the whole system, whilst at the same time relevant control accounts would still agree. The sub-divison of work should do much to obviate this, whilst it also serves to emphasise the attention the auditor should pay to original records.

5. Variations in the system. Should the system be varied in any way, the alteration should be fully examined by the auditor. The method employed in the correction of errors should be ascertained. Where operators are allowed to do this, there is considerable danger of *defalcation*, and the auditor should request that an adjustment journal be maintained. If this is not kept he should ascertain whether every adjustment is verified at the time of the adjustment by a responsible official. Furthermore, the work entailed in maintaining an adjustment journal could be kept to a minimum by the filing of relevant documents or slips in respect of adjustments made.

6. The danger of fraudulent manipulation. It is felt that fraud may be facilitated by the use of mechanised systems. This should not be the case provided suitable safeguards are instituted. Some of these have been mentioned, others arise from the nature of system itself:

(a) The rigid application of internal control and check systems.

Where "general purpose" machines are used by one operator, an internal check system must be laid down at the commencement and strictly maintained.

(b) The difficulty of alterations of records. To alter records may mean the reproduction of complete sheets, but on the other hand some machines can be manipulated regarding total figures.

(c) The necessity of collusion where a sound system of internal check prevails. This type of fraud would necessitate the manipulation of such an area of the whole system that access would be difficult to obtain.

(d) Likewise, where systems are properly installed and audited, it would require considerable knowledge by those likely to perpetrate such fraud whilst not engaged on the actual work. Where such systems have been in operation for some time, however, it is possible to gain such a knowledge.

SPECIFIC AUDIT DIFFICULTIES

In the Institute of Chartered Accountants' publication, *Mechanised Accounting and the Auditor*, a section was devoted to "Specific audit difficulties". Although no longer forming part of the handbook its usefulness warrants mention here.

7. The elimination of books of prime entry. Slip systems have been mentioned earlier (*see* p. 63). Original documents are utilised, avoiding the use of day books.

If documents are numbered serially, the number may be used for cross-referencing purposes with ledger accounts and otherwise. If these are suitably pre-listed and totalled and the resulting batches of documents are again serially numbered, the tracing back of items should be facilitated. Likewise, the totalling of such batches for the purpose of sectional balancing is advantageous.

It follows that the operation of efficient filing systems is essential for the subsequent checking of records.

8. The use of code numbers. These may be used extensively in machine accounting systems and clients' staff may experience no difficulty in identifying them as they are familiar with them through constant use. The auditor, on the other hand, may find his work made difficult because of the lack of narrative, particularly in the checking of nominal accounts.

Whilst there is no easy remedy for this, the auditor's work may be facilitated as follows:

(*a*) On the commencement of his work he should acquaint himself with the system under which the code references are applied. Code numbers are usually allocated on a specified basis and broken down under various sections.

(*b*) He should be supplied with clearly referenced lists for his use on the audit.

(*c*) In particular instances, he should request that the narrations should be appended to entries such as those in certain nominal ledger accounts. The advantage to the client should be pointed out. Some more obvious entries, such as those in the sales account, need not be in narrative form.

(*d*) Specially designed stationery with headings showing the content of each document should be advocated.

9. The composition of ledger balances. From the auditor's standpoint, the composition of ledger account columns is most important. Where mechanised systems are used, there may not exist an easily identifiable method of applying debits against credits. This may cause serious difficulty in analysis of the makeup of balances when the auditor is concerned with:

(*a*) bad and doubtful debts;

(*b*) the veracity of the amount shown as outstanding;

(*c*) the constitution of nominal ledger accounts where transfers are put through from one account to another.

The auditor has the advantage here when requesting his client to show the undermentioned matters; he can point out the danger inherent in leaving balances in an inexplicable state. He should request therefore that the items should be cross referenced by code symbol to the items on the other side of the account. It should be part of the normal accounting procedure to identify the composition of balances at relevant dates.

The Institute's recommendation covers the employment of *query* or *credit control* staff to be employed on this where the amount of the work involved warrants it.

10. Absence of normal ledger accounts. For the systems to be employed where payment is made direct against documents, *see* p. 63.

It is obvious that for this system to prove satisfactory not only from the auditor's point of view but also in the interest of effective working, there should be efficient filing, the maintenance of control accounts, and, where the "complexity and value of the transactions are considerable", the maintenance of normal ledger accounts.

11. Misuse of accounting terms. Where control accounts are maintained, it should be ascertained that they constitute control accounts in the accounting sense, and do not merely prove mechanical accuracy (*see* p. 83).

Because of the method of operation of these machines, the terms *debit* and *credit* are sometimes used in ways likely to lead to misunderstanding. It really rests with the auditor here to make himself so thoroughly acquainted with the system that he can make recommendations regarding its operation which will obviate any possible misunderstandings.

PUNCHED CARD ACCOUNTING

12. Differences from all-purpose machines. Punched-card accounting systems differ fundamentally from the all-purpose type of accounting machine, for this is similar to a typewriter in the way that it prints the information at once on to the final records, whereas punched-card accounting machines, whilst finally printing the information fed in, in the first instance only produce holes at intervals on a card.

13. Punching on information. The holes punched may be read from the card since the cards are pre-printed and sub-divided under various headings. This would only be used for examination purposes, however, since it can only be done slowly, and the punching may be checked much more quickly and efficiently by means of a verifier.

14. Verifying the punching. As the whole system is mechanised from the first punching of the information on the cards, it is essential that the original information shall be punched correctly. To check this, the only human activity, the cards pass after their first punching, to a second operator who, from the original documents, re-punches the cards. Any difference in the punching is revealed by two round holes being punched over the original oval hole. It is not necessary, however, to examine the cards visually, as, when put through the sorter a coloured card will automatically be inserted where any difference arises. In some cases the verifier when finding a card punched differently, will automatically lock, so revealing the difference.

15. Automatic sorting and printing. Once the holes have been punched on to the cards, the cards may be sorted into any order required for statistical as well as accounting purposes.

The actual printing of invoices, statements, etc., is carried out automatically by the tabulator when the cards are put through the machine.

16. Auditor's duties. From the foregoing it is apparent that, being automatic, whatever is put into the machine in the first place will go right through the system, e.g. printing the sales invoice to the monthly statement and to the total sales for posting to the sales account and for the sales control account. The auditor should, therefore:

(*a*) verify the soundness of the internal check system, ensuring that the *original* documents are dealt with by the machine operators;

(*b*) ensure that the lists of documents are pre-listed and added, e.g. on a simple adding/listing machine;

(*c*) ascertain that all original punching is checked from the original documents on the verifier;

(*d*) select a number of cards and request the operator to put them through the machine, thereby testing the punching with the information revealed on the original documents;

(*e*) test all sections of the work as in (*d*) above. The auditor should concern himself particularly with the purchases and sales control accounts, the balances shown on the control accounts being compared with the list of balances;

(*f*) check the nominal ledger accounts in detail.

PROGRESS TEST 5

1. What is the particular danger likely to arise on the installation of a mechanised system of accounting? **(2)**

2. Illustrate briefly the work carried out on an *all-purpose* accounting machine. **(3)**

3. When machine accounting systems are varied, what should the auditor do? **(5)**

4. Is there greater chance of fraudulent manipulation by the use of machines than by normal accounting methods? **(6)**

5. In what ways may the danger of fraud in the use of mechanical systems be avoided? **(6)**

6. Mention specific audit difficulties encountered in the use of machine accounting. (7–9)

7. How may the difficulties mentioned in 6 above be overcome? (7–9)

8. In what ways does punched-card accounting differ from the other types of machine accounting? (12)

9. Explain briefly the methods employed in punched-card accounting. (13–15)

10. What are the auditor's duties regarding punched-card accounting? (16)

SPECIMEN QUESTIONS

1. In auditing the accounts of a company having a fully mechanised accounting system (but not utilising punched cards) what are:

(a) The main difficulties peculiar to such a system?

(b) The safeguards available to overcome these difficulties?

(c) The special points to which attention should be directed? *I.C.A.*

2. The accountant of a company has asked you, as auditor, to examine his draft instructions for the operation of a system of mechanised accounting (not punched cards) which is being installed in the sales ledger section.

Set out the matters to which you would give your particular attention both as regards internal control and the conduct of the audit. *I.C.A.* (*E.W.*)

3. Peanuts Ltd., of which company you are the auditor, has converted its sales ledgers from manual to machine methods, employing code numbers in place of names and descriptions.

You are required:

(a) To indicate the difficulties you would expect to meet as the result of the change.

(b) To state how the difficulties might be overcome.

I.C.A. (*E.W.*)

4. A limited company of which you are the auditor has recently introduced keyboard accounting machines for the sales ledgers.

State the main points to which you would direct attention when examining the system of internal control. *I.C.A.* (*E.W.*)

5. Describe in detail the procedure you would adopt in the

audit of the purchase day book and bought ledger of a company employing a mechanised system of accounts. *A.C.A.* (*Inter.*)

6. It is not infrequently stated that the institution of a system of mechanised accounts increases the possibility of fraud. State the arguments for and against this statement. *A.C.A.*

7. You are auditor of a company which carries out a large volume of small transactions and, at present, has a staff of six book-keepers who keep a manual set of books. Your client asks you whether their system should be mechanised and you are required to draft a report stating the factors to be borne in mind when making a decision. *A.C.A.*

8. Discuss:

(*a*) Modern trends in auditing practice.

(*b*) The contention that the installation of a mechanical accounting system will increase the possibility of fraud. *A.C.A.*

9. Discuss briefly the special features which arise in the audit of accounts kept by a punched card system. *I.C.A.* (*E.W.*)

10. Explain the special problems with which an auditor is confronted when dealing with punched-card accounting records and indicate the steps he should take to meet them. *A.C.A.*

CHAPTER VI

Electronic Data Processing

The first part of this chapter provides an overall assessment of the work involved in dealing with computer-based systems from the auditor's point of view; the second part gives a summary of the two Recommendations of the I.C.A. concerning this subject.

1. Co-operation with management. The established use of computers means that auditors must know the procedures involved when auditing their output and investigating their control. In this chapter, some acquaintance with computer techniques is assumed. The methods outlined are of general application; in practice it would be necessary for the auditor to acquaint himself fully with the particular installation concerned.

Wherever possible, the auditor should be in close consultation with the management from the installation of the machine. He may then request the incorporation of various checks which may be expensive to add later. Experience may necessitate certain alterations later, but these can be minimised by early co-operation with management.

In the first instance, the auditor should seek to gain an overall picture of the system either operating, or to be operated, and to do this he should request the client to supply him with:

(*a*) any data outlining the system that may be presented by the company installing the system on its installation, or that may be given to new staff;

(*b*) flow charts—if these have not been prepared by the client, the auditor may find it most useful to compile his own;

(*c*) designations and names of all staff engaged on the various phases of the work;

(*d*) the instruction manual given to staff engaged on the various stages.

PROCEDURAL CONTROLS

A computer will, subject to breakdown, give the answer required of it; the likelihood of error or fraud will arise from:

(*a*) the feed-in of incorrect information;

(*b*) incorrect programming.

2. The auditor and internal control. Commencing with procedural controls, the auditor will be concerned with internal control in general and internal check in particular.

The auditor should ensure the efficient operation of the internal control by seeing that the system provides for:

(*a*) the control of all input by a section devoted to this (if at all possible);

(*b*) the control section to be responsible for ensuring that the designated flow of work is processed and that input is authentic;

(*c*) operators having no access to computer files and programmes. Test runs should be the job of operators and not programmers;

(*d*) proper authorisation of all programme alterations by a responsible official;

(*e*) input data not being altered by operators, any queries being referred back to the control;

(*f*) operator's duties to be, if possible, interchanged, subject to safeguards as work passes from one operator to the next.

3. Control section and log book. The control section should, if possible, be separate from staff engaged on the working of the computer. If such a section exists, the auditor's work may be greatly facilitated if he is satisfied as to the effectiveness of the operation of the section. It should be the duty of the staff to reconcile output with information supplied and also to maintain the computer records. This includes the maintenance of a log book. The information contained in the log book should reveal that:

(*a*) correct programmes are used with relevant files;

(*b*) no unauthorised alterations are made to programmes;

(*c*) reconciliations are made with manual totals prepared prior to input.

The auditor should examine the log book, which may be kept in a printed control form, and ensure that it is properly maintained.

4. Original input data control. As computers will only supply accurate information, if accurate information is fed in, the strictest control should be observed to ensure that input data is correct. Such control will involve the use of mechanised devices as mentioned in the previous chapter, including the use of a verifier punch in the case of punched cards or duplicate verified tape where paper tape is used. Comparison of pre-list totals with those on processing runs should be made. The computer itself may be made to operate other controls by means of editing (*see* 10–12 below).

5. Processing controls. The efficient operation of a system of internal check should mean that the operator can deal with the setting up of runs, control these either by console typewriter or by the manual control of switches, and can deal with any errors or exceptional items. It is possible for the operator to influence the system, so the auditor must satisfy himself completely that the internal check is both clearly defined in writing and properly maintained. The matters involved include the following:

(*a*) Proper recording of work executed referenced to programmes and master files and the maintenance of a computer log.

(*b*) The recording of action taken on errors or exception reports.

(*c*) Definite instructions as to the examination and certification of the computer log book by a responsible official at regular intervals.

(*d*) Strictly enforced rules whereby only computer processing staff may have access to the computer room and only authorised staff may withdraw files from the library.

6. Master file control. Although they contain standing data (*see* 11(*a*), (*iii*)), such files have nevertheless to be frequently updated, for example, changes in staff will require updating of the wages programme. Whilst first ensuring the operation of a sound internal check system, the auditor will be particularly concerned to see that the following safeguards are operated:

(*a*) Only authorised staff may incorporate changes.

(*b*) Detailed print-outs are made for amendments to be checked by the control section.

(*c*) Amendments are only made on receipt of forms specially printed and serially numbered for the purpose.

(*d*) Cross-checks are made of output with information contained in other departments, such as control accounts compiled from pre-input lists.

(*e*) Verification of output is made by examination of information produced with identifiable items, e.g. in the case of debtors, balances with monthly statements.

(*f*) The clear and unambiguous labelling of spools, containers, etc.

(*g*) Comparison of output with information maintained in user departments, e.g. print-outs being compared with records of employees kept in the wages department.

7. Output control. The internal control of interest to the auditor would cover such matters as:

(*a*) efficient overall supervision by control section;

(*b*) comparison of output with originating data, e.g. pre-list totals;

(*c*) checking that queries have been dealt with properly, and, where errors have been found, that these have been dealt with;

(*d*) the proper distribution of output to departments and checking with department information as deemed necessary.

8. Standby procedures. The auditor will be concerned to ensure the efficient maintenance of internal control, and although the actual running of the computer is not so much his concern, he will nevertheless be interested to see that a proper standby system is prepared in case of breakdown by the computer, as records might suffer if a proper system was not ready for use.

It is often advantageous to postpone various operations rather than obtain the use of another computer. Other processes might be carried out manually on an approximate basis, e.g. the payment of set sums for wages, correction being made later.

9. Service bureaux. If the client uses the services available on an outside computer, the controls mentioned above for input and output of data should still be operated. The procedural controls may be assumed to be effective if the auditor is satisfied that no collusion is possible between the client's staff and those of the bureau. If there is the slightest possibility of this, the auditor will have to investigate the internal check thoroughly.

COMPUTER SYSTEM CONTROLS

Having dealt with the controls to be exercised over the processing operations, we must consider those matters of importance to the auditor regarding controls over the actual computer. These include such matters as:

(*a*) programme checks within the system;

(*b*) adequacy and frequency of print-outs;

(*c*) error correcting procedures.

10. Programme checks. Computers may be programmed to incorporate checks of an "editing" nature, and, wherever possible, the auditor should request their inclusion from the commencement. These may include the following:

(*a*) *Limit checks:* limits may be set whereby no item may fall outside the limit, e.g. sixty hours' working in week.

(*b*) *Validity checks:* where punched cards or paper tape are used any malfunctioning due to an operating error (or breakdown in the machine) is revealed.

(*c*) *Parity checks:* these guard against the rendering of incorrect information due, for example, to tape damage.

(*d*) *Reference checks:* these may be sub-divided as to the following:

(*i*) *Cross-referencing.* Print-outs may be obtained of each programme as it is brought into use ensuring not only that authorised programmes are used, but also the continuous activity of the machine.

(*ii*) *Serial numbering of forms.* This applies to invoices, cheques, or similar documents. The computer can be made to match the numbers on the pre-numbered forms, so ensuring that no numbers are inserted or withdrawn.

(*iii*) *New items counts.* Where master files are transferred, the number of items on the new file can be counted, so facilitating agreement with the old master file and the adjustments made on updating.

(*iv*) *Compiling a log.* Where there is an automatic typewriter on the operator's console, any item fed into the machine from the console will be automatically typed, so compiling a log serving as a double check in conjunction with the operator's manual log. The possibility of cutting out the typing exists, but internal check by supervision should obviate this.

11. Print-outs.

(*a*) *Computer output.* These print-outs constitute the end products for which the computer is used, for example:

(*i*) documents of a financial nature, e.g. invoices, orders, accounts, etc.;

(*ii*) management control reports. These include statistical accounting, and other data, as well as "exception" reports, covering overdue accounts, excess stock usage, etc.;

(*iii*) print-out of data from master files for computer control.

It may be mentioned that data contained on files may be either:

(*i*) standing data—this may be used for repeated operations and includes a certain number of related items, e.g. stock price lists; or

(*ii*) data referring to a particular transaction, e.g. number of hours worked.

(*b*) *Auditor's examination of print-outs.* It will be necessary for the auditor to ensure that the information contained on the files is kept up to date and regularly printed out and verified with the items to which it refers, for example, comparison of stock figures with balances held. This will involve an examination of both the print-outs and the internal control operated.

Provided the overall internal control is efficiently operated the auditor need only make some checks on the most important matters, but he must see that such information is *available* for examination.

As master files are of particular interest to the auditor he may reasonably ask the client to have special print-outs made of matters which are his particular concern, such as lists of debtors' or creditors' ledger accounts for the purpose of examining the makeup of certain accounts. He may also request certain tests to be made to ascertain whether master files have been properly updated.

(*c*) *Test packs.* Print-outs may be obtained by the use of test packs, which can be used to test programme controls. These consist of whatever input media is used, and are expensive to prepare, requiring a detailed knowledge of the procedures and considerable preparation time. The information produced may also have to be translated for audit purposes, which is time-consuming.

The actual method of testing involves introducing specified transactions into the operations concerned and checking the results with previously prepared information. If they are available, the auditor may use them to good advantage, but for him to insist on their production seems unjustifiable in normal circumstances in view of the difficulties mentioned above, especially as other methods of testing the operation of the procedures are available.

(*d*) *Random tests.* Having made exhaustive enquiries and various tests on taking up the audit, the auditor may thereafter confine his testing to items of special importance on a random sampling basis. For example, a payroll print-out for a selected week may be retained and compared with that for a later selected week, the differences which have arisen within the period being investigated.

The computer itself may be usefully applied to select certain items at mathematically determined intervals, and to eliminate less important items. For example, the debtors ledger balances below a certain amount may be omitted, and a selection made of the remainder, while at the same time for control account purposes the total of all balances, those both selected and omitted, may be obtained.

(*e*) *Stopping and re-starting the computer.* To ensure that no unauthorised change is made between stopping and re-starting the computer, the auditor should request that print-outs be made each time, examining the log book to make sure no print-out has been omitted.

12. Error correction procedures. Where the computer reveals that errors have arisen, it is usual to programme it to reject these. The process of correction, however, may prove expensive if the system has to be interrupted, and it is therefore usual to deal with such errors manually. For example, if a mistake is made in an employee's wage, the correct data is prepared manually, and it is then necessary to feed this in to bring the record up to date, care being taken to avoid making the payment twice.

If errors are discovered prior to feed-in, the data may be sent back for correction and re-presentation. If incorrect data has been fed in, however, it may be allowed to continue through the system, being marked for examination prior to dispatch to the relevant department.

The auditor will be concerned to see that the internal control operating is efficiently maintained to ensure that the records are properly recorded, checked and cleared by the control section.

13. I.C.A. Recommendations. An addition to the overall summary of the auditor's work regarding computer-based systems given in **1–12** above, we should consider briefly the Institute of Chartered Accountants' Recommendations U.14 and U.15 on this subject. A more detailed consideration is given in Taylor and Perry's *Principles of Auditing*, Leslie R. Howard, nineteenth edition, Macdonald and Evans Ltd.

INTERNAL CONTROL IN A COMPUTER-BASED ACCOUNTING SYSTEM (U.14)

The I.C.A. list the main controls affecting a computer-based accounting system as administrative, systems development and procedural.

14. Administrative controls. These may be sub-divided according to the following:

(*a*) *Division of responsibilities.* Although the size of the organisation will be a determining factor, nevertheless internal control must be efficiently organised and applied. Safeguards should be operated to ensure this:

(*i*) Only control and preparation sections should have access to original data. Only computer staff should have access to the computer during production runs, and they and the librarian to files and current programmes.

(*ii*) Only use department staff and the control section should be allowed to amend input data.

(*iii*) The staff of the control section and the librarian should not have any other duties within the computer department.

(*iv*) Computer department staff should not initiate transactions and changes to master files, while access to the computer room should be restricted to authorised persons at authorised times.

(*b*) *Control over computer operators.* Generally, the following controls may be exercised:

(*i*) The use of work manuals and detailed work scheduling.

(*ii*) Frequent and independent review of computer usage by reference to time and fault logs, and, where a console typewriter is used, by reference to operating logs produced.

(*iii*) Not less than two operators to be employed, with proper rotation of operators' duties.

(*iv*) Programming so that all operator intervention appears on print-outs shown on pre-numbered paper, or interventions to be numbered consecutively by the computer.

(*c*) *File control.* Where possible, a librarian should be employed, but otherwise specified staff should be held responsible for such duties as storage identification and reconstruction procedures. These duties will include control of issue and return of files.

The file identification procedures cover the following:

(*i*) Allocation of file identification numbers.

(*ii*) The use of file protection rings—to be attached (in the case of tape files) before any writing can be made on the tape.

(*iii*) Inclusion of identification data on the file header label. This would be checked by the computer programme on set-up, results usually being printed out on the console.

File reconstruction procedures usually include specific retention periods for maintaining tape data. Where direct access devices are used, so that new data is written in the same location as that from which the old was read, then provision must be made for re-creating files. This usually involves data being copied on to another file, together with subsequent transactions which have been processed.

(*d*) *Fire precautions and standby arrangements.* Rules should be laid down to limit fire risks, and others to be applied in the event of breakdown. Because of the complexity of procedures, it is often of no advantage to employ another computer. Rather, some operations should be postponed, e.g. the preparation of invoices and statements. Other operations might be carried out on an approximate basis, e.g. the payment of wages, corrections being made later. Such specified procedures should periodically be reviewed.

15. Systems development controls. The headings for such controls are specified in U.14 as:

(*a*) standard procedures and documentation;

(*b*) systems and programme testing;

(*c*) file conversion;

(*d*) acceptance and authorisation procedures;

(*e*) systems and programme amendments.

(*a*) *Standard procedures and documentation.* Documentation to support each application and procedures for developing the system must be given careful consideration, otherwise the system of internal control may lapse. At the outset, the internal control system must be organised so that adequate information will be available to the auditor for his subsequent tests.

After broad agreement on the system, a detailed description

of the computer programme should be compiled. Procedure manuals for staff in the user department(s) should be prepared, including methods of providing input and dealing with output. Programmes are then written and documented and master files set up.

Internal control must be maintained by ensuring that documentation is properly prepared and kept up to date for any subsequent changes.

(b) *Systems and programme testing.* Before becoming operational, the system must be fully tested, to make sure that all individual programmes have been desk-checked and tested with test and "live" data, that a pilot run is made or a run is made in parallel with the existing system and that the user departments can carry out their specified operations within the designated time cycle.

(c) *File conversion.* Before a computer system becomes operational, care must be taken that correct data is set up in the master files and that the setting-up operation itself is complete and accurate.

(d) *Acceptance and authorisation procedures.* After the setting up of the master files with a complete print-out and check of contents, each major stage of development should be reviewed by a responsible official, while the user departments should ensure that the system will satisfy their requirements as specified.

(e) *Systems and programme amendments.* Changes and adjustments in the system, no matter how seemingly unimportant, may appear; all such matters should be subject to a definitive system of authorisation and control. All changes must be dealt with in conjunction with the necessary documentation and tested before being put into use.

16. Procedural controls. Data to be controlled falls under two headings:

(a) *Standing data.* This is incorporated in the master file and affects the accounting of all transactions of a similar nature, e.g. selling prices, wage rates.

(b) *Transaction data.* Such data relates only to one particular transaction, e.g. number of hours worked in a period or number of items ordered. The effect of any mistake arising in respect of standing data will be far more wide-ranging than that of transaction data, and for this reason higher standards of control must be exercised in respect of standing data. Likewise, more stringent controls are exercised where input data is concerned than for data to be included in file data retained for reference purposes.

The procedural controls are included under four headings:

(*a*) input controls;
(*b*) processing controls;
(*c*) output controls;
(*d*) master file controls;

although it is emphasised that control over data is a continuous process and the general overall aspect must be considered when dealing with any particular aspect.

(*a*) *Input controls.* To ensure that authorised, and only authorised data is processed, controls must extend back to the user department, to the movement of data to the computer department and eventually to its conversion within the data preparation section.

(*i*) *Establishment of control.* To ensure complete and accurate processing of data it is necessary to establish a control with which the final output can be verified. This may be done by—

(1) the use of controls from prime procedures (e.g. the totalling of cash received on opening the post would provide a control for the subsequent processing of cash to the sales ledger);

(2) clerical sequence checks (e.g. accounting for serially-numbered stores issue notes before passing to the computer department);

(3) the retention of copies of important documents sent for processing (e.g. amendments to standing data) for subsequent checking with output;

(4) establishment, either clerically or by the computer, of batch control totals. These totals might be document counts, item counts (e.g. the different items on a sales order), sterling totals, quantity totals (e.g., goods dispatched or hours worked) or hash totals (e.g. aggregation of stock code numbers);

(5) programme controls (e.g. sequence checks, check digit verification or matching with master file records).

It is not claimed that any one of the foregoing procedures would be sufficient in itself to secure accuracy, often a combination of two techniques may be employed, e.g. in processing clock cards a double check might be made with total hours worked.

Unlike the procedure adopted when compiling control accounts for accounting purposes, it is unusual for control totals to be established over reference data, as this is normally controlled within the computer by check digit verification and by matching with master file records.

(*ii*) *Verification of conversion.* The techniques of control vary between installations but usually include:

(1) separation of the duties of punching and verifying;

(2) physical control over the source documents and the input media produced therefrom;

(3) procedures for recording and investigating errors detected at the verification stage and controlling their correction;

(4) control of the progress of punching and verifying.

If control is established after the conversion of data into input media (e.g. by control totals established by the computer) the verification of conversion is normally an important part of the control structure, as otherwise conversion errors would not normally be revealed.

(*iii*) *Authorisation of input.* While the manual of procedures will normally apply, any change must be properly authorised. With regard to actual processing, authorisation will not of itself ensure only authorised data will be processed. This will apply only after control has been established, e.g. approval of purchases invoices in pre-listed batches. Where control is established after authorisation, it will be necessary, if the data is important, to check that the authorised data has not been changed or suppressed, or that unauthorised data has not been introduced before control is established. In certain cases, authorisation functions previously carried out clerically may be exercised by programme controls in the form of limit and reasonableness checks (e.g. excessive hours worked identified and reported for action).

(*b*) *Processing controls.* The three main types of processing control available within the computer system itself are:

(*i*) editing;

(*ii*) control over rejections;

(*iii*) run to run controls.

(*i*) Editing. Checks against a pre-determined standard are made, and any data falling outside the limits may be rejected or held on suspense file, or if accepted, reported for investigation.

The tests include:

(1) check digit verification (e.g., testing that a check digit included in a reference number bears the required relationship to

the rest of the number. This protects against most transposition and transcription errors);

(2) reasonableness checks (e.g. ensuring that data lies within pre-determined limits—that hours worked are between nil and fifty);

(3) existence checks (e.g. comparing data codes with pre-determined lists of codes—that stock codes range from 1,000–5,000);

(4) sequence checks (e.g. detecting sequence failures or duplicate records);

(5) format checks (e.g. testing that characters are alphabetic, numeric or blank—that invoice value fields are numeric);

(6) the matching of transactions with master file records.

(*ii*) *Control over rejections.* If totals are obtained clerically prior to computer runs, then control over rejection is high-lighted by the need to adjust the control total. Where, however, no such clerical checks exist, then rejections will not be auto-matically revealed and a greater degree of care will have to be exercised. Where certain items are held in backing storage on a suspense file and not rejected, procedures must be specified to ensure that such items are printed out and corrected. Correction procedures may be carried out clerically or the computer may be programmed to transfer such items from suspense. In either case all such transfers should be printed and reviewed and a periodic review should be made of the suspense file.

(*iii*) *Run-to-run controls—intermediate print-out of control data.* As most computer applications require more than one run, to ensure that no data shall be lost, the computer may be made to accumulate control tests during each run for comparison with totals held on the file or for clerical agreement with input totals or print-outs from previous runs. Where the computer carries out such agreements, it is advisable to have these printed out and checked clerically.

(*c*) *Output controls.* Output may be directly related to input, e.g. sales invoices produced from dispatch notes and prices, and may then be verified clerically with control accounts or by checking individual items with copies of input documents.

Output may be only indirectly related to input, such as in the case of:

(*i*) current input data (e.g. reports of unmatched and missing items);

(*ii*) previous or latest input data (e.g. overdue debtor reminder procedures);

(*iii*) all input for a given period (e.g. personal and nominal ledgers, interest charges and cumulative totals);

then this may be verified clerically with cumulative totals established over input, e.g. debtors' control account, reliance here being put upon the computer program more than with output *directly* related to input data.

The computer can be programmed to scrutinise input data and to report on exceptional items (exception reports), e.g. pay outside given limits.

Control must be maintained over distribution of output. The user department may carry out the tests mentioned above, but where control is kept by the computer itself, then the user department will have to verify the receipt of all output by such means as output registers or sequential numbering of exception reports.

Proper instructions must be laid down to make sure that all exception reports are investigated by an independent investigator.

(*d*) *Master file controls.* The utmost care is necessary to ensure that standing data can only be altered on proper authority. To prevent any unauthorised change, periodic print-outs should be checked with clerically-held information while independent control totals should be checked periodically with equivalent totals maintained in the file.

Often regular print-outs of individual balances will form an automatic part of the processing routine (e.g. debtors, creditors and stock). Conventional controls will often involve the verification of individual balances (e.g. comparison of creditors' balances with statements and comparison of stock balances with physical stock counts).

17. Service bureaux. It is expedient to have definitive rules to be applied in the event of breakdown, for at such a time there is a risk of abuse because of the possible lapsing of the system of internal check. Often with complex systems it is better to carry out certain operations on a simplified basis, e.g. payment of wages at a fixed amount until repairs have been carried out.

The Recommendations mention a number of practical requirements concerning the use of service bureaux.

(*a*) *Clearly-defined liaison between bureau and user.* Normally a senior member of the user's staff should be appointed as liaison officer.

(b) *System testing* involving all clerical procedures at the user company.

(c) *Adequate file conversion checking procedures* by the user.

(d) *Additional controls over the physical movement of data.* It is often appropriate to keep a copy or microfilm of documents sent to the service bureau.

(e) *Carefully planned rejection procedures.* The bureau must provide sufficient documentation for the error to be identified. The user must ensure the prompt correction and re-submission of rejections to meet the bureau's processing schedules.

(f) *Output distribution controls.* In particular, there should be procedures in the user company to ensure that all exception reports are received from the bureau.

(g) *Additional clerical controls at the company* to verify the accuracy of computer processing (e.g. test-checking of details on output).

(h) If there are significant programme checks, a *review of reports* by the user to ensure the check is functioning regularly.

(i) A high degree of control over the *maintenance of data on master files.* This is necessary because the user has no physical control over the files.

THE AUDIT OF COMPUTER-BASED ACCOUNTING SYSTEMS (U.15)

Statement on Auditing U.15 considers the adjustments which may be required in internal control, as well as the audit procedures involved, in four sections:

(a) Timing of audit work and review of the system of internal control.

(b) Audit tests on the system of internal control.

(c) Balance sheet and profit and loss account verification.

(d) Special audit techniques.

18. Audit work timing and review of internal control.

(a) *Timing of audit work.*

(i) *Initial approach.* If the auditor is consulted at the outset, he can discuss matters on a broad basis. He may thereafter carry out his more detailed review before programming is too advanced, when systems specifications are substantially complete and controls decided.

(*ii*) *Timing of audit tests*. Tests on an interim audit basis may not always be practical; it is easier to confine tests to recent data, as previous data may have been overprinted, etc. If there is an internal audit department, continuous test evidence will be available.

Often data is not retained, so the auditor may have to request that certain print-outs be retained, e.g. error requests subsequently corrected.

Document filing may also affect the timing of tests, e.g. if invoices are filed in supplier order, detailed checking may not be practical after a short time.

(*b*) *Review of internal control system*. The main objective must always be kept in mind; to become immersed in detailed programme documentation, often of a technical nature, is inadvisable. The overall system should be examined in conjunction with flow charts, lists of programme controls, etc.

Briefly, the methods of approach to be adopted are, first, if there are exhaustive clerical procedure controls, then it should only be necessary to examine the administrative controls in detail if the clerical controls are exercised in the actual computer department, and second, if the overall system of control is significantly reliant on programme controls, then these should be examined in detail. (7–9)

The use of internal control questionnaires is mentioned as being valuable in evaluating the whole system. (10–11)

19. Audit tests on the system of internal control. The general principles regarding the nature and tests are as stated in Statement on Auditing No. 1; changes, however, will be necessitated where:

(*a*) there are changes in the system of procedural controls;

(*b*) there is any significant loss of, or change in, audit trail;

(*c*) it is necessary to test the administrative and systems development controls.

(*a*) *Changes in system of procedural controls.*

(*i*) *Establishment and verification of control*. Most computer applications use batching techniques, whereby control totals are established at an early stage. These totals are often used to verify the accuracy of subsequent processing, so here the control of batches and agreement of totals is of greater significance than the control relating to individual items. This is contrary to conventional accounting systems, where control totals are only established at a late stage in processing and individual items are more particularly controlled.

Where batching takes place at an early stage in processing, it is normally appropriate to select a number of batches and test the effectiveness of the total controls exercised over them, reducing the number of individual items traced through the system.

This reflects the greater reliability which may be placed on computer processing.

(*ii*) *Intermediate print-outs of control data.* It is necessary to assess the overall significance of run-to-run controls and intermediate print-outs, with tests to be restricted to those of prime importance. Run-to-run controls may be of such importance where control totals are established initially or during processing, as in the case of sales from quantities dispatched. These will be either printed out intermediately (e.g. on audit listing), or will be be held on file and verified internally by the computer.

(*iii*) *Amendment and maintenance of standing data.* It is normal to establish adequate control over standing data, so if the auditor satisfies himself as to the adequacy of this, then the testing of final results may be reduced.

(*iv*) *Programme controls.*

(1) *Individual items.* It will be necessary to test that these have been correctly treated by the programme control, e.g. if sales orders are compared with a credit limit by the programme, it will be necessary to test that sales orders selected for audit tests have been correctly treated by the programme. Because of the difficulty in selecting a variety of source documents, tests are often supplemented by scrutiny of rejection or exception reports. If a more positive assurance of correct functioning is required, test packs may be used.

(2) *Groups of data.* Testing correctness of totals accumulated is simple when print-outs are available, but where there may be a loss of audit trail, then the following procedure is necessary.

(*b*) *Loss of, or change in, audit trail.* The audit trail refers to the ability to trace individual items through the whole system. This ability may be lost, however, where changes take place or more advanced computer systems are used.

Conventional audit tests may not be possible when computer-generated totals, balances, etc. are not printed out, or when no totals are printed from which to test the completeness of output.

In such cases, it will be necessary for the auditor to apply such techniques as:

(*i*) arranging for special print-outs of additional information for the auditor's use;

(*ii*) programmed interrogation facilities, whereby records held on magnetic or card files are printed out on a selective basis by means of a direct request to that file;

(*iii*) clerical re-creation (e.g. to verify a sales total when no detailed lists have been printed out, the copy invoices might be add listed and the total thereof compared with the computer total);

(*iv*) testing a total basis and ignoring individual items (e.g. comparing analyses which can be verified in total, but to which individual items cannot be traced, with previous periods and budgets);

(*v*) relying on alternative tests (e.g. if the movements making up stock balances cannot be tested, but the balances are checked regularly with physical stock, testing the stocktaking procedures and examining the procedure for dealing with discrepancies);

(*vi*) using special audit techniques (*see* 21 below).

Special audit techniques will be required where no visible evidence is given that all items have been processed, e.g. on exception reports of slow-moving stock items.

(*c*) *Administrative and systems development controls.* If the overall system of procedural controls is mainly within the computer department, then audit tests might include verification:

(*i*) by observation that staff are complying with specified duties;

(*ii*) that time and fault logs and console print-outs are being independently reviewed;

(*iii*) on a test basis, that library records are being properly maintained;

(*iv*) that storage regulations of programme documentation, master files, etc., are being applied.

The foregoing tests cover administrative controls, the systems development controls might be checked by selecting some new systems and programmes and amendments to existing programmes.

(*d*) *Internal audit.* The Council point out that the internal auditor is in a position not only to see the efficient working of the system, but also that proper testing takes place prior to implementation of developments; also that the independent auditor should be consulted during the institution of various developments.

20. Balance sheet and profit and loss account verification. The general principles of auditing verification are as in Statement on Auditing U.1, subject to various changes necessitated by computer-based accounting systems.

If control over the accounting records is exercised to a large extent by programme controls, it is necessary to consider whether to alter the verification tests to ensure that the relevant computer programmes are functioning correctly. Examples of significant programme controls include reliance on the computer to maintain and agree control accounts on magnetic or card files, to generate important profit and loss items such as service charges, interest, rentals and commission, to compare purchase invoices and goods received records and calculate the liability for outstanding purchases and to write down stock automatically according to usage details.

There is a tendency in computer-based accounting systems to produce less detailed lists of balances and more exception reports. It is necessary, therefore, to ensure that print-outs provide sufficient information and that maximum audit benefit is obtained from exception reports.

If additional information is required, special print-outs may be needed or programmed interrogation facilities used.

21. Special audit techniques: test packs. These involve chiefly the use of test packs and computer audit programmes, and are used to assure correct functioning of programme controls and to overcome loss of audit trail, while at the same time reducing audit costs.

The use of test packs is expensive and they should be used only where essential. They are suited for such matters as verifying specific programme controls, e.g. audit checks carried out on input data. They are not really suitable for verification of profit and loss and balance sheet items, save where the system of internal control is sound in principle, and this has been confirmed by audit tests.

The advantages of using test packs in mechanised accounting are:

(*a*) they provide a positive assurance of the correct functioning of the programme controls tested;

(*b*) they can be used on a continuing basis until the programmes are changed;

(*c*) if restricted to testing particular programme controls (especially if master files are not required), they are not expensive to develop;

(*d*) once set up, "running" costs from year to year are low;

(*e*) additional tests can be "grafted" on to basic test packs fairly easily;

(*f*) their contents are variable at will.

The difficulties in the use of test packs are:

(*a*) to ensure that the test data is processed as expected, a more detailed knowledge is required of the programmes than is usual;

(*b*) to test certain programme controls may entail either "passing the data through" previous parts of the system that do not require testing, or writing additional programmes to by-pass those parts of the processing;

(*c*) computer time is often difficult to obtain;

(*d*) processing halts often occur due to the artificial type and small quantity of data used;

(*e*) initial set-up costs can be high;

(*f*) amendment may be required for programme changes.

The limitations of test packs are:

(*a*) the difficulty in establishing whether the programme tested is the current operational programme;

(*b*) unless "live" data is used, they do not test actual transactions;

(*c*) the security risks involved normally make it impracticable to use them against "live" files.

Test packs are thus usually supplemented by audit tests on actual data and by tests on the organisational controls.

Provided care is exercised to avoid affecting the company's financial records, it is possible to set up records on the operational files against which the auditor can process test data. By this means, the need to obtain computer time and to create copy master files for use with test packs is avoided. At the same time, there is the assurance of the use of a current operational programme.

Computer audit programmes may be used by the auditor to read and extract information or to audit the contents of files.

These "inquiry" or "interrogation" programmes can be used to read and examine a single file or to compare two files (e.g. wages files six months apart).

Special computer audit programmes may be utilised to assist the audit work:

(a) As regards tests on the system of internal control:

(i) to select representative types of transactions for audit tests;

(ii) to scrutinise files and select exceptional items for examination;

(iii) to compare two files and select normal or exceptional changes.

(b) As regards balance sheet and profit and loss account verification:

(i) to select transactions for further testing by means of random sampling;

(ii) to prepare exception reports;

(iii) to stratify data as an aid to its investigation;

(iv) to carry out certain detailed tests and calculations.

SPECIMEN QUESTIONS FOR EVALUATING THE SYSTEM OF CONTROL IN A COMPUTER-BASED ACCOUNTING SYSTEM

These questions, dealt with in an appendix to U.15, are stated to be "some of the principal questions that the auditor will wish to ask in evaluating the system of internal control in a computer-based accounting system".

It is stated that "the approach to be adopted in evaluating the system of internal control is summarised in paragraph 9 of the main text". The questions in this questionnaire have been designed bearing this approach in mind.

I. ADMINISTRATIVE CONTROLS

NOTE: The questions in this section relate to the computer installation as a whole.

(A) *Division of responsibilities* (9 and 10)

1. Is the head of the computer department responsible to an appropriate senior official in the company?

2. Is the following work carried out by separate sections or departments:

(a) development;

(b) data preparation;

(c) computer operating;

(d) file library;

(e) control?

3. Have organisation charts and job descriptions been prepared?

4. Do the following basic restrictions apply:

(a) access to documents containing original data is limited to the control section and data preparation staff;

(b) computer department staff do not have access to any of the company's clerically maintained financial records;

(c) access to the computer during production runs is limited to computer operators;

(d) access to files and current programmes is limited to computer operators and file librarian;

(e) computer operators and programmers do not amend input data;

(f) control section staff and the librarian do not have other duties within the computer department;

(g) computer department staff do not initiate transactions and changes to master files;

(h) unauthorised access to the computer room is forbidden (state how this is achieved)?

5. Do the restrictions in 4 apply at all times?

(B) *Control over computer operators* (11)

6. Is the work of computer operators controlled by the use of (describe):

(a) administrative procedure manuals;

(b) work schedules;

(c) operating instructions for each programme;

(d) computer usage reports (e.g. operating logs and console print-outs);

(e) minimum of two operators *per* shift;

(f) rotation of duties;

(g) any other method (describe)?

7. Is all operator intervention recorded on the console print-out?

8. Are computer usage reports, including console print-outs reviewed by a responsible official?

NOTE: If the procedural controls rely on operator intervention to a significant degree, this control is important.

(C) File control (12)

File storage procedures (13 and 14) (refer to questions 2(*d*) and 4(*c*)).

9. Is a permanent record of files maintained (describe)?

10. Are movements of files recorded (describe)?

11. On what authority are files issued?

12. Are master copies of important files (e.g. programmes and documentation) kept at outside locations?

(D) File identification procedures (15)

13. Are there adequate file identification procedures by use of (describe):

    (*a*) visible reference numbers;

    (*b*) protection rings;

    (*c*) header label checks on set-up;

    (*d*) any other method (describe)?

(E) File reconstruction procedures (16)

14. Are there adequate reconstruction procedures by use of (describe):

    (*a*) the establishment of retention periods for files, input media and documents;

    (*b*) file generation systems;

    (*c*) copying of disc files at appropriate intervals;

    (*d*) any other method (describe)?

(F) Fire precautions and standby arrangements (17)

15. (*a*) Are there adequate fire precautions (describe)?

    (*b*) Are there adequate standby arrangements for processing in case of equipment failure (describe)?

    (*c*) If so, have these arrangements been tested?

II. SYSTEMS DEVELOPMENT CONTROLS

NOTES:

(1) The questions in this section relate to the computer installation as a whole.

(2) In many installations standards have been established for many of the controls and procedures concerned with systems development work. The auditor should be aware of their existence, or otherwise, because this is likely to affect the quality of the systems work.

(*A*) *Standard procedures and documentation* (19–22)

1. Does the documentation produced for an application include the following:

(*a*) narrative description of the system;
(*b*) flow charts and block diagrams;
(*c*) input and output data descriptions;
(*d*) file record layouts;
(*e*) control procedures;
(*f*) programme listing;
(*g*) test data and results of testing;
(*h*) output distribution instructions;
(*i*) operating instructions;
(*j*) procedure manuals?

2. How does the system ensure that the documentation in 1 is:

(*a*) properly prepared;
(*b*) properly altered for system and programme changes?

(*B*) *Systems and programme testing* (23)

3. Are programmes adequately tested by means of:

(*a*) desk checking;
(*b*) processing with test data;
(*c*) use of operating instructions without programmers being present;
(*d*) any other method (describe)?

4. Are systems adequately tested by means of:

(*a*) processing test data;
(*b*) pilot running;
(*c*) parallel running;
(*d*) involving the clerical and control procedures in all user departments concerned with the system;
(*e*) any other method (describe)?

Specimen question:

5. Who evaluates the results of testing and what report is prepared?

(*C*) *File conversion* (24)

6. Are the contents of master files checked before a system becomes operational (describe)?

(*D*) *Acceptance and authorisation procedures* (25)

7. Is completed work reviewed and approved and further progress authorised by responsible officials in both user and computer departments at the following stages in development:

(*a*) completion of outline systems report;
(*b*) completion of systems specification;
(*c*) completion of programme and systems testing;
(*d*) accepting new systems into operational use?

(*E*) *Systems and programme amendments* (26)
8. Do all changes to operational systems and programmes require to be authorised?
9. Are all changes:

(*a*) documented;
(*b*) tested;

in the same manner as new systems and programmes?
10. How does the system ensure that all changes are notified to all concerned, including user departments?

III. PROCEDURAL CONTROLS

NOTES:
(1) The questions in this section relate to each application.
(2) The questions in this section should be asked separately for each input document, print-out and master file.

(*A*) *Input controls: establishment of control* (35 and 36)
1. Is control for complete and accurate processing first established:

(*a*) before the documents are batched by use of:
  (*i*) controls from prior procedures (describe);
  (*ii*) clerical sequence checks;
  (*iii*) retention of copies;
  (*iv*) any other method (describe)?

(*b*) clerically after batching by use of:
  (*i*) control totals (describe)?
  (*ii*) any other method (describe)?

(*c*) by the computer by use of:
  (*i*) control totals (describe);
  (*ii*) sequence checks;
  (*iii*) any other method (describe)?

NOTES:
(1) Question 1 would be applied to all data fields on the documents that contain or create financial data. It is important to distinguish between controls for completeness and controls for accuracy.

(2) In 1(*b*) it is important to distinguish whether control is first established in the user or computer department. If established in the computer department, the administrative controls are important.

(3) If control is first established by the computer (1(*c*)) the systems development and administrative controls are important.

2. What controls are established over data fields that contain significant reference data (e.g. check digit verification and matching with master file records)?

(*B*) *Input controls: verification of conversion* (27 and 38)

3. (*a*) Is the conversion of data independently verified?

(*b*) How does the system ensure that all errors are corrected?

NOTE: If control is first established after conversion, this control is important.

(*C*) *Input controls: authorisation of input* (39)

4. Is all input data adequately authorised?

5. If the documents are authorised before control is established, is the authorisation checked after control is established (i.e. to guard against the introduction of unauthorised documents)?

Specimen question:

6. Is the computer programmed to carry out significant authorising functions (e.g. limit and reasonableness checks)?

NOTE: If authorising functions are carried out by the computer (6 above), the systems development and administrative controls are important.

(*D*) *Processing controls: rejections* (45 and 46)

7. Obtain a list of the reasons for which data can be rejected.

8. What are the procedures for investigating, correcting and re-submitting the rejected data and recording the action taken?

9. How does the system ensure that all rejections are promptly re-processed (e.g. maintaining suspense control records, independent scrutiny of rejection listings)?

NOTE: Similar questions would be asked for rejected items held on suspense files.

10. (*a*) If control is established prior to processing (1(*a–b*)) is this control used to verify all (or some) accounting data on final output (describe)?

(*b*) If not, is it used to verify processing to a certain stage by checking intermediate output (e.g. input totals printed and checked on edit list) (describe)?

11. If the control used to verify final output is established by the computer either on input (1(c)) or during processing:

(a) Is it first printed out as intermediate output for subsequent clerical verification with final output (e.g. computer totals printed on edit list) (describe)?

(b) If so, are there adequate programme controls to ensure the completeness and accuracy of the data at each stage of processing until printed out (describe)?

NOTE: If programme controls are relied on (11(b)), the systems development and administrative controls are important.

(E) *Output controls: general*

12. What is the print-out used for (e.g. to originate or support entries in the books for control purposes)?

13. Does the print-out contain sufficient information to:

(a) trace source documents to it,

(b) verify computer-generated calculations and totals?

NOTE: This question is designed to ascertain whether an audit trail exists. Lack of an audit trail does not of itself indicate that a weakness in internal control exists.

(F) *Output controls: output directly related to input* (51)

14. (a) Are the totals and details checked clerically with controls established prior to processing (1(a–b)), or obtained from intermediate print-out (11(a))?

(b) If not, are there adequate programme controls to ensure the completeness and accuracy of the data printed out (describe)?

(G) *Output controls: output indirectly related to input* (52)

15. (a) Are the totals and details checked clerically to external information (describe)?

(b) If not, are there adequate programme controls to ensure the completeness and accuracy of the data printed out (describe)?

(H) *Output controls: exception reports* (53 and 55)

16. Is the completeness of the report verified clerically? If so, give details.

17. Are there adequate programme controls to ensure the completeness (if applicable) and accuracy of the data printed out (describe)?

18. What are the procedures for investigating and taking action on exception reports and recording the action taken?

(*I*) *Output controls: distribution of output* (54)

19. If receipt of output is not controlled by the user department, how does the system ensure it receives *all* print-outs intact?

NOTES:

(1) In questions 14(*a*) and 15(*a*) it is important to distinguish whether the verification is carried out in the user or computer department. If verified in the computer department, administrative controls are important.

(2) If programme controls are relied on (questions 14(*b*), 15(*b*) and 17), the systems development and administrative controls are important.

(*J*) *Master file controls: amendments to standing data* (57)

20. (*a*) How are amendments authorised;

(*b*) Is this authorisation adequate?

21. Are processed amendments checked in detail (describe)?

22. How does the system ensure that all amendments are processed:

(*a*) by control totals (describe);

(*b*) by retention of copies;

(*c*) by any other method (describe)?

(*K*) *Master file controls: maintenance of standing data* (58)

23. How, and how often, is standing data verified:

(*a*) by print-outs of individual items for checking with external information;

(*b*) by print-outs of totals for reconciliation with an independently, or computer-established, record of totals;

(*c*) by establishment and reconciliation of totals by the computer;

(*d*) by any other method (describe)?

(*L*) *Master file control: maintenance of transaction data* (59 and 60)

24. How, and how often, is transaction data on the file verified on a total basis:

(*a*) by print-outs of totals for reconciliation with a record of independently or computer-established totals;

(*b*) by establishment and reconciliation of totals by the computer;

(*c*) by any other method (describe)?

25. Are individual balances printed out and externally verified (describe)?

PROGRESS TEST 6

1. By what means should the auditor seek to gain an overall picture on first commencing an audit involving a computer?   (1)

2. For what matters should an efficient system of internal control provide?   (2)

3. What information of interest to the auditor would be normally found in a computer log book?   (3)

4. Specify the main aspects of internal check covering processing controls.   (5)

5. What procedures should be operated with regard to the safeguarding of master files?   (6)

6. Are there any controls which may be exercised over output?   (7)

7. Are standby procedures of any interest to the auditor?   (8)

8. Enumerate the controls of an "editing" nature which may be incorporated in the computer.   (10)

9. In what ways are print-outs of interest to the auditor?   (11(b))

10. It has been advocated that auditors should make extensive use of test packs. Do you agree with this statement?   (11(c))

11. To what information may the auditor apply random tests?   (11(d))

12. By what means may correction of errors be carried out?   (12)

SPECIMEN QUESTIONS

1. "The auditor will need to adapt his technique to the conditions of electronic data processing." Discuss this statement.

A.C.A.

2. Where a system of electronic data processing is in use:

(a) state in what chief respects the problems likely to be encountered by an auditor differ from those met with in other forms of mechanised accounting;

(b) describe any three important controls or checks that might be found in or around such a system as an essential part of the internal control; and

(c) outline a further independent check that the auditor might carry out to satisfy himself that a programme has been properly prepared and fed into the equipment, and that the internal controls have been properly applied. *I.C.A. (E.W.)*

3. Where a system of E.D.P. is in operation:

(*a*) explain how an auditor's choice of approach to his task may be influenced by the current trend towards elimination of batch totals and intermediate print-outs; and

(*b*) suggest three specific applications for which he might consider employing his own computer programmes for audit purposes. *I.C.A. (E.W.)*

4. Where a business has transferred part of its accounting procedures to a computer, state:

(*a*) whether in your opinion the work of the auditor becomes less or more important than before, briefly giving your reasons;

(*b*) how the planning of the auditor's tests in relation to the processing of data will be affected;

(*c*) the ways in which the ability of the computer to report by exception can be helpful to him;

(*d*) the principal precautions relating to provision for recovery in the event of a system failure that should be embodied in the instruction manual or other form of permanent documentation; and

(*e*) the matters that need to be established immediately should a main file be found to have been corrupted. *I.C.A. (E.W.)*

5. A company, of which you are an auditor, informs you that it has decided to introduce a computer system.

(*a*) What effect will this decision have on your rights and duties as the external auditor?

(*b*) What matters will require particular attention in determining the programme of work to be carried out in the course of the audit? *A.C.A.*

6. What are the chief practical matters to be considered by an auditor when first evaluating the system of internal control as regards data processed for his client by a computer service bureau? *I.C.A. (E.W.)*

7. You have been appointed auditor of a company which uses a computer to prepare its factory payroll.

You are required to draft a questionnaire to assess the internal control established in the wages system.

The following information is provided:

(*a*) the payroll consists of 5,000 persons;

(*b*) an hourly time rate with a premium for overtime is the sole method of remuneration;

(*c*) a wages department exists at the factory which collects clock cards and receives output from the computer department in addition to dealing with enquiries from factory personnel.

I.C.A. (E.W.)

8. What would you expect to find included in an audit control file that has been built up by an auditor in order to provide him self with useful details of a particular E.D.P. system?

I.C.A. (E.W.)

CHAPTER VII

Verification of Balance Sheet Items

INITIAL PROCEDURE

1. Verification of existence of assets. After having vouched the entries in the books, the auditor may be satisfied as to the authenticity of the transactions by which assets may have been acquired or liabilities incurred, but his examination thus far will not have proved the existence of the actual items, nor, in the case of assets, that they are actually held by the body concerned.

Since an audit consists primarily of the examination of the books, accounts and vouchers of an establishment, it is easy for the auditor to lose sight of the more practical aspect of the work; but to omit to verify the existence of assets or liabilities is to run the risk of being liable for damages in negligence in the execution of the work, as was held in the case of *London Oil Storage Co., Ltd.* v. *Seear Hasluck & Co.* (1904) (*see* p. 273).

In a number of instances it will be possible for the auditor to inspect the assets personally, but where documents are held by solicitors or banks a relevant certificate may be obtained.

2. Precautionary measures. Certain general precautions have to be taken in order to ascertain that there is no manipulation of assets in order to cover the absence of certain items. For example, where a number of petty cash floats are maintained, the auditor should insist on the production of all the balances held at one time. Likewise, where verification takes place after the balance sheet date and various items, such as current assets, have changed since the closing date, then the transactions resulting in the change will have to be vouched back in order to verify the item at the original date.

3. Disposal of assets. Where assets are disposed of, the auditor should vouch the authority in writing authorising the sale and he should ascertain that the amount received on disposal is adequate and is likewise approved. Great care should be exercised here, as there is a possibility that those having authority in any department might dispose of assets, before their condition warrants, to outsiders, with whom agreement may be reached for the payment of a commission or of the private payment of part of the price.

VERIFICATION OF ASSETS

4. Goodwill. Goodwill may arise on the purchase of a business, and where this is so, the original agreement on acquisition of the liabilities and assets concerned should be available. On the other hand, goodwill may be created on the retirement of a partner in a firm, and again the relevant agreement affecting the transactions should be inspected.

Goodwill may be written off, and where this has been done and it is proposed to restore goodwill or to increase its value as shown on the balance sheet by an amount already written off, no objection can be raised to this, e.g. *Stapley* v. *Read Bros., Ltd.* (1924) (*see* pp. 174 and 210).

5. Patents. Patents may be taken out only by individuals and in most cases have a life of sixteen years. Where corporate bodies are concerned, patents may be acquired by assignment only and when examining actual patents, the auditor should also ascertain that they have been properly transferred by means of a registered assignment.

In certain companies a comparatively large number of patents may be held, in which case the auditor should request that a list giving details of the patents, including their expiry dates, is compiled. If such a schedule is kept up to date, much of the auditor's time may be saved.

Renewal certificates should be examined, as failure to renew will allow the patent to lapse; where any have lapsed the auditor should ascertain that this has been agreed by those responsible.

6. Trade marks. Certificates are issued in respect of trade marks by the Patent Office if registered direct; where obtained by transfer this should be properly assigned, and the auditor should therefore examine the document applicable. The costs incurred in obtaining the trade mark may be capitalised as an asset and the expenses, whether on assignment or in designing and registering, should be checked.

7. Copyrights. Under the Copyrights Act 1956, a copyright subsists until the end of fifty years after the year in which the author dies, or in the case of films, recordings or works other than those of a literary nature, until fifty years after the year in which the publication first took place.

Where the client is the author there should be a signed copy of the contract available for inspection. If he has assigned the copyright he will normally retain a copy of the contract giving details of the terms on which the copyright has been assigned. The auditor should then vouch any documents received when royalties are paid by the publisher.

If a copyright has been purchased, then the assignment should be examined and compliance with the terms as to payment of royalties, etc., checked.

8. Land and buildings. The responsibilities of the auditor here are as follows:

(a) *Freehold property.*

(i) *Examination of title deeds.* Where freehold property is owned, the title deeds should be inspected. The auditor need only be satisfied that they appear to be in order, since it is for the legal advisers of the organisation concerned to deal with the actual validity of title. However, there are obvious facts with which the auditor should be conversant, for example, that the sequence of deeds is complete and that the last conveyance duly passes the title to his client.

If the title deeds have been deposited with a bank or a solicitor for safe custody, he should obtain a certificate to this effect, requesting that he should be notified if they are held under any charge or lien. Where property has been mortgaged, then the title deeds will be held by the mortgagee or his representative, from whom a certificate should be obtained.

If there are a number of deeds covering various titles, rather than inspect them on every audit, much time may be saved if they are carefully inspected and immediately thereafter are sealed in the auditor's presence. Subsequently, they may be inspected *en bloc* by examination of the unbroken seals.

(ii) *Registered land.* Increasingly, land is being registered under the Land Registration Acts, and where this is so, the Land Registry Certificate should be inspected, noting any incumbrances thereon as well as examining the details mentioned above with regard to deeds of title. The certificate is dated and may be returned to the Registry for the purposes of updating. Therefore if the auditor feels it is necessary to investigate further, he may request that the certificate be sent back for this purpose.

If a certain part of the freehold is leased, a so-called *freehold ground rent* is receivable. The auditor should examine the counterpart of the lease, taking note of its expiration date as well as the amount receivable from the lessee; at the same time the due receipt of the freehold ground rent on the relevant dates should be checked.

(*iii*) *Depreciation.* An increase in value of land or buildings does not remove the need for charging depreciation on the buildings when the causes of depreciation are applicable, whether or not the value of the asset has increased in the past (*see* VIII).

(*b*) *Leasehold property.*

(*i*) *Leases granted.* The title deeds should be inspected and the counterpart of the lease examined, noting the details of the ground rent receivable.

(*ii*) *Leases acquired.* Leases may be acquired direct from the owner of the freehold or by assignment. The auditor should examine the lease, and if so acquired, the assignment thereof, noting the terms of the lease and its expiry date. Compliance by the client with the terms of the lease, such as the agreed rent on the due date, should be ascertained, for non-compliance may involve forfeiture.

(*c*) *Sub-tenants.* If property has been sub-let, whether in respect of a freehold or a leasehold property, the agreement should be examined and note taken of the rent receivable, due receipt of which should be checked.

9. Plant and machinery.

(*a*) *Vouching and inspection.* The original invoices from the suppliers should be vouched where possible. If on taking up a new audit these cannot be produced, the auditor will have to check back from the records available. Furthermore, in the case of a new audit, it has proved most useful in practice actually to inspect the assets held, for it has been discovered that income tax allowances have been claimed even on assets no longer held. Such inspection should be carried out at intervals deemed necessary by the auditor, and in any case of doubt.

Where plant registers are maintained the verification of the assets is greatly facilitated, as well as the checking of the depreciation written off; if the number of machines or plant held is considerable, then the auditor should strongly recommend that such a register be kept if this is not done.

(*b*) *Retention of own records*. The auditor should retain a list in his working papers of the plant and machinery owned, and this should be kept up to date. It should give brief particulars of the number of the machine, date of purchase and depreciation rate. Selected items should then be checked by inspection, and although the auditor may not be expected to value the machines, nevertheless by comparison with the purchase date and the depreciation rate, he may obtain some idea of the expected life of the machine and when verifying the existence of the asset may form his opinion as to the adequacy or otherwise of the depreciation rate.

(*c*) *Checking accounting entries*. The accounting entries with regard to the plant and machinery account and the depreciation account should be checked with the details as maintained in the plant register and any discrepancies queried.

The cross-checking of the assets actually held with the taxation records has already been touched on above and the list maintained in the audit records should facilitate this. Likewise the insurance cover may prove a useful check, not only for valuation, but also for verification purposes.

10. Loose tools. Stock should be checked each year and the auditor should examine the original stock sheets. Where a proper system of requisitioning is in operation, the auditor should test-check a number of items, ascertaining that loose tools are returned to stock if it is possible to re-use them. The consumption of loose tools will no doubt vary from year to year, but any abnormal consumption should be accounted for by such matters as increased production or a change in production methods.

11. Furniture, fittings and office equipment. No great difficuly may arise in verifying the existence of the furniture and fittings of a small business, but in larger organisations the auditor should request the maintenance of adequate records. These need not be so detailed as in the case of plant and machinery, and furthermore, as the acquisition and disposal is not so frequent, the maintenance of up-to-date records should not be an onerous task.

With regard to office machinery, records similar to a plant register are justified, care being taken to ensure that the numbers of all machines are shown. The expense involved on certain types of machines will justify actual inspection of selected items from time to time.

The remarks with regard to plant and machinery are applicable here about ascertaining that due authority for purchase and sale of items is obtained in writing, although the risk of any collusion with outside purchasers is less likely in these cases.

12. Motor vehicles. Where the number of vehicles held justifies it, records similar to a plant register should be maintained. If these are not kept, full details of make, year, registration numbers, etc., should be shown in the ledger accounts, subdivided as to transport vehicles, travellers' cars, directors' cars, etc.

The auditor should vouch the registration books, noting particularly whether the vehicles are registered under the name of the client; where this is not the case, the auditor must be sure to vouch a written statement from the person shown as owner that he has no charge over the vehicle which he confirms is the property of the client.

Acquisition and disposal authorities should be vouched, care being exercised to ensure that no collusion with outside agents exists on cheap sale prices. Actual physical verification on a test basis and comparison of repairs and petrol bills with car numbers is advisable, while road fund licences and insurance payments may evidence ownership on a particular date.

The checking of the assets held with the taxation records is again of relevance.

INTERNAL CONTROL QUESTIONNAIRE

FIXED ASSETS

(A) Acquisitions and disposals

1. Are all applications for capital expenditure required in writing in a specified manner stating cost, reasons, any items to be replaced, and possible return on capital?

2. List officials who authorise capital expenditure and their authority limits.

3. Is any comparison made with actual and authorised expenditure, and, if so, who is responsible for this?

4. What is the procedure if the authority limit is exceeded?

5. Who authorises work of a capital nature to be carried out by the company's employees?

6. What records are maintained in respect of such work?

7. Who authorises work of repair to capital items, and what is his authority limit?

8. Who authorises the disposal of assets; is any independent check made thereof?

9. Are any inter-company or branch sales made of fixed assets and is any inter-company or branch profit eliminated from the group accounts?

10. Is any reconciliation made between company records and those on the returns to the Inland Revenue in respect of fixed assets?

(B) *Depreciation and appreciation*

11. Are registers kept in respect of:

(a) plant and machinery,
(b) motor vehicles,
(c) other fixed assets? (state which).

12. Who fixes rates in respect of the foregoing for depreciation, or revalues them? (list).

(C) *Verification*

13. Where are the documents of title retained in respect of:

(a) freehold and leasehold properties,
(b) motor vehicles?

14. Which officials have access to the foregoing?

15. Is a period inspection made or certification received in respect of these?

16. How often is a physical check made with the records as to fixed assets held, and is this shown on the records concerned?

STANDARD AUDIT PROGRAMME

FIXED ASSETS

(A) *General*

1. Prepare or obtain full details of all fixed assets as to cost, aggregate depreciation and net value, reconcile with figures on previous year's balance sheet.

2. Verify all items of a material sum, and test others, with completion statements, suppliers' invoices, architects' certificates, and costing or other records as to expenditure on works orders, etc.

3. Any additions during year test with authorisations, investigating any marked differences.

4. Investigate the whole procedure with respect to any disposals of material sums, checking authorisation for disposal and the reasonableness of any amounts received.

5. Where inter-company or branch acquisitions have been made, ascertain whether there is any uplift, and ensure that it is eliminated from the group accounts.

6. Inspect title deeds in respect of freehold and leasehold properties, or inspect seals where inspected previously and sealed, or obtain bankers' certificates with statement as to freedom from lien or charge.

7. Inspect as many fixed assets as deemed necessary and in consideration of their nature, especially any new capital projects, ensuring in the last case the correct allocation between buildings and plant and machinery.

8. In respect of motor vehicles:

(a) Verify that the registration books are held.

(b) If any vehicles held in names of employees or others, obtain certificate as to ownership by client.

(c) Prepare reconciliation of vehicles at opening and closing dates.

(B) *Depreciation*

9. Obtain a list giving details of rates applied to the various classes of assets for permanent file. This list should be checked annually as to suitability of rates in view of prevailing circumstances.

10. Check that all such rates have been properly authorised.

11. Where any change in the basis of calculation of depreciation is made, investigate as to reasonableness and also as to whether this will have to be specially disclosed in the accounts.

13. Debtors. The amounts due from debtors should be verified in the course of the normal audit procedure. The agreement of debtors' schedules with control accounts should be ascertained.

The verification of debtors' balances is considered of such importance as to justify the issue of Recommendation U.7, from which the following extracts are taken.

The auditor will use his individual judgment as to the tests he makes but

in the absence of any similar properly controlled procedure carried out by the company itself, the auditors should consider direct communication with debtors as one of the means by which they can form an opinion as to the adequacy of the system of internal control over

sales and its operation in practice. It may also be useful as a check
on the accuracy of the cut-off procedures ... and the test will be
useful in ascertaining whether the balances are genuine, accurately
stated and not in dispute.

The decision to request the client to carry out a test circularisation
of debtors should not be construed as an assumption by the auditors
of the directors' duties. Circularisation is essentially an act of the
client, who alone can authorise third parties to divulge information
to the auditors.

When circularisation is undertaken the method of requesting
information from the debtor may be either positive or negative.
Under the positive method the debtor is requested to confirm the
accuracy of the balance shown or state in what respect he is in disagreement. Under the negative method the debtor is requested to
reply if the amount stated is disputed. In either case the debtor is
requested to reply direct to the auditor. Both methods may be used
in conjunction.

Weak internal control, the suspicion of irregularities or that
amounts may be in dispute, or the existence of numerous book-
keeping errors are circumstances which indicate that the positive
method is preferable as it is designed to encourage definite replies
from those circularised.

Good internal control, with a large number of small accounts,
would suggest the negative method as likely to be appropriate. However, in some circumstances, e.g. where there is a small number of
large accounts and a large number of small accounts, a combination
of both methods, as noted above, may be appropriate.

It is seldom desirable to circularise all debtors and it is therefore
necessary to establish an adequate sample, ... based upon a complete list of all debtor accounts.

The request sent to debtors may be either a specially prepared
form of letter or an attachment to the client's statement giving a
copy of the debtor's ledger account for an appropriate period and,
in the case of a "positive" request, being accompanied by a pre-paid
reply form.

14. Loans.

(a) *Ascertaining security*. Where loans are granted, it is usual
to require some security to ensure their repayment. Therefore,
the auditor, when verifying the loan, should ascertain whether
any security has been given, in which case it will also be necessary
to verify this, ensuring at the same time that it constitutes an
adequate safeguard, being of sufficient value to cover the amount
of the loan.

On his first visit after the loan has been granted the auditor should inspect the documents which have arisen, such as an application for the loan and a receipt for it when it is paid over. A proper authority for granting the loan must be inspected, which in the case of a company should take the form of a resolution passed at a director's meeting, or in the case of a partnership, should be authorised by all the partners. It should also be ascertained that the terms of the loan have been properly recorded and agreed by both parties.

(*b*) *Receipt of interest*. Due receipts of interest and repayments should be checked, care being taken to note any deviation from the agreement which might lead to forfeiture of the loan and the right to utilise the security.

Where it is part of the normal course of business to make loans, then the auditor should operate the procedure mentioned above with regard to sales ledger balances, and send requests direct to the borrowers for confirmation of the outstanding debts due.

15. Loans to directors. The Companies Act 1948, s. 190, forbids a company from making a loan to any person who is a director or a director of its holding company, or to enter into a guarantee or provide security in connection with a loan. The exceptions are briefly:

(*a*) anything done by a subsidiary where the director is a holding company;

(*b*) advances to meet expenses for fulfilment of duties;

(*c*) where the ordinary business of the company is the lending of money or the giving of guarantees.

There is a proviso with regard to the foregoing, namely, that the loan or guarantee may be given provided:

(*a*) prior approval is given at a general meeting where the purposes and amount are disclosed;

(*b*) if approval is not given at or before the next annual general meeting, the loan or guarantee shall be discharged within six months from the conclusion of the meeting.

The auditor should pay careful attention therefore to any loan to a director to make sure that the foregoing requirements have been complied with.

16. Loans to subsidiary companies. Where it is necessary for the auditor of the holding company to audit this item, no difficulty will arise if he is also auditor of the subsidiary. If he is not, however, he should request certification from the auditors of the other company. This item would be covered in the total responsibility of the auditor to ascertain the true position affecting the relationship between the two companies. (*See Group accounts—reliance on other auditors*, p. 262.)

17. Loans on mortgage. The mortgage deed should be inspected and the following matters ascertained:

(*a*) The mortgagee's name, which should be either that of the client or his nominee. In the latter case the nominee should be requested to confirm that he has no beneficial interest in the mortgage.

(*b*) The nature of the property mortgaged, which should accord with that of the title deeds accompanying the mortgage.

(*c*) The details of the loan, as to amount, interest rate and date from which payable.

(*d*) In the case of a loan made to an employee, there should be an agreement in writing for deduction from salary, if such applies, and a certificate should be obtained as to the agreement of the amount still due at the end of the financial period.

NOTES:

(1) If notes of the foregoing are inserted in the audit notebook and the deeds are deposited for safe custody, a covering certificate will be sufficient for future audits.

(2) If the registration of title has taken place, particulars of the charge will be shown on the Land Registry Certificate in the relevant charges section.

(3) The auditor should ascertain that the value of the property is sufficient cover for the loan; with rising prices in respect of land and property, this should not require re-checking in the case of freehold properties, but he should request that the fire insurance receipt be made available for inspection. In the case of a leasehold property, he should ascertain that the adequacy of the cover is maintained and that the last receipt for the payment of ground rent is available for inspection.

(4) Where a second mortgage is given as security, the deed should state the prior charge, the title deeds being in possession of the first mortgagee. The auditor should request certificates as to the holding of the deeds from the first mortgagee and also as to his knowledge of the second charge.

18. Loans on security of investments. The procedure for the verification of the investments concerned will follow that described above (*see* 14).

Valuation of the investments is necessary to ensure that the cover for the loan is adequate.

19. Loans on security of life policies. The auditor should inspect the life policy and the receipt in respect of the latest premium due. Where the policy has not been assigned, confirmation should be requested from the insurance company as to their knowledge of the deposit for the loan. The surrender value should be ascertained, which should be sufficient to cover the loan.

20. Loans on guarantees from third parties. Such guarantees in respect of loans must be in writing and the auditor should inspect this and also satisfy himself as to the standing of the third party. It is essential that some provision should be made in order to be able to ensure the guarantor's continuing ability to meet any loss arising, such as the supplying of a bank reference from time to time.

Compliance with the terms of the guarantee should be checked in order to make certain that no provision has been broken which would invalidate the guarantee.

21. Checking investments.

(*a*) *Adequate recording.* Where holdings of investments are considerable, a proper system of recording of holdings and their acquisition and disposal should be in operation and verification will be facilitated if carried out with reference to these. In any case, the auditor should request that a list be supplied of all holdings with cost and market values shown.

(*b*) *Retention of documents of title.* Frequently the investments will be held by banks or other recognised institutions from whom certificates should be obtained direct, requesting that the presence of any charges on the documents be stated.

Where the documents are held by the client, the auditor should ensure that he is able to examine all the investments at one and the same time to prevent any substitution for missing documents, and where any investments are not shown to be held in the name of the client, as in the case of nominee holdings, he should require that a deed of trust be produced.

22. Types of investment. The following are the most common types of investment held:

(a) *Inscribed stocks.* These stocks have now been superseded by registration and the issue of certificates.

(b) *Registered stocks and shares.*

(i) *Verification of title.* Registered stocks and shares imply that the title of the owner has been entered on the register of the company. A certificate under the seal of the company is granted giving details as to the numbers of the shares held and the owner's name. The auditor should examine this.

Where stock has been sold before the close of the financial period but delivery has not been completed, the auditor should examine the certificate still held and the broker's sold note. If delivery has been effected, then the receipt of the proceeds should be ascertained, although this may be shown in the following financial period.

If part of the holding has been sold and the certificate has been handed over but no new certificate has been received, the auditor should request the stockbroker who handled the matter that a new certificate be issued for the balance.

On the other hand, when shares have been purchased but no certificate has been received, the auditor should likewise request the stockbroker to issue a certificate for the shares.

(ii) *Bonus issues and rights issues.* Where investments are held in companies, bonus issues are sometimes made. It may be difficult for the auditor to know of such matters, but enquiries must be made in order to ensure that any such issues have been duly brought into the books. This will also apply with respect to rights issues. Shareholders may be given the right to take up shares at a lower rate than that prevailing on the market.

(iii) *Sale of rights.* Renounceable allotment letters are often forwarded with the notification since if the shareholder does not wish to take up the rights he may renounce the allotment and sell the rights on the market by transfer of the allotment letter duly renounced.

The difficulties arising in such transactions from the auditor's point of view must be apparent, since rights could be received and sold without any entries in the books to reveal the transaction. It will be necessary for the auditor to acquaint himself with securities when any movements are likely to take place, and also to make full enquiries with the clients or other stockbrokers.

(c) *Bearer securities.* These must, under the Exchange Control

Act 1947 be lodged with an "authorised depository", which normally would be a bank, although they may be deposited with solicitors or insurance companies, stock exchanges, or others. This is required as bearer securities are transferable on delivery and are subject to easy misappropriation.

The auditor should obtain a certificate from the bank, or otherwise, on which is shown the details of the securities concerned and stating that coupons are attached which must be surrendered when the interest or dividend payable is received.

In the case of bonds only recently acquired, where the actual certificate or bond has not been received, the auditor should vouch allotment letters and receipts for calls paid to date.

(d) *Tax reserve certificates.* Where these are held by the client they should be examined to see that they are held in the client's name and are not out of date. If they have been deposited with a bank, a certificate should be obtained to that effect.

If the certificates have been surrendered for settlement of tax prior to the attendance of the auditor, the receipt issued by the Inland Revenue should be vouched, the interest credit being checked as to the amount. As the interest is not paid over to the client but is used in reduction of the tax payable, care should be taken to ensure that the sum is duly entered in the taxation account and credited to the profit and loss account as interest received.

(e) *Treasury bills.* As these bills are payable to bearer they are normally deposited with a bank and where this is the case the auditor should obtain a certificate to that effect from the bank, requesting that their value and date be stated, and that they are free from any charge.

If they are in the client's possession they should be examined, care being taken to ensure that they are not out of date. Where the bills have matured prior to his attendance, the receipt of the proceeds should be vouched with the bank statement and the bank's notification.

(f) *Investments in building societies.* Where shares or deposits are made in building societies a pass book is issued. The auditor should examine this, noting due receipts of interest; but as with bank pass sheets, the deposit book should not be accepted as final evidence but a certificate to be forwarded direct to the auditor should be requested from the building society.

(g) *Loans to local authorities.* The relevant documents stating the terms of the loan should be inspected. A receipt for the loan should be vouched and a certificate should be applied for from the local authority concerned confirming the amount on loan.

INTERNAL CONTROL QUESTIONNAIRE

INVESTMENTS AND INVESTMENT INCOME

(A) *Control of investments*

1. Are securities held:

    (a) as investments,

    (b) on customers' behalf,

    (c) as collateral for bonus or otherwise?

2. Where are securities held?

3. Are adequate records kept differentiating between own securities and otherwise?

4. Are not less than two responsible officials required to have access at any one time?   Name these.

5. Who has control of keys or is otherwise empowered to gain access to the securities?

6. Are requests in writing required before withdrawal of securities is permitted?

7. What procedure ensures that all withdrawals of securities are properly recorded?

(B) *Verification of investments*

8. Are verifications, as to holdings, made regularly by staff?

9. What procedures are operated on verification?

10. Are securities verified compared with securities records?

11. Are verifications made by persons other than those maintaining the securities records, or cash transactions?

(C) *Investment income*

12. Is a record maintained showing the dates on which income is receivable?

13. Are the receipts checked and marked with these records?

14. Is this checking carried out by a person independent of cash receipts duties and security control?

15. By what means is it ensured that notification of rights or bonus issues is received and acted upon?

16. Do the records ensure that dividends are received when sales *ex div* or purchases *cum div* take place?

17. If securities are sold *cum div* and due to non-registration before books are closed the dividends are subsequently received,

what procedure operates to ensure such dividends are forwarded to the holder?

18. What procedure is laid down about receiving income from bearer securities?

STANDARD AUDIT PROGRAMME

INVESTMENTS AND INVESTMENT INCOME

(A) *Investment holdings*

1. Request list of present holding of investments, distinguishing between quoted and unquoted, and reconciling present book value with that on last balance sheet. Request also market value at end date be shown.

2. Verify purchase or sale of investments during year with documentary evidence, e.g. contract notes or agreements.

3. Examine minute book for proper authorisation of purchase or sales.

4. Check list as to market values shown with stock exchange list where quoted. If unquoted, inspect companies' accounts.

5. Enquire as to any material falls in value since end date.

6. Inspect certificates or bonds, ensuring that transfers and declarations of trust are attached in the case of nominee holdings. If deposited with bank, obtain certificate stating in whose name they are registered and whether they are free from lien.

(B) *Investment income.* To ensure that all income due is actually received:

7. Where interest fixed, scrutinise to ensure amount due is received.

8. Verify a proportion of the equity holdings as to income received, especially in respect of those purchased or sold during the period. This may be done in conjunction with Stock Exchange lists or company accounts in respect of unquoted investments. At the same time information should be obtained as to bonus and rights issues during year and where these apply to the companies holding the due receipt of bonus issues or action taken as to rights issues should be investigated.

23. Cash and bank balances.

(a) *Petty cash.* In verifying the amount of petty cash in hand, where more than one balance is maintained it is essential that all of them should be produced simultaneously. If this is not done

one balance may be used to make up a missing or deficient balance on another account.

It is not necessary for the auditor to attend on the last day of the financial period, but he may request that any such balances be banked on that date. However, this should not be necessary for he may check through the vouchers for payments made since and verify the balances still in hand on the day of his attendance. Where IOUs are shown amongst the vouchers he should have these certified by a responsible official. If any of these IOUs have been outstanding for any length of time he should pay particular attention to them, querying whether they should not rather be regarded as loans and so shown in the accounts.

When verifying petty cash balances through to the date of the audit, the amounts paid over from the main to the petty cash book should be checked.

(b) *Bank balances.* The balances shown on the bank pass sheets are not sufficient evidence as to the balance at the bank on the final date. Such sheets have been altered and others have been forged from time to time. Although the pass sheets should be checked with the cash book receipts and payments, the auditor should write direct to the bank requesting certification of all balances shown on the books of the bank in the name of the company.

Recommendation U.22 (*Bank Reports for Audit Purposes*) has been issued, which gives an illustration of a standard form and outlines procedures to be followed when applying to the bank for certificates as to balances and securities held.

(c) *Foreign balances.* In the case of balances held abroad, a certificate should be obtained from the agent concerned.

For S.A.P. for bank reconciliation, *see* p. 54.

24. Deposits including customs duty.

(a) *Exclusion from revenue.* Deposits may be required in a number of instances where a service is supplied, for example, in respect of electricity or telephone charges. Such deposits may easily be overlooked and charged with the amount transferred to the revenue account for the year. Where this is done the business may lose the benefit of a refund on removal or otherwise.

The auditor should ensure that the sum is properly segregated on the original bill and is carried forward as a balance, details of the deposit being given on the heading of the account.

(b) *Customs duty.* Deposits in respect of customs duty may

represent a considerable amount, and where these are made the auditor should pay careful attention to this matter, especially in view of the fact that the customs authorities do not normally issue receipts for the actual deposits.

The system prevails where goods are subject to duty that they may be left in bonded warehouses from which they are released on payment of the necessary duty. To obviate numerous separate payments and the work involved, a deposit may be made against which the duty is set on release of the goods by the authorities.

(c) *Internal check on customs duty.* The auditor should first ascertain that the internal system with regard to the recording of deposits and subsequent releases is adequate. He should also obtain a certificate from the authorities with respect to each deposit balance, as the authorities are prepared to certify the balance remaining at any date.

Where payment is made in respect of transactions, the customs authorities are prepared to acknowledge the payment, and the auditor should request that such acknowledgments be obtained and retained for future examination.

PROPRIETORS' FUNDS AND LIABILITIES

The items included in the balance sheet which require verification in respect of proprietors' funds or amounts due to creditors include the following:

(a) Share capital.
(b) Capital and revenue reserves.
(c) Loan capital.
(d) Liabilities and provisions.

25. Share capital.

(a) *Verification.* The authorised and issued share capital of a business must be shown on the balance sheet as required by the Companies Act 1948. The authorised share capital is stated in the Memorandum of the company. Its division into shares of a certain amount and into various classes may be stated in either the Memorandum or the Articles.

On the occasion of the first audit a note may be made of these particulars in the audit notebook and thereafter any changes may be checked as they arise.

It is not considered necessary for the balances on the share registers to be checked on every audit with the amounts on the share capital, and provided the auditor examines the lists of balances maintained by the staff of the business and notes that these total the amount of shares issued, this should be sufficient. But if movements of shares warrant it, a share transfer audit may be undertaken (*see* p. 225).

If during the period under review some major capital changes take place, then it will be necessary to check these.

(*b*) *New issues.* In the case of a new issue the receipt of application and allotment moneys should be vouched and the entries into the relevant accounts checked. If a bonus issue takes place, the auditor should check the entries in the accounts and ensure that the share register balances agree with them.

The minutes in respect of such capital issues should be examined and likewise if any forfeiture of shares takes place, the minutes as well as the adjustments required in the accounts should be checked. If any shares are issued for consideration other than cash, the relevant minutes and the copy of the contract should be examined, ascertaining that the contract has been filed with the Registrar of Companies.

(*c*) *Redeemable preference shares.* The special treatment to be accorded to this type of capital may conveniently be dealt with in the section concerned with the capital redemption reserve fund (*see* 30). The matter of dividends payable on such shares is discussed on p. 211.

(*d*) *Shares issued at a discount.* It is unlikely that the auditor will have much to do with such shares; there are more effective ways of issuing shares than offering them at a discount, since this in itself would militate against the success of the issue. Nevertheless, he should be aware of the clauses in the Companies Act 1948, s. 57, which specifies that a company may issue such shares, provided:

(*i*) they are of a class already issued;

(*ii*) it has passed a resolution in general meeting to that effect, and obtained the sanction of the court;

(*iii*) the resolution specifies the maximum rate of discount;

(*iv*) the issue is made more than one year after the company was entitled to commence business;

(*v*) the issue is made within one month (or extended time) of the date of the court sanction.

Every prospectus of the issue must show particulars of the

discount or as much as has not been written off at the date of the prospectus.

The amount of the discount not written off must be shown in every balance sheet of the company.

26. Capital and revenue reserves. When verifying the various items shown on the balance sheet, the auditor will not be so much concerned with the amounts set aside to reserves from the point of view of prudent policy or otherwise; he will be concerned, however, to see that such items reflect a true and fair view as to what has taken place, and also that, where applicable, certain requirements of the Companies Act 1967 are complied with.

27. Classification of reserves. Before dealing more specifically with various types of reserve, the following extract from the Institute of Chartered Accountants' publication, *Terms used in the Published Accounts of Limited Companies* should be considered:

(*a*) The descriptions CAPITAL RESERVE(S) and REVENUE RESERVE are normally appropriate as headings to groups of reserves or as descriptions of single items.

(*b*) The expression CAPITAL RESERVE is appropriate for a reserve which for statutory reasons or because of the provisions of the Memorandum or Articles of Association of a company or for other legal reasons is not free for distribution through the profit and loss account.

(*c*) The expression CAPITAL RESERVE may also be applied to any other reserve which although legally distributable is regarded by the directors as not available for distribution through the profit and loss account at the date of the balance sheet.

(*d*) Subject to any provision in the Articles of Association prescribing another name, it will normally be appropriate to describe a reserve as GENERAL to distinguish it from another reserve specifically described, or in the case of a revenue reserve to distinguish it from the profit and loss account balance.

(*e*) The description RESERVE FUND is not appropriate unless the reserve is represented by specifically earmarked investments (or other assets) realisable as and when required at not less than the amount of the "reserve fund". Exceptions arise from the statutory requirement to describe a "capital redemption reserve fund" as such and from any provision of the Memorandum or Articles of Association, or other instrument constituting or regulating a company, requiring a reserve to be described as a "fund".

28. Distinction between capital and revenue reserves. The distinction made between capital and revenue reserves is not required under the Companies Act 1967, but the aggregate amounts of reserves and provisions must be shown and any material movements therein. Although amounts may be set aside to capital reserves for reasons in accordance with the Articles of a company, it is possible to transfer amounts so set aside back to a revenue reserve for subsequent distribution.

Concerning the various types of reserve which may be created, the following matters are of particular interest to the auditor. He should ascertain either that the legal requirements have been observed or that the reserves comply with the articles of the company.

29. Share premium account. When shares are issued at a premium, it is a requirement of s. 56 of the Companies Act 1948 that the amount received in respect of the premium shall be placed to the credit of a share premium account and shown as a separate item on the balance sheet. The same section specifies that the share premium account may only be used for the following purposes:

(*a*) In paying up unissued shares of the company to be issued to the members as fully paid bonus shares.

(*b*) In writing off preliminary expenses.

(*c*) In writing off the expenses of, or the commission paid or discount allowed on, any issue of shares or debentures.

(*d*) In providing for the premium payable on redemption of any redeemable preference shares or debentures.

30. Capital redemption reserve fund (and redeemable preference shares). A capital redemption reserve fund may arise on the redemption of redeemable preference shares. Such shares may be issued by a company if so authorised by its Articles, provided that:

(*a*) no such shares shall be redeemed except out of profits available for dividend, or out of the proceeds of a fresh issue of shares made for the purpose;

(*b*) at the date of redemption the shares must be fully paid;

(*c*) where any such shares are redeemed otherwise than out of the proceeds of a fresh issue, there shall, out of profits which would otherwise have been available for dividend, be transferred to a reserve fund, to be called the *capital redemption reserve fund,* a sum equal to the nominal amount of the shares redeemed, and the provisions of this Act relating to the reduction of the share capital of a company shall, except as provided in this section, apply as if the capital redemption reserve fund were paid up share capital;

(d) any premium payable on redemption must have been provided, before the redemption, out of profits, or out of the company's share premium account.

If so desired, the capital redemption reserve fund may be used for the purpose of paying up unissued shares of the company to be issued as fully paid bonus shares to the members.

If new shares are issued for the purpose of redemption of the old shares, no *ad valorum* stamp duty will be payable provided the old shares are redeemed within one month of the issue of the new shares: s. 58, Companies Act 1948.

The Companies Act 1967, Sch. 2, requires disclosure of

> any part of the issued capital that consists of redeemable preference shares, the earliest and latest dates on which the company has power to redeem those shares, whether those shares must be redeemed in any event or are liable to be redeemed at the option of the company, and whether any (and if so, what) premium is payable on redemption.

31. Reserve funds. In the quotation from the Institute of Chartered Accountants' publication given above, it will be observed that the description reserve fund should normally be applied only to such reserves where the profits which they represent have been applied in the purchase of investments earmarked specially for the purpose.

The auditor is particularly concerned with such reserve funds since, although there is no statutory requirement as to the specific investment of funds set aside out of profits for a particular purpose, often such conditions are required under a deed or in accordance with a provision in the Memorandum or Articles of a company. The most common of these is the *debenture redemption reserve fund.*

32. Debenture redemption reserve fund.

(a) *Funds available for redemption.* This type of reserve is frequently met, for where debentures are redeemable, in certain circumstances, as specified in the debenture deed, or more particularly on a specified date, it is a matter of expediency to ensure that the necessary funds are available as required. This being stated in the deed, the auditor should make himself

conversant with the terms of the deed and should satisfy himself
that its requirements are carried out. If the sums set aside are to
be invested in specially earmarked securities, the auditor should
ascertain that this is being done. He should also be satisfied that
the sums set aside are adequate having regard to the redemption
date.

Such matters as the amounts to be invested and the rate of
yield to be received are calculated prior to issue of the debentures
to ensure that with interest received on the investments the
necessary sum due on redemption will be forthcoming.

(b) *Redemption.* Where debentures are redeemed during their
lifetime and investments are realised for the purpose, the auditor
should ascertain that any profits or losses arising on realisation
or on the redemption of the debentures is carried to the reserve
fund and not to the general profit and loss account.

On redemption of the debentures, the nominal value of the
debentures redeemed, or if on final redemption, the balance
shown on the reserve fund account, should be transferred to a
general reserve as the profits the fund represent will have been
absorbed into the general assets of the business.

33. Company taxation. The auditor will need to ascertain that
the amounts provided for taxation are adequate, which will
involve checking the draft computations, and if received, their
agreement by the Inland Revenue. At the same time he will need
to ensure that proper records of fixed assets are kept. Checking
of claims made in respect of writing-down allowances can sometimes be revealing as compared with the records maintained in
respect of fixed assets (*see* p. 126).

The Standard issued under *Accounting for deferred taxation,*
S.S.A.P. M.15, has been necessitated by the need to ensure
uniformity of presentation. Taxation on profits for a period may
bear little relationship to the income and expenditure dis-
allowable, or certain items in the period of the accounts may fall
into a different period for taxation purposes. The Standard
recommends that the liability method of provision should be
adopted.

The auditor will be concerned to see that deferred taxation
should be accounted for in all short-term timing differences and
in respect of the tax effects arising from other timing differences
of material amount which can be shown to have a reasonable
probability of continuing in the future.

(a) Profit and Loss Account.

The taxation effect of timing differences dealt with in the profit and loss account should be shown separately as a component of the total taxation charge or credit in the profit and loss account, or by way of note to the accounts. To the extent that amounts of deferred taxation arise which relate to extraordinary items these should be shown separately as part of such items. Adjustments to the balance of the deferred taxation account consequent (under the liability method) upon a change in the rate of tax should be separately disclosed as part of the taxation charge unless the change in rate is associated with a fundamental change in the basis of taxation, in which case the adjustment should itself be treated as an extraordinary item.

(b) Balance Sheet.

Deferred taxation account balances should be shown separately in the balance sheet and described as "deferred taxation". They should not be shown as part of shareholders' funds nor included under current assets or current liabilities. A note to the accounts should indicate the nature and amount of the major elements of which the net balance is composed and a description of the method of calculation adopted.

Where amounts of deferred taxation arise which relate to movements on reserves (e.g. resulting from a revaluation of assets) the amounts transferred to or from the deferred taxation account should be shown separately as part of such movements.

Where the value of an asset is shown by way of note on the face of or annexed to the accounts and that value differs from the book value of the asset, the note should also show, if material, the tax implications which would result from the realisation of the asset at the balance sheet data at the stated value.

The Standard is in agreement with the Companies Act 1967, Sch. 2, 27(1)(b), which states:

The expression reserve shall not . . . include any sum set aside for the purpose of its being used to prevent undue fluctuation in charges for taxation.

Paragraph 7A:

If an amount is set aside for the purpose of its being used to prevent undue fluctuations in charges for taxation, it shall be stated.

Paragraph 11(8A):

If a sum set aside for the purpose of its being used to prevent undue fluctuations in charges for taxation has been used during the financial year for another purpose, the amount thereof and the fact that it has been so used . . . shall be stated.

Paragraph 12(1)(*c*):

> ... the amount of the charge to revenue for U.K. corporation tax
> and, if that amount would have been greater but for relief from
> double taxation, the amount which it would have been but for such
> relief, the amount of the charge for U.K. income tax and the amount
> of the charge for taxation imposed outside the U.K. of profits,
> income and (so far as charged to revenue) capital gains.

34. Dividend equalisation reserve. A dividend equalisation
reserve is formed by the setting aside of profits to enable the
payment of dividends in a year when profits do not warrant the
payment out of current funds, or to maintain a regular distribution of dividends from year to year when profits earned are of a
fluctuating nature.

Since share prices are largely governed by dividend payments
it is prudent policy to maintain regular dividends and to prevent
undue variations. This reserve may be especially applicable in the
following circumstances:

(*a*) Where companies are operating in business subject to
sudden changes in income, e.g. those dealing in agricultural
crops, or are dependent on overseas harvests.

(*b*) Where raw materials forming a large proportion of prime
cost of manufacture are subject to wide price fluctuations.

(*c*) Where sales are subject to fluctuations through changes of
fashion or taste.

(*d*) Where the business is of a hazardous nature, such as
financing new business undertakings.

Where such reserves are created, it is always advisable to
ensure that they are represented by investments outside the
business. These should be easily realisable and as income on them
is not the main consideration, they should be in the nature of
gilt-edged securities.

35. Loan capital: debentures.

(*a*) *Definition.* A debenture is a written acknowledgment under
seal of a debt due by a company undertaking to pay the debt in
certain circumstances or on a specified date and to pay a specified
rate of interest in the meantime.

Such debentures may be *simple* or *naked* debentures, giving no
security for the loan; or, more usually, they may give security
either as a *fixed* or *floating* charge over the assets of the company
—a fixed charge being in respect of certain assets and a floating

charge being over the whole assets of the company at the date on which the charge crystallises, i.e. when the debenture holders, on the occurrence of a certain event, enforce their security, e.g. on the non-payment of interest or principal.

(*b*) *Issue of debentures*. If an issue of debentures takes place during the period under audit, the auditor should ascertain that the issue is in accordance with any clauses contained in the articles of the company. If no such clauses exist, then a trading company has implied power to borrow money and to give security therefor.

(*c*) *Issue at a discount*. The receipt of the cash should be vouched, and if the debentures are issued at a discount, the transfer to the debenture discount account should be checked, so ensuring that the debenture will be shown at the full value of indebtedness both in the account and on the balance sheet.

The discount should also be shown on the balance sheet until written off. In compliance with the Companies Acts, the auditor should ascertain that such debentures are duly registered with the Registrar of Companies, and that they are entered in the Register of Charges.

(*d*) *Issue at a premium*. If the debentures are issued at a premium, there is no restriction on the use of the premium, but being in the nature of a capital profit, it would be preferably used for some capital purpose, such as the writing-off of any fictitious assets or otherwise used for the purpose of augmenting a debenture redemption reserve fund (*see* 32).

The auditor should take notes of the terms of the debentures for inclusion in the audit notebook as well as confirming such matters as the rate of interest payable and the redemption date and any premium payable on redemption.

36. Loan capital: convertible loan notes. These may, or may not, give a charge on the assets of the company. The terms of their issue should be ascertained, noting the interest rate and the conversion date. There may be a prospectus in respect of their issue where they are offered by a quoted company to the public, but in the first instance the shareholders must be given the right to take them up. This right may be waived by the company in general meeting, however.

If they give a charge over the assets, the auditor should ascertain that this is duly registered with the Registrar of Joint Stock Companies.

37. Liabilities and provisions.

(*a*) *Liabilities.*

(*i*) *Trade creditors.* The method of ensuring that all liabilities in respect of goods purchased has already been dealth with (*see p.* 64).

(*ii*) *Taxation.* The liability in respect of taxation is a matter of importance to the auditor.

The amount set aside in respect for liability to tax can materially affect profits available for distribution; it is essential, therefore, that the auditor should check the computation of the amount set aside for taxation purposes. If the sum has been agreed it should be shown as a liability, otherwise it should be considered a provision.

(*iii*) *Accruals.* These will include the amounts due on the various nominal accounts, such as rent, rates, lighting, heating, loan interest, etc. These should be checked when examining the accounts in the nominal ledger, and by their nature should reveal amounts due. The calculations involved should be checked and vouched with relevant documents as necessary. Changes in recurring charges, such as rent, should be watched for, and enquiries made to ensure that any new or non-recurring items have been accounted for, especially if invoices in respect of these have not been received.

Wages and salaries are not always paid up to the balance sheet date, and any liability in respect thereof should be obtained.

(*b*) *Contingent liabilities.* The subject of contingent liabilities can prove a difficult one for the auditor. In their very nature they are *contingent* and therefore may not accrue. On the other hand, if they do subsequently arise because of some event relevant to the period covered by the auditor's report, then to ignore them might tend towards an untrue view of the company's revenue position.

Such liabilities as may arise can be rather easily concealed. This difficulty of ascertainment has prompted the I.C.A. to issue their Statement of Auditing U.16, *The ascertainment and confirmation of contingent liabilities arising from pending legal matters.*

The duty of directors to ensure that proper account is taken of all liabilities is mentioned, but audit procedures which may be applied are given. Briefly summarised these are:

(*i*) reviewing the client's system of recording claims and how they are brought to the attention of the board;

(*ii*) discussing the arrangement for instructing solicitors with the official(s) responsible;

(*iii*) examining the minutes of the board of directors or other committees;

(*iv*) examining correspondence with solicitors and bills rendered by them, and also requesting that they be asked to furnish bills outstanding and to confirm they have no unbilled charges;

(*v*) Obtaining a list of matters referred to solicitors with estimates of possible ultimate liabilities; also requesting a statement that the relevant official is unaware of any further matters other than those disclosed.

In appropriate circumstances, confirmation of certain representations made by directors may be deemed necessary, and where confirmation is sought from the clients' legal advisers, the solicitor/client relationship must be respected. This will necessitate the client writing to the legal adviser with a request that reply be made to the auditors direct.

The Law Society and the I.C.A. have agreed on a specific form of wording in order that confirmation may be made by the legal advisers of estimated amounts submitted for their verification (*see* U.16).

If significant matters not previously disclosed are discovered by the auditors, then they may request their clients to address further enquires, to, or arrange a meeting with, the solicitors.

In extreme cases, it may be necessary for the auditors to qualify their report.

(*c*) *Provisions*. These are dealt with on p. 202, where certain legal decisions affecting them are quoted.

PROGRESS TEST 7

1. What precautionary measures should the auditor take when verifying assets?   **(1–3)**

2. In what way may goodwill be verified?   **(4)**

3. How may costs on acquisition of trade-marks be dealt with?   **(6)**

4. How should freehold properties be verified?   **(8)**

5. What is signified by the term *registered land*?   **(8)**

6. With regard to freehold properties, what should the auditor

particularly concern himself with to ensure complete ownership? (8)

7. How may plant and machinery be verified? Is it expedient
in any case personally to inspect such assets? (9)

8. How may ownership of motor vehicles be verified? (12)

9. How may debtor balances be verified? (13)

10. State the requirements of the Companies Act 1948, with
regard to loans made to directors. (15)

11. What are the most common types of loans made on
security? (17–20)

12. When inspecting a mortgage deed, what matters should
receive particular attention? (17)

13. What is an essential part of audit procedure when inspecting investments actually held by the client? (21)

14. What special difficulty arises in auditing *rights issues*?
(22)

15. How is interest received on tax reserve certificates? (22)

16. Where various petty cash balances are held, what procedures should the auditor observe? Should he attend on the last
day of the financial period? (23)

17. Are bank pass sheets sufficient evidence of balances held
at the bank? (23)

18. State the procedures to be observed in the case of a new
share issue. (25)

19. Give a definition of a capital reserve. What is a reserve
fund? (26, 27)

20. In what ways may a share premium account be used? (29)

21. For what reason is it important to invest the funds set
aside for debenture redemption reserve funds outside the
business? (32)

22. In what circumstances may dividend equalisation funds be
set up? (34)

23. What is a debenture? Are there different kinds of debentures? (35)

24. In what way should accruals be verified? (37)

SPECIMEN QUESTIONS

1. Write brief notes on the points to be observed in the
verification of the following assets of a limited company:

(a) Freehold properties.
(b) Motor vehicles.

(c) Plant.

(d) Trade debtors.   *I.C.A.* (*E.W.*)

2. As auditor of a limited company, you ascertain that, during the year under review, the company had purchased:

(a) A plot of freehold land adjacent to the factory.

(b) £25,000 of Uptown Corporation 5% Stock 1968–73.

(c) Tax reserve certificates.

(d) A fork-lift truck for use in the works.

State how you would vouch these purchases and verify the assets.   *I.C.A.* (*E.W.*)

3. In the course of your audit of the accounts of a limited company you ask for the title deeds to a freehold building purchased during the year under review.

State:

(a) Four points appearing in the conveyance to your client which you would require to note.

(b) How you would vouch the payments for the acquisition of the property including the incidental costs.

I.C.A. (*E.W.*) (*Inter.*)

4. How would you verify the following items included in the balance sheet of a limited company:

(a) Machinery being acquired on hire purchase.

(b) Loans to employees (not officers of the company).

(c) Leasehold premises?   *I.C.A.* (*E.W.*)

5. State what steps you would take to verify the amounts shown in the annual accounts, for:

(a) Plant and machinery.

(b) Additions and alterations to factory premises carried out by own employees.

(c) Motor vehicles.

(d) Loose tools.   *I.C.A.* (*E.W.*)

6. A limited company, whose accounts you are auditing, has made a loan to a director.

You are required to tabulate the provisions of the Companies Act 1948, relating to such a loan.   *I.C.A.* (*E.W.*)

7. You are auditor of a limited company. State how you would verify the existence of the following assets and liabilities, and ensure that they appear at a proper value in the accounts:

(a) A motor vehicle purchased seven years ago.

(b) The balance due at the end of the financial year to a finance company in respect of a machine bought on hire purchase.

(c) The amount of the telephone account which is accrued at the balancing date.

(d) The petty cash float held at the company's store twenty miles away.

(e) A life policy on the life of the managing director assigned to the company. *A.C.A. (Inter.)*

8. (a) How would you verify the valuation of loose tools manufactured by a company for its own use and what steps would you take to verify the quantity on hand at the balancing data?

(b) What steps would you take to verify the existence of all the information required by the Companies Acts relating to investments made by a company in shares of a quoted company?

(c) Give your views on a proposal by the directors of a contracting company to establish a dividend equalisation reserve.

A.C.A.

9. In connection with your audit of a large firm of builders' merchants, you have been supplied with a schedule of debtors' balances at the year end, and with a list of the various items making up the amount set aside in the accounts against bad and doubtful debts. Arrangements have also been made with the client for you to carry out a sample verification of debtors' balances by direct communication. You are asked:

(a) to state the circumstances in which you would consider the positive method of verification of such balances to be preferable to the use of the negative method, and

(b) to state the evidence that you would expect to be obtained from an examination of the individual sales ledger accounts which would assist you to form an opinion as to the adequacy or otherwise of the bad and doubtful debts provision that has been made. *I.C.A. (E.W.)*

10. State the particular points to which you would direct your attention in carrying out the audit of an issue of debentures to the public by a limited company. *I.C.A.*

11. How would you verify the amount appearing in the balance sheet of a limited company for current taxation?

I.C.A. (E.W.)

12. As auditor of Parent Ltd., a holding company, you are examining the consolidation schedules with the accounts of the

individual companies in the group in order to make your report to the members of the holding company on the consolidated accounts relating to the year ended 31st December, 1961.

During 1961 Parent Ltd. acquired for cash, three new wholly-owned subsidiaries; the accounting year of each ends on 31st December.

You are required to state how you would expect the following matters relating to the three new subsidiaries to have been dealt with in the consolidated accounts:

(a) The amounts paid for the shares of those companies.

(b) The dividends paid or proposed to be paid by them since acquisition.

(c) The revenue reserves, including the balance on profit and loss account, appearing in their balance sheets on 31st December, 1961. *I.C.A. (E.W.)*

13. When verifying debtors' balances:

(a) In what circumstances might an auditor consider adopting the procedure of confirmation by direct communication?

(b) What factors will influence his choice between the negative and the positive request methods?

(c) What considerations should he take into account when selecting a sample of the debtors' accounts for test circularisation?

(d) Draft a suitable form of letter to be sent to the debtors selected. *I.C.A. (E.W.)*

14. Your firm is preparing a manual of outline audit programmes and has assigned to you the task of preparing the programme for trade debtors.

Draft the required programme, which is to include the circularisation of debtors. *A.C.A.*

CHAPTER VIII

Depreciation and Appreciation

DEPRECIATION

Before proceeding to the subject of the valuation of the items included on a balance sheet, we must consider a factor which vitally affects the ultimate valuation of assets, namely, depreciation.

1. Definition. Depreciation may be defined briefly as the diminution in the value of an asset over a period. No one particular cause is reckoned to reduce the value of an asset by depreciation, rather, a combination of factors. Internally, there are those inherent in the asset itself, such as wear and tear, and externally there are such things as technological obsolescence. In itself, therefore, depreciation might be thought to cause no great difficulty from the auditing point of view. There are, however, various aspects which require careful attention.

2. No actual expenditure involved. As opposed to other charges made against the revenue of a business or other undertaking, the charge made for depreciation, whilst reducing the profit, does not entail any actual expenditure on the sum currently set against profits. The initial capital outlay having been made, no further amount is actually expended, nevertheless the business is suffering a real loss in the diminution of the value of the asset being retained for the purpose of earning profits.

3. Auditor's responsibility. Since the figure set against the profits will affect the resultant excess or deficiency, it is the auditor's responsibility to ascertain that this sum is adequate, being neither too small nor too great. Should the figure be understated, then profits may be shown as distributable, which if paid out would cause the value of the business to decrease, and at the same time cause an inadequate sum to be set aside for the future replacement of the asset or assets concerned.

It may be argued that even if an adequate sum is shown in the accounts it does not follow that the profits which would otherwise have been shown as available for distribution will be set aside specifically for the replacement of the assets, as the amount of profit made available may be expended on some other item, and be lost in the general assets of the business. This is true, but nevertheless the amount set against profits will ensure that the amount is retained within the business in whatever form. The argument does reveal, however, the importance of setting aside the amount of depreciation shown in the accounts by the maintenance of a sinking fund with the investment of the funds in a manner which will make them readily available when the replacement date falls due.

4. Replacement reserves. The additional complication now arises as to the actual sum to be made available for the replacement of assets. With the operation of inflationary tendencies, an annual amount set aside for the diminution of asset values, even if invested, may on the date for replacement only ensure that the original cost figure is available. For this reason it is now considered prudent policy to invest additional sums, so building up an asset replacement reserve. In compliance with the Companies Act 1967, such sums set aside are properly shown under a reserve as any amount in excess of the depreciation provision is rightly considered an appropriation of profits rather than a charge against them. In this respect, the auditor will need to have some particular information as to the nature of the assets being dealt with, for it is possible to transfer a more than adequate amount to replacement reserves, though this would not be of such moment as the contrary policy of under-providing for depreciation on assets.

APPRECIATION

5. Adjustment of balance sheet values. We have been concerned thus far with the problems arising when it is necessary to replace assets after a period of inflation, but as some assets, such as freehold land and properties, are often held over considerable periods, inflationary and other economic effects have to be dealt with during the period over which such assets are retained. Though, as in the case of freehold properties, some assets may suffer loss in value due to normal wear and tear, owing to economic factors, their intrinsic value may quite rapidly increase.

Accountants, however, are rightly hesitant to bring into

consideration profits of an estimated nature which have not actually been realised, and which may make such profits appear available for distribution, or expendable purposes. Nevertheless, although unrealised, the increase in value of an asset, which if disposed of could bring in a considerable profit, cannot be ignored. This has led to the writing-up of assets on balance sheets, with the creation of corresponding reserves. Furthermore, pressure due to such matters as take-over bids and share valuation have forced some companies to revalue their assets, putting the resulting increase to reserves, thereby showing the assets at their current value, and so improving the "appearance" of the balance sheet, where the full value of the company as a whole is shown (*see also* Recommendation N.12).

6. Capital nature of reserves. Still wishing to preserve an attitude of prudence with respect to such reserves, accountants have generally considered it advisable to designate the amounts created on revaluation as capital reserves. By this it is hoped to mitigate the desire to appropriate unrealised profits by way of revenue distributions while at the same time encouraging the capitalisation of distributions to shareholders by means of bonus issues. Legally, however, there are only two capital reserves which it is not possible to appropriate for revenue purposes, namely, the share premium account and a capital redemption reserve fund. Therefore, from the auditor's point of view, provided the revaluation is to his satisfaction, he can only offer advice as to that which is considered prudent policy, but thereafter his duty would extend only to compliance with the requirements of the Companies Acts. This subject is also dealt with in Chapter XI.

ACCOUNTING FOR DEPRECIATION

7. Introduction. As S.S.A.P. M.12 is an important but short Standard, it is quoted below complete (**8–12**).

8. Explanatory Note. Depreciation is a measure of the wearing out, consumption or other loss of value of a fixed asset whether arising from use, effluxion of time or obsolescence through technology and market changes. Depreciation should be allocated to accounting periods so as to charge a fair proportion to each accounting period during the expected useful life of the asset. Depreciation includes amortisation of fixed assets whose useful life is predetermined (e.g. leases) and depletion of wasting assets (e.g. mines).   (1)

Assessment of depreciation, and its allocation to accounting periods, involves in the first instance consideration of three factors: (*a*) cost (or valuation when an asset has been revalued in the financial statements); (*b*) the nature of the asset and the length of its expected useful life to the business having due regard to the incidence of obsolescence; (*c*) estimated residual value.   (2)

An asset's useful life may be: (*a*) predetermined, as in leaseholds; (*b*) directly governed by extraction or consumption; (*c*) dependent on the extent of use; (*d*) reduced by obsolescence or physical deterioration. (3)

The precise assessment of residual value is normally a difficult matter. Where it is likely to be small in relation to cost, it is convenient to regard it as "nil" and to deal with any proceeds on eventual disposal in the same way as depreciation over-provided on disposal as referred to in para. (6) below.   (4)

The allocation of depreciation to accounting periods involves the exercise of judgment by management in the light of technical, commercial and accounting considerations and accordingly requires annual review. When, as the result of experience or of changed circumstances, it is considered that the original estimate of useful life of an asset requires to be revised, the unamortised cost of the asset should be charged to revenue over the revised remaining useful life. If at any time the unamortised cost is seen to be irrecoverable in full (perhaps as a result of obsolescence or a fall in demand for a product), it should be written down immediately to the estimated recoverable amount which should be charged over the remaining useful life.   (5)

Where fixed assets are disposed of for an amount which is greater or less than their book value, the surplus or deficiency should be reflected in the results of the year and disclosed separately if material.   (6)

The management of a business has a duty to allocate depreciation as fairly as possible to the periods expected to benefit from the use of the asset and should select the method regarded as most appropriate to the type of asset and its use in the business.   (7)

A change from one method of providing depreciation to another is permissible only on the grounds that the new method will give a fairer representation of the results and of the financial position. In these circumstances the unamortised cost should be written off over the remaining useful life commencing with the period in which the change is made.   (8)

Where assets are revalued and effect is given to the revaluation in the financial statements, the charge for depreciation thereafter should be based on the revalued amount and, in the year of change, there should be disclosed by way of note to the financial statements the subdivision of the charge between that applicable to original cost (or valuation if previously revalued) and that applicable to the change in value on the current revaluation, if material.   (9)

It is not appropriate to omit charging depreciation of a fixed asset on the grounds that its market value is greater than its net book value. If account is taken of such increased value by writing up the net book value of a fixed asset then, as indicated in para. (9), an increased charge for depreciation will become necessary. (10)

Freehold land, unless subject to depletion by, for example, the extraction of minerals or to reduction in value due to other circumstances, will not normally require a provision for depreciation. However, the value of freehold land may be adversely affected by considersations such as the desirability of its location either socially or in relation available sources of material, labour or sales and in these circumstance it should be written down. (11)

Buildings have a limited life which may be materially affected by technological and environmental changes and they should be depreciated having regard to the same criteria as in the case of other fixed assets. (12)

As in the case of other assets an increase in the value of land or buildings does not remove the necessity for charging depreciation on the buildings whenever any of the causes mentioned in para. (1) are applicable, whether or not the value of the asset has increased in the past. (13)

9. Transitional arrangements. Where existing buildings are depreciated for the first time under the terms of this standard it will represent a change in accounting policy and therefore the amount of depreciation charged which relates to prior years should properly be treated as a prior year adjustment and charged against the opening balance of retained profits. (14)

10. Definition of terms. The following definition is used for the purpose of this statement: *depreciation* is the measure of the wearing out, consumption or other loss of value of a fixed asset whether arising from use, effluxion of time or obsolescence through technology and market changes. (15)

11. Standard accounting practice: accounting treatment. Provision for depreciation of fixed assets having a finite useful life should be made by allocating the cost (or revalued amount) less estimated residual values of the assets as fairly as possible to the periods expected to benefit from their use. (16)

Where there is a revision of the estimated useful life of an asset, the unamortised cost should be charged over the revised remaining useful life. (17)

However, if at any time unamortised cost of an asset is seen to be irrecoverable in full, it should be written down immediately to the estimated recoverable amount which should be charged over the remaining useful life. (18)

Where there is a change from one method of depreciation to another, the unamortised cost of the asset should be written off over the remaining useful life on the new basis commencing with the period in which the change is made. The effect should be disclosed in the year of change, if material.   (19)

Where assets are revalued in the financial statements, the provision for depreciation should be based on the revalued amount and current estimate of remaining useful life, with disclosure in the year of change, of the effect of the revaluation, if material.   (20)

12. Disclosure. The following should be disclosed in the financial statements for each major class of depreciable asset: (*a*) the depreciation methods used; (*b*) the useful lives or the depreciation rates used; (*c*) total depreciation allocated for the period; (*d*) the gross amount of depreciable assets and the related accumulated depreciation.   (21)

Date from which effective
The accounting and disclosure requirements set out in this statement should be adopted as soon as possible and regarded as standard in respect of financial statements relating to periods starting on or after 1st January, 1978, except that the provisions of the standard need not be applied to investment properties in respect of periods starting before 1st January, 1979.   (22)

Compliance with International Standard No. 4 Depreciation Accounting
Compliance with the requirements of Statement of Standard Accounting Practice No. 12 Accounting for Depreciation will automatically ensure compliance with International Accounting Standard No. 4 Depreciation Accounting.

LEGAL ASPECTS OF DEPRECIATION

13. Introduction. Certain specific assets have been mentioned in the foregoing extract which are dealt with again (*see* IX), when dealing with the valuation of particular types of assets. The legal aspect of depreciation is closely bound up with the consideration of profits and the amount which may be properly used for distribution purposes, but whilst the following cases are of importance to the auditor from the latter point of view, they are also relevant as to the charge which should, or should not, be included for depreciation purposes.

14. Verner v. General and Commercial Investment Trust (1894).
In this case, the capital value of some of the company's investments had fallen considerably, and the company proposed to pay a dividend without providing for the obvious depreciation of its main assets. The aid of the court was sought to restrain the company from carrying out its proposal. The injunction was refused as it was held that the company was solvent and acting within its Articles.

An important statement from the auditor's point of view was made during the course of the judgment, namely:

> Fixed capital may be sunk and lost, and yet the excess of current receipts over current payments may be divided; but floating or circulating capital must be kept up, as otherwise it will enter into and form part of such excess, in which case to divide such excess without deducting the capital which forms part of it will be contrary to law.

15. Lee v. Neuchatel Asphalte Co. Ltd. (1889). Here, the company's main asset consisted of a concession to mine a bituminous substance in Switzerland.

The company had been formed specifically to acquire and work the asset and a clause had been inserted in the Articles stating that no provision for depreciation or wastage of fixed assets need be made before payment of dividends. An ordinary shareholder sought the aid of the court to restrain the payment of a dividend on the preference shares.

It was held that a company may, by its Articles, provide for the distribution of profits before making good the depreciation of fixed assets.

During the course of judgment it was stated that:

> If a company is formed to acquire or work property of a wasting nature, e.g. a mine, quarry or patent, the capital expended in acquiring the property may be regarded as sunk and gone, and . . . any excess of money obtained by working the mine over the cost of working it may be divided among the shareholders; and this is true, although some portion of the property itself is sold and in one sense the capital is thereby diminished.

The principle applied in the foregoing cases makes it clear that it is not necessary to provide for depreciation of fixed assets before declaring a dividend out of current profits. The following cases are also relevant, but it will be observed they are all still concerned with the aspect of depreciation on *fixed* assets.

16. Bolton *v*. Natal Land and Colonisation Co., Ltd. (1892). Ten years earlier, in 1882, the company had suffered a heavy bad debt of £70,000 but had avoided showing a loss for the year by writing up the value of the lands to approximately the same amount. In 1885, current profits were made and a dividend was then paid out of these profits.

It was held that, despite the fact of there having been no justification for the writing-up of the land, and that it was excessively valued in the accounts, following the decision in *Lee* v. *Neuchatel Asphalte Co., Ltd.*, it was not illegal to distribute the current profits without making any adjustment for the loss of the capital.

17. Wilmer *v*. McNamara and Co., Ltd. (1895). The principle that a company may distribute dividends out of current profits without providing for depreciation of fixed assets, was maintained in this case. Having been formed to acquire an existing business including its goodwill, amounts were written off the assets taken over. On revaluation, however, it was discovered that there was a deficiency of £43,000 in the value of the assets as against capital of £120,000. It was proposed to declare a dividend on the preference shares which would entail the distribution of the current year's profits.

Although the sufficiency of the depreciation charge for the year was questioned, it was held that this had little relevance with regard to the proposed payment of the dividend since the principle as applied to the *Lee* v. *Neuchatel* case applied here.

18. Brown *v*. Gaumont British Picture Corporation Ltd. (1937). Where a company has holdings in subsidiary companies and these have depreciated, it is not necessary to provide against this before payment of dividends on cumulative preference shares. Whilst the balance sheet of the holding company showed a large reserve mostly in the form of a share premium account, the consolidated balance sheet of the group showed that heavy losses had been made by the subsidiary companies. Here again the *Lee* v. *Neuchatel* principle was maintained.

BUSINESS POLICY AND DEPRECIATION

19. The accountant's view-point. The foregoing constitute sound legal decisions, but from the accounting point of view do not constitute prudent business policy. If the desire is to maintain a continuing business where assets are depreciating, they must at some stage be renewed. Therefore, to run down the fixed assets and to make no provision for their replacement is to invite disaster. The courts are not so much concerned with prudent business policy as are accountants, and as the money expended on fixed assets has to be disposed of, then current profits are available for distribution purposes.

Obviously, such a policy could not be pursued by a continuing company which had to face the necessity of renewing its assets, but there are instances of companies, such as those engaged in gold mining, where it is realised that the capital has been sunk in a wasting asset and when this has been exhausted, the company has no purpose for continuing to exist. The distribution of profits in such cases, which might otherwise seem excessive, are then looked upon as not only including the current profits, but an element of return of capital, which will ultimately be written off on liquidation, although in normal circumstances no reduction of the capital of the business would be allowed.

20. Losses on current assets. The courts do, however, maintain a very different attitude with respect to losses sustained on current assets, since these must always be provided against, as was stated by the judge in the extract given from the *Verner* v. *General and Commercial Investment Trust* (*see* **14**).

This distinction between fixed and current assets the court will decide in accordance with the circumstances of the particular case and in conjunction with the provisions contained in the company's Memorandum and Articles. (The expressions, *floating* or *circulating* assets often used in the cases quoted are merely the earlier designations of *current* assets.)

21. Bond v. The Barrow Haematite Steel Co., Ltd. (1902). Although still concerned with mining, in this case there was the important distinction that the company was not an actual mining company but purchased certain mines to supply raw material for its manufacturing purposes. It was held here that the mines owned must be regarded as floating assets and therefore depreciation must be provided.

The judge stated:

> I think that the money invested in those items (mining leases) is properly regarded as circulating capital. Suppose the company had bought enormous stocks of ore sufficient to last for ten years, it

could hardly be said that the true value of so much of this as remained from time to time ought not to be brought into the Balance Sheet, and I can see no difference for the purpose of the account between ore *in situ* and ore so bought in advance.

22. Companies Act 1967 requirements. The Companies Act 1967, is quite clear in its requirement that the auditor reporting must state that the balance sheet gives a true and fair view of the company's affairs as well as requiring that the following specific matters be shown:

(*a*) The amount charged to revenue by way of provision for depreciation, renewals or diminution in the value of fixed assets (para. 12(1)(*a*)).

(*b*) The amounts charged for provision for renewal of assets for which there has *also* been a depreciation charge.

(*c*) Where the depreciation charge has *not* been determined by reference to value of assets shown in the balance sheet, this must be stated.

(*d*) The method of providing for depreciation, if other than by a depreciation charge or provision for renewals, or the fact that it is not provided for.

PROGRESS TEST 8

1. What is depreciation?   **(1)**

2. In what way does depreciation differ from other charges against profits?   **(2)**

3. What is the auditor's responsibility regarding depreciation?   **(3)**

4. In what way is the difficulty arising on the replacement of assets at inflated prices overcome?   **(4)**

5. Where reserves are created on revaluation, why do accountants advocate that these should be considered *capital* reserves?   **(6)**

6. Enumerate the factors involved in providing depreciation.   **(7)**

7. Which method of calculating depreciation is advocated by the Institute of Chartered Accountants and why?   **(7)**

8. Is it a legal necessity to write off depreciation on fixed assets before distributing profits?   **(15)**

9. Is business policy always in accord with legal considerations regarding depreciation of fixed assets?   **(19)**

10. Where losses are sustained on current assets, may profit distributions be made despite the excess of current expenditure over receipts? If not, why not? **(19, 20)**

SPECIMEN QUESTIONS

1. Draft your reply to the following letter which, as auditor of XY Co., Ltd., you have received from the Secretary of the company:

> At the last meeting of the Board one of the directors proposed that the heritable properties and plant should be shown in the financial accounts at their present-day values in order to present to the shareholders a fair statement of the worth of the company. My Board would be glad to have your views on this proposal before considering it further. *I.C.A.*

2. Discuss the statement that "The Balance Sheet of a company as it is normally drawn up in accordance with the Companies Acts, is inadequate as a guide to the value of the share capital in a period of fluctuating money values". In your solution deal in particular with the relevancy or otherwise of the above statement in relation to fixed assets. *A.C.A.*

3. State the principal considerations to be borne in mind by the auditor of a manufacturing company in determining the adequacy or otherwise of the provisions made in the annual accounts for depreciation of plant and machinery. *I.C.A.*

4. Discuss:

(a) The main advantages and disadvantages of the principal methods of providing for depreciation of the plant and machinery of a manufacturing concern.

(b) The matters to be considered in determining whether the depreciation provided is adequate. *I.C.A. (E.W.) (Inter.)*

5. Discuss the considerations which should guide the auditor of a manufacturing concern in deciding whether the provision for depreciation on plant and machinery is, or is not, adequate.

Your answer should be in the form of an essay and should indicate the main features of the principal methods of providing for depreciation. *I.C.A. (E.W.) (Inter.)*

6. The Board of a limited company propose not to make any further provision for depreciation of their freehold and leasehold properties on the grounds that "no depreciation is necessary as

site values have increased by more than the amount of the decrease in the value of the buildings themselves".

Indicate the considerations that you, as the company's auditor, would bear in mind in deciding upon your attitude towards this proposal.   *I.C.A.* (*E.W.*)

CHAPTER IX

Valuation of Assets

VALUATION

1. Difficulties of valuation. In times when price levels were stable, it was not a difficult task for the auditor to ascertain whether correct valuations had been placed upon the majority of assets; the cost figure was vouched on acquisition, and thereafter an amount for depreciation was deducted each year. Fluctuating price levels and continuous inflation have made the task much more difficult.

The matter of depreciation and appreciation of assets was purposely dealt with in the previous chapter before proceeding to consider the various aspects of valuation.

2. Accounting for changes in the purchasing power of money. Under this title the Councils of the accountancy bodies issued their Statement of Standard Accounting Practice M.7, which offered guidelines to assist accountants in the difficulties experienced in showing a true and fair view when it came to matters affected by inflationary pressure. The recommendations made were superseded by the recommendation of the Sandilands Committee appointed to consider whether, and if so how, company accounts should allow for changes in costs and prices. The report of the Sandilands Committee caused a great deal of controversy, and subsequently the Morpeth Committee also made certain pronouncements. In December 1977 the Accounting Standards Committee issued its Interim Recommendation (S22) on inflation accounting, the so called Hyde Guidelines.

We are concerned here with such matters from the viewpoint of the auditor. The most that can be said in the present circumstances is that it will be necessary for the auditor to ensure that his knowledge is kept up to date when considering the true and fair view reflected in accounts and balance sheets. However, he cannot exercise a purely personal viewpoint on how such matters brought about by inflation should be shown, rather he must be acquainted with the recognised and agreed methods as considered by the accounting profession best to be employed. The auditor may then see whether he can give his unqualified opinion or otherwise as to the application of those methods in revealing the true and fair view.

3. Inflation accounting—an interim recommendation (S.22). The auditor should acquaint himself with the recommendation in S.22. The Guidelines show the effect of price changes on the profit and loss account as specified by means of three separate adjustments:

It is recommended that three adjustments should be made to the financial results as computed on the historical cost convention. Each adjustment should be shown separately.

Depreciation: an adjustment should be made for the difference between depreciation based upon the current cost of fixed assets and the depreciation charged in computing the historical cost result.

Cost of sales: an adjustment should be made for the difference between the current cost of stock at the date of sale and the amount charged in computing the historical cost result.

"Gearing": it is recognised that there are differing views on the question of how monetary items should be dealt with in inflation adjusted statements and that such differences are unlikely to be resolved quickly or without experiment. Nevertheless, it is considered that it would not be acceptable for the statement recommended to be limited to adjustments for depreciation and cost of sales. Such limitation would result in an incomplete and potentially misleading picture being given to shareholders and other users of accounts. There are two different situations to be met, each of which calls for a different treatment:

(a) If the total liabilities of the business, including for this purpose preference share capital, exceed its total monetary assets, so that part of its operating capability is effectively financed by the net monetary liabilities, an adjustment should be made to reflect the extent to which the depreciation and cost of sales adjustments do not need to be provided in full from the current revenues of the business in showing the profit attributable to the shareholders.

(b) If the total monetary assets of the business exceed its total liabilities, an adjustment should be made to reflect the increase in the net monetary assets needed to maintain its scale of operation.

Bulletin No. 8 of the Auditing Practices Committee states:

Although it is not mandatory, auditors are encouraged to report on the supplementary statement published in accordance with the Guidelines. The Auditing Practices Committee recommends that the auditor's report on the supplementary statement should read: "We have examined the current cost statements together with the notes thereon on pages . . . to . . . for the year ended. . . . In our opinion the statement has been properly prepared in accordance with the methods set out in the notes to give the information set out in the A.S.C.'s interim recommendation on inflation accounting in November 1977".

TYPES OF ASSET

We must now consider some specific types of asset:

(*a*) Fixed assets.
(*b*) Investments.
(*c*) Current assets.
(*d*) Fictitious assets.

4. Fixed assets. Inflationary price increases are most obviously felt on assets retained for lengthy periods of use and they are likely to cause the most difficulty in valuation. The need to provide sufficient finance for replacement of assets at increased prices is not of concern to the auditor, although he should ensure that where assets are depreciated at a greater rate than is justified in order to effect the setting aside of profits for replacement purposes, such excess depreciation is properly shown as a replacement reserve.

Where assets, on the other hand, increase in value it is the auditor's duty to see that any new value placed upon them is justified, and that the excess on revaluation is placed to a reserve. Where depreciation has been written off this may be transferred back to the appropriation section of the profit and loss account, or to a reserve.

(*a*) Valuation of company property assets and their disclosures in directors' reports of accounts of companies: Recommendation s. 20.

(*i*) *Basis of valuation.* Although issued prior to the report of the Sandilands Committee this Recommendation is still apposite. To quote from the summary of the Sandilands Report as shown above "Property assets should be independently valued at regular intervals". Here s. 20 states:

Members are recommended to take particular note of the following and to adopt the procedures in all appropriate cases:

(*a*) Basis of valuation.

(*i*) Any valuation of land and buildings has regard to evidence of current open market transactions in similar property. Such valuations may affect either:

(*a*) the use of the property for the same purpose as hitherto ("existing use valuation"); or

(*b*) the prospective use of the property for some other purpose ("alternative use valuation").

(*ii*) *Going concern valuation*. This method of valuation is not advocated in s. 20.

Because the value of business as a going concern must take account of intangibles (particularly goodwill) and reflect overall earning capacity, such value cannot be properly apportioned to any particular property assets of the entity, except to the extent that the special element of value enters into the open market value as in (*i*) (*a*) above. It follows therefore that the expression "going concern valuation" in relation to company property should not be used.

(*iii*) *Disclosure in directors' reports or accounts*. For disclosure purposes, the methods are set out in (*a*)(*i*) and (*ii*) above, and where these may differ from one another to any material extent, the value of both should be given under the existing use valuation and the alternative use valuation.

While Sandilands states:

The "value to the business" of any asset owned by a company is the loss the company would suffer if it were deprived of the asset. In the great majority of cases this is equal to the amount it would cost the company to replace the asset in its existing condition. It will therefore normally be appropriate to value assets in the balance sheet by reference to their current replacement cost (allowing for depreciation where appropriate), taking any holding gains arising to a fixed asset revaluation reserve.

This does not invalidate s. 20 quoted above where the going concern basis is condemned, and Sandilands particularly mentions here replacement cost.

(*c*) *Freehold and leasehold land and buildings*. Appreciation in value has been a feature of this type of asset. The remarks as to transfer to a reserve made above apply particularly here.

Valuation by experts is necessary and the auditor will wish to examine the documents concerned. *Accounting for Depreciation* S.S.A.P. 12 is relevant, for where assets are revalued upwards, it is recommended that depreciation be charged on the revalued amount.

With the idea of retaining a hidden reserve on the balance sheet in the form of the non-revaluation of such assets, some businesses prefer to maintain such assets at their cost or written-down figure. The auditor has no right to insist on revaluation, but he should point out the dangers of under-valuation of assets, such as take-over bids, lower valuation of shares, etc., and also mentioning that the Companies Acts forbid by implication the maintenance of secret reserves in company's affairs. Should his advice be ignored and the sum involved warrant it, he should qualify his report accordingly.

In the case of leaseholds, the auditor should ascertain that the amortisation charge is adequate, bearing in mind the life of the lease.

(d) *Plant and machinery.* The cost of such assets will have been vouched on acquisition, but the auditor will not be in a position to know the expected life of such an asset; he may therefore request that a certified assessment be supplied by a responsible official of the organisation. Such certification may be shown on each folio sheet giving details of the plant or machinery in the plant register. Where some time has elapsed since the last certification, he may request that this be brought up to date.

In S.22 it has been mentioned that for assets held in the United Kingdom, indexes may be selected from those contained in the booklet *Price Index Numbers for Current Cost Accounting*, published by the government's Central Statistical Office.

Plant and machinery can be very expensive and from the auditor's point of view, it is essential to ensure that the true valuation is stated. The going-concern basis has been condemned in s. 20 and this is easily understandable as the method of valuation would be too indefinite. But the auditor's responsibility now extends to a careful investigation as to adequate depreciation, current replacement cost and the requisite indices which may be used in revaluation.

Obsolescence may intervene with expensive machinery, and any material sudden losses in value should be checked, with exceptional depreciation being shown apart from the normal annual charge.

Frequently, the company's own employees may be engaged on erection of machines, in which case their wages may properly be charged to the cost of the asset, together with the value of any parts supplied. In confirming the asset value the auditor should check the original documents arising, such as time sheets, etc., and the costing records maintained in respect of any capital project.

(e) *Furniture and fittings.* No real difficulty should exist in the valuation of such assets which the auditor may ascertain when verifying their existence.

Whilst furniture will be written off at an agreed annual rate, fittings may be of varying types, and where changes are frequently made in installations for advertising purposes, e.g. in reception rooms for companies selling various types of office machinery, it may be necessary to write off such fittings over a short period.

(f) *Office machinery*. The more usual types of office machinery may be valued, as mentioned above, for furniture and fittings, but where expensive punched card, or even computer systems are involved, the auditor should endeavour to obtain an authoritative valuation figure from an outside source. Usually the suppliers are helpful in supplying details regarding their machines, although the temptation may exist for them to quote a higher figure than might be justified by the wear and tear, or obsolescence factor, involved. However, the auditor has the original cost and an expected life estimate should be obtainable.

5. Investments. This type of asset is shown here separately as it may be classified as either a fixed asset or a current asset. Where investments are obtained with the purpose of holding them continuously, as in the case of an investment company, they should be viewed as fixed assets, whereas if it is not intended to retain them but rather to set aside surplus funds for a short period in view of earning a higher interest rate, or, as in the case of a finance company, their resale at a profit is envisaged, then they should be treated as current assets.

The Companies Acts require that there shall be shown under separate headings the company's trade investments and other investments, with the aggregate amounts respectively of the company's quoted and unquoted investments.

Where investments may be properly viewed as fixed assets, there is no legal necessity to provide for their diminution in value, but whilst this is the *legal* position, this would not be counted as prudent business policy and adjustment would more correctly be made.

The investment of funds in other businesses is now undertaken on such a large scale that rights and duties as to the auditing of the valuation of such items have to be considered on a specialised basis. This is especially true with regard to investment in subsidiary and associated companies, necessitating both statutory requirements and professional recommendations as to auditors' rights and duties (*see Group accounts—reliance on other auditors*, p. 262). Although Recommendation s. 18 refers to group accounts, the duty is likewise laid upon the auditor to make sure that investments in companies or other types of business are of the value shown on the balance sheet of the investing company. The auditor will therefore wish to study the information supplied regarding any such investment and to see if it is sufficient for his purposes, otherwise he will need to request further details, and if not satisfied, will need to qualify his report.

6. Trade investments. These occur where the investment has been made in order to secure some trading advantage, such as in the case of vertical integration. It follows that the investment, to afford some advantage, has to be of such an amount proportionately that the company must be able to gain some effective power in the company concerned. Such investments will be shown normally at cost, but to quote a useful passage from an earlier Recommendation, N. 5:

> Exceptional circumstances may arise in which an undertaking, wherein an important trade investment is held, has retained and accumulated profits on such a scale that the income which reaches the investor company and the amount at which the investment is carried in the accounts are a wholly inadequate reflection of the value of the investment, although this fact is not apparent from the trade investments item in the Balance Sheet or from the accounts as a whole. In such circumstances consideration should be given to the question whether the relative importance of the matter is such that without some explanation in the accounts they would fail to show a fair view.

7. Investments in subsidiary companies. Investments in subsidiary companies and indebtedness to and by subsidiaries must be shown separately in the holding company's balance sheet (Companies Act 1948, Sch. 8, Part 2), and therefore, in order to ensure that a true and fair view is given, the auditor must satisfy himself that the values shown are true. This will involve examination of the balance sheet and accounts of the subsidiaries. The auditing aspect regarding subsidiary companies is dealt with in Chapter XIV, 11, p. 262.

The auditor should ensure that dividends received after acquisition of controlling interests, if paid out of pre-acquisition profits, are credited against the cost of the shares, so reducing their value, as the holding company has since received part of the value which it originally purchased as a separate item.

8. Quoted and unquoted investments. In the case of quoted shares the Stock Exchange official list should be consulted and the value fixed at the mid-market price, i.e. the figure between the quoted buying and selling prices.

To obtain a valuation figure where investments are made in companies whose shares are not quoted, it will be necessary to obtain past final accounts and balance sheets, and to request the secretary of the company to give information as to the value at which recent share transactions have taken place. Some idea of the valuation may also be obtained by computation on a dividend yield basis, as compared with companies of a similar nature.

The Companies Act 1967 requires that the matters referred to in the following heads shall, if not otherwise shown, be stated by way of note or in a statement or report annexed (in the case of investments consisting in equity share capital other than any whose values as estimated by the directors are separately shown). Schedule 2, Para. 5A:

(a) the aggregate amount of the company's income for the financial year that is ascribable to the investments;

(b) the amount of the company's share before taxation, and the amount of that share after taxation, of the net aggregate amount of the profits of the bodies in which the investments are held, being profits for the several periods to which accounts sent by them during the financial year to the company related, after deducting those bodies' losses for those periods (or vice-versa);

(c) the amount of the company's share of the net aggregate amount of the undistributed profits accumulated by the bodies in which the investments are held since the time when the investments were acquired, after deducting the losses accumulated by them since that time (or vice-versa);

(d) the manner in which any losses incurred by the said bodies have been dealt with in the company's accounts.

9. Current assets. Current assets are more often of an obvious nature, such as liquid funds. Book debts should be dealt with on their verification concerning any bad debts to be written off or provision against such to be made.

Stock-in-trade and work-in-progress are dealt with in Chapter X.

10. Intangible and fictitious assets. Because an asset is intangible, it does not signify that it may be of no value; goodwill is an example of this.

(a) *Goodwill.* There is no legal liability to write off goodwill, and if this is done, there is nothing against writing it back at a fair value, so making the profits originally written off available for distribution: *Stapley* v. *Read Bros., Ltd.* (1924). It is usual to show goodwill at its cost value until written off, however, and as in such circumstances where goodwill has been paid on acquisition of a branch since disposed of, it would be misleading to leave such an asset on the balance sheet. The auditor should use his discretion in considering whether goodwill shown at cost is really of the value shown, and would be wise to comment in his report if he considers that what he finds is misleading to any degree.

(b) *Preliminary expenses, discount on issue of debentures and other fictitious assets.* Fictitious assets such as these should be written off as soon as possible, for they are of no value. In any case, they should not be left on the balance sheet at the same time as the inclusion of reserves, since the true excess of assets over liabilities cannot be said to be represented in part by such fictitious assets.

PROGRESS TEST 9

1. What one main cause has made valuation from the auditing point of view more difficult in recent years? **(1)**

2. What are the recommendations of the Accounting Standards Committee to maintain consistency and avoid confusion during the interim period until definitive recommendations are made regarding inflation accounting? **(3)**

3. Where it is decided to revalue freehold properties, what is the auditor's duty regarding this? **(4)**

4. Where the company's own employees are engaged on work in erection of machines, how should the expenditure involved be treated? **(4)**

5. How may expenditure such as that shown in Question 4 be vouched? **(4)**

6. Under what heading should investments be shown on the balance sheet? **(5)**

7. If investments are considered as fixed assets, is there any necessity to provide for their diminution in value? **(5)**

8. How should investments in subsidiary companies be valued?
(7)

9. At what value is it usual to show goodwill?   **(10)**

SPECIMEN QUESTIONS

1. To what extent, if any, do you consider that an auditor should take into account events which happen after the balance sheet date but before the completion of the audit?   Reasons and examples should be given for your explanations.   *A.C.A.*

2. Discuss the extent to which an auditor should have regard to events occurring after the balance sheet date when auditing the following items in a company's balance sheet:

(*a*) Fixed assets.
(*b*) Debtors.
(*c*) Stock-in-trade.   *I.C.A.* (*E.W.*)

3. To what extent should an auditor have regard to events that take place between the balance sheet date of a client's business and the date of the completion of his audit?   *I.C.A.*(*E.W.*)(*Inter.*)

CHAPTER X

Verification and Valuation of Stock and Work-in-Progress

The verification of stock-in-trade and work-in-progress held and their proper valuation is of the utmost importance to the auditor.

The case of *Kingston Cotton Mill Company* (1896), is taken as exemplifying the governing principle regarding the auditor and his general responsibility thereto. In this case it was held *not to be the duty of the auditor to take stock, and that he is not guilty of negligence if he accepts the certificate of a responsible official in the absence of suspicious circumstances.* This does not absolve the auditor from his responsibility to exercise his professional skill in ascertaining that stocks are what they are stated to be. The defalcations arising by means of the manipulation of stocks and the moneys expended upon them have been numerous and the auditor must apply the utmost care in investigating the procedures governing these and the true position with end-of-period stocks on hand.

VERIFICATION

1. Auditing difficulties. In the first instance where raw materials or other goods are purchased the procedures operating must be sound. These have been dealt with (*see* pp. 63–5), covering the ordering of goods and the subsequent receipt of invoices. But to illustrate the difficulties which may arise it may be mentioned that where collusion took place in a business, sums of money were paid away to a fictitious company having its own bank account and for which invoices were specially printed, while stocks were purported to be held in various outside warehouses for which certificates were supplied. Such a case as this is exceptional and difficult to discover but does serve to emphasise the necessity of sound audit procedures to ascertain that not only are payments made on properly authenticated documents but also that goods are duly received.

Furthermore, the double entry book figures which are

normally available to the auditor may not be applicable in the case of stocks, since the figures are in effect introduced into the system after verification and valuation of the physical stocks. This fact is sufficient to make it possible to manipulate the amount of profits or losses shown in a business by inflation or deflation of the figures for stocks held.

2. The auditor and physical stock-taking. Although it is not part of the auditor's duty to take stock, the application of auditing in depth has caused attention to be given to the physical aspects of stock control. In recognition of this the I.C.A. have issued Recommendation U.9 in which it is advocated that in examining the effectiveness of the internal control of stock the auditor should observe personally how the procedures involved are carried out, not completely, but on a test basis. Measures to ensure efficient stock control within the business are mentioned and suggested audit procedures are outlined, including the following:

(a) *Before stock-taking.* The client's stock-taking instructions should be examined. After familiarising himself with the procedures the auditor should discuss any weaknesses with the client.

(b) *During stock-taking.* In order to ensure efficient stock-checking, counts or recounts should be made in the employees' presence of certain items by selecting mainly objects of high value and checking these back from records to warehouse or vice-versa. Notes should be taken of any important matters, such as slow-moving stocks, for later examination.

(c) *After stock-taking.* The "cut-off" should be checked, especially with regard to any movements of stock near the end date.

Where physical attendance is not possible, the auditor should exercise his skill to obtain additional evidence such as independent confirmation, but in any case responsibility rests with management to provide stock figures and the auditors should make it clear that they are not attending for the purposes of taking stock but to examine the effectiveness of the client's procedures.

3. Cut-off procedures. Cut-off procedures are those arrangements made in order to ensure that at a particular point of time, e.g. the end of the financial period, there will be agreement between the

physical stock-in-trade and work-in-progress and the figures
shown in the accounts, as obtained from the records of purchases, sales, debtors and creditors.

Briefly, the relevant considerations are:

(a) the linking of sales and stock records to ensure goods sold
but not dispatched are excluded from stock;

(b) the linking of purchases and stock records to ensure that
all invoices are included for stock held wherever situated;

(c) where physical stock-taking is at a date other than the
balance sheet date that the movements of stock in or out are
properly added or deducted as required;

(d) that stocks held on others' behalf are excluded from stock
figures.

4. Auditing procedures. In Recommendation U.11 the Council
of the I.C.A. have pointed out that in order to satisfy themselves
as to the validity of the amount attributed to stock it will be
necessary for the auditors to check the soundness of the procedures adopted and to test the competence of their execution.
However, responsibility still rests with the directors to ensure
that stock is properly recorded and that the physical quantities
and condition of stock are ascertained, and that the amount
shown on the balance sheet has been properly determined by
suitable methods.

Audit procedures, in addition to attendance at stock-taking,
should cover the following:

(a) General scrutiny of stock records and comparison with the
previous year, attention being given to the possibility of material
omissions or inclusion of items, such as loose tools, which
should appear elsewhere in the accounts.

(b) Where applicable, tests by reference to statistical information covering matters such as yields which may be expected from
given quantities and normal losses or gains by evaporation or
absorption of moisture.

Where stock is defective or is obsolete or slow-moving, these
factors must be taken into account. Audit tests of the company's
procedure for judging the physical condition will normally
include the following:

(a) Scrutiny of stock records to ascertain what information as
to condition and slow-moving stocks has been recorded and
what action has been taken on that information.

(*b*) Comparison with the stock records relating to the previous balance sheet date.

(*c*) Examination by reference to normal experience of wastage due to rejects and deterioration.

(*d*) Examination of the relationship between stocks and turnover, including consideration of current trading conditions and any changes in sales or stock-piling policies.

(*e*) Discussion with the management.

5. Amount at which stock is stated. Valuation of stock is dealt with hereafter but further procedures mentioned in U.11 are as follows.

After examining the principles adopted by the management, the audit procedure to test the application of those principles will normally include:

(*a*) test of the stock sheets or continuous stock records with relevant documents such as invoices, costing records and other sources for the ascertainment of "cost";

(*b*) examination and testing of the treatment of overhead expenses;

(*c*) tests of "net realisable value";

(*d*) careful enquiry of responsible officials and examination of evidence supporting the assessment of net realisable value, with particular reference to defective, obsolete or slow-moving stock, and consideration of the reasonableness of the replies from officials to the enquiries made;

(*e*) tests of the arithmetic accuracy of the calculations;

(*f*) tests of the consistency, in principle and in detail, with which the amounts have been computed;

(*g*) consideration of the adequacy of the description applied to stock-in-trade and work-in-progress in the accounts.

6. Work-in-progress. Costing records, work tickets attached to unfinished work, relevant contracts, and, in fact, any financial or statistical data likely to be of help, should be examined, every time it is not possible to identify physical quantities of stock in work-in-progress.

Where such difficulties arise the auditor will wish to ascertain:

(*a*) the nature and reliability of the costing records;

(*b*) the extent to which checks are made by reference to statistical information concerning outputs of main products and of by-products (if any) which ought to be obtained from materials used;

(c) the system of inspection and reporting thereon to enable allowance to be made in the costing records for scrapping and rectification;

(d) the basis upon which overheads and profit elements are dealt with later in the chapter.

7. Overall tests. Audit tests which may often be appropriate by way of overall assessment of the reliability of the records will include, according to circumstances, the following:

(a) Reconciliation of changes in stock quantities as between the beginning and end of the financial year with the records of purchases, productions and sales.

(b) Comparison of the quantities and amounts of stocks in the various categories with those included at the previous balance sheet date and with current sales and purchases.

(c) Consideration of the gross profit ratio shown by the accounts, and its comparison with the ratio shown in previous years.

(d) Consideration of the rate of turnover of stocks, and its comparison with previous years.

(e) Consideration of the relationship of the quantities ready for sale and in course of production with the quantities shown in operating and sales budgets.

(f) Where applicable, examination of standard costing records and consideration of the variances shown thereby and their treatment in the accounts.

8. Independent stock-takers. The auditors should ascertain direct with the stock-taking firm the basis of valuation used, and assure themselves that proper cut-off procedures have been operated. Although it may be that stock count and valuation are virtually one operation, for example, in the inventory of a stock of precious stones, nevertheless the auditors must still accept their own responsibility in forming an opinion.

9. Inventory letters. It is usual and desirable to obtain from a director or other responsible official a written statement outlining in detail stock quantities and bases of valuation. This constitutes both a record of action taken by management and a reminder of their responsibility, but this in no way relieves the auditors of their own responsibility to form their own opinion as to the stock being reported upon and presented in the accounts.

VALUATION

10. External influences. We now consider the actual valuation of stocks and work in progress. This difficult aspect of the auditor's work has been made even more complicated by the change in values brought about by the effects of such factors as inflation and trade recession. This last-named may affect a violent fall in stock values when it is not possible to dispose of stocks on hand. More especially, however, we are concerned here with the increase in stock values due to the effects of inflation.

The Statement of Standard Accounting Practice M.9 has been published under the title *Stocks and Work-in-Progress*. Briefly, for valuation purposes it advocates chiefly the use of "the lower cost and net realisable value". In view of the report of the Sandilands Committee it may be queried as to whether these recommendations are relevant in view of the requirement to apply the accounting system termed Current Cost Accounting (*see* p. 167). This is, however, to overlook the fact that the employment of CCA requires the application of price indices to figures obtained by means of precise methods of calculation. Stock appreciation will still be calculated from figures obtained from historical cost with the addition of any justifiable overheads.

11. The Accounting Standards. In dealing with S.S.A.P. M.9 it is necessary to consider the International Accounting Standard *Valuation and Presentation of Inventories in the Context of the Historical Cost System* (I.A.S.2). This agrees very closely with S.S.A.P. M.9 except that recognition is also afforded to the lifo or base-stock method of valuation provided that disclosure is made of the difference of the amount as arrived at by using (*a*) the lower of lifo or the weighted average method and net realisable value or (*b*) the lower of current cost at balance sheet date or net realisable value.

We shall consider both statements, commencing with M.9, which recognises at once the difficulties inherent in stock valuation—

> no area of accounting has produced wider differences in practice than the computation of the amount at which stocks and work-in-progress are stated in financial accounts.

(a) Introduction.

The determination of profit for an accounting year requires the matching of costs with related revenues. The cost of unsold or unconsumed stocks and work-in-progress will have been incurred in the expectation of future revenue, and when this will not arise until a year later it is appropriate to carry forward this cost to be matched with the revenue when it arises; the applicable concept is the matching of cost and revenue in the year in which the revenue arises rather than in the year in which the cost is incurred.

If there is no reasonable expectation of sufficient future revenue to cover cost incurred (e.g. as a result of deterioration, obsolescence or change in demand), the irrecoverable cost should be charged to revenue in the year under review. *Thus, stocks and work-in-progress normally need to be stated at cost, or if lower, at net realisable value.*

The comparison of cost and net realisable value needs to be made in respect of each item of stock separately. Where this is impracticable, groups or categories of stock items which are similar will need to be taken together. To compare the total realisable value of stocks with the total cost could result in an unacceptable setting off of foreseeable losses against unrealised profits.

In order to match costs and revenue, "costs" of stocks of work-in-progress should comprise that expenditure which has been incurred in the *normal course of business* in bringing the product or service to its present location and condition. Such costs will include all related production overheads, even though these may accrue on a time basis.

Formerly it was strongly maintained that no overhead expenses incurred on a time basis should be included in stock values. The reason for this objection can be illustrated by the case of radios held for sale in a rented warehouse; if these were unsold at the end of a period the rent overhead might be added to cost so increasing their value, whereas in fact as obsolescence is very present with such items they would probably be worth less. However, S.S.A.P. M.9 covers this point in advocating valuation in such cases at net realisable value. From the auditor's point of view, however, the addition of such costs incurred on a time basis must be considered very carefully.

The methods used in allocating costs to stocks and work-in-progress need to be selected with a view to providing the fairest possible approximation to the expenditure actually incurred in bringing the product to its present location and condition. For example, in the case of retail stores holding a large number of rapidly changing individual items, stocks on the shelves have often been stated at current selling prices less the normal gross profit margin. In these particular circumstances, this may be acceptable as being the only practical method of arriving at a figure which approximates to cost.

(b) Net realisable value.

Net realisable value is the amount at which it is expected that items of stocks and work-in-progress can be disposed of without creating either profit or loss in the year of sale, i.e. the estimated proceeds of sale less all further costs to completion and less all costs to be incurred in marketing, selling and distributing directly related to the items in question.

(c) Replacement cost.

Items of stock and work-in-progress have sometimes been stated in accounts at estimated replacement cost where this is lower than net realisable value. Where the effect is to take account of a loss greater than that which is expected to be incurred, the use of replacement cost is not regarded as acceptable. However, in some circumstances (e.g. in the case of materials whose price has fluctuated considerably and which have not become the subject of firm sales contracts by the time the accounts are prepared) replacement cost may be the best measure of net realisable value.

(d) Long-term contract work-in-progress.

The Standard here deals with the taking to profit and loss account the amount which may be done so justifiably where long-term contracts are in question. Not so much the activities of a company are to be considered as rather the results of completed contracts during the year. The student should consult textbooks on contract costing for the formulae applied where work on contracts is divided according to architects' certificates received.

The profit, if any, taken needs to reflect the proportion of the work carried out and to consider any inequalities of profitability in the various stages of a contract. Where the outcome of contracts cannot reasonably be assessed, then no profit should be taken.

If, however, it is expected that there will be a loss on a contract as a whole, provision needs to be made (in accordance with the prudence concept), for the whole of the loss as soon as it is recognised. This has the effect of reducing the work done to date to its net realisable value. Where unprofitable contracts are of such magnitude that they can be expected to absorb a considerable part of the company's capacity for a substantial period, related administration overheads to be incurred during the period to the completion of these contracts should also be included in the calculation of the provision for losses.

Thus, the gross amount of long-term contract work-in-progress should be stated in accounts at cost plus attributable profits (if any) less foreseeable losses (if any). In arriving at a decision as to whether there are attributable profits, a company should consider whether, having regard to the nature of the contracts undertaken, it is reasonable to foresee profits in advance of the completion of the contracts.

(e) Disclosure in accounts.

A suitable description of the amount at which stocks and work-in-progress are stated in accounts might be "at the lower of cost and net realisable value" or, in the case of long-term contract work in progress, "at cost plus attributable profit (if any) less foreseeable losses (if any) and progress payments received and receivable".

Where differing bases have been adopted for different types of stocks and work-in-progress the amount included in the accounts in respect of each type will need to be stated by way of a note.

In the case of long-term contract work-in-progress the terms of a contract usually involve progress payments which reduce the amount at which the contract is stated in the accounts. The financial position of a company may be materially dependent on the outcome of such contracts despite this lessening of their apparent significance . A related note should, therefore, indicate the amount of progress payments received and receivable separately from the net amount of cost plus attributable profit, less foreseeable losses as appropriate.

General guidance is given in Appendix I to S.S.A.P. M.9 where net realisable value is likely to be less than cost and with respect to matters to be considered regarding long-term contracts.

12. Definition of terms.

The following definitions of terms are used for the purpose of this statement. Stocks and work-in-progress comprise:

(a) goods or other assets purchased for resale;
(b) consumable stores;
(c) raw materials and components purchased for incorporation into productions for sale;
(d) products and services in intermediate stages of completion;
(e) finished goods.

Cost is defined in relation to the different categories of stocks and work-in-progress as being that expenditure which has been incurred in the normal course of business in bringing the product or service *to its present location and condition.* This expenditure should include, in addition to cost of purchase, such costs of conversion *(see (i)* and *(ii)* below) as are appropriate to that location and condition.

(i) *Cost of purchase* comprises purchase price including import duties, transport and handling costs and any other directly attributable costs, less trade discounts, rebates and subsidies.

(*ii*) *Cost of conversion* comprises:
(*a*) costs which are specifically attributable to units of production, i.e. direct labour, direct expenses and sub-contracted work;
(*b*) production overheads;
(*c*) other overheads, if any, attributable in the particular circumstances of the business to bringing the product or service to its present location and condition.

(*iii*) *Production overheads* are overheads incurred in respect of materials, labour or services for production, based on the normal level of activity, taking one year with another. For this purpose, each overhead should be classified according to function (e.g. production, selling or administration) so as to ensure the inclusion in cost of conversion of those overheads (including depreciation) which relate to production, notwithstanding that these may accrue wholly or partly on a time basis.

(*iv*) *Net realisable value* is the actual or estimated selling price (net of trade but before settlement discounts) less:
(*a*) all further costs to completion; and
(*b*) all costs to be incurred in marketing, selling and distributing.

(*v*) *Long-term contract* is a contract entered into for manufacture or building of a single substantial entity or the provision of a service where the time taken to manufacture, build or provide is such that a substantial proportion of all such contract work will extend for a period exceeding one year.

(*vi*) *Attributable profit* is that part of the total profit currently estimated to arise over the duration of the contract (after allowing for likely increases in costs so far as not recoverable under the terms of the contract) which fairly reflects the profit attributable to that part of the work performed at the accounting date. (There can be no attributable profit until the outcome of the contract can be assessed with reasonable certainty.)

(*vii*) *Foreseeable losses* are losses which are currently estimated to arise over the duration of the contract (after allowing for estimated remedial and maintenance costs, and increase in costs so far as not recoverable under the terms of the contract).
This estimate is required irrespective of:
(*a*) whether or not work has yet commenced on such contracts;
(*b*) the proportion of work carried out at the accounting date; and
(*c*) the amount of profits expected to arise on other contracts.

13. Standard accounting practice.

(*a*) *Stocks and work-in-progress other than long-term contract work-in-progress.*

The amount at which stocks and work-in-progress, other than long-term contract work-in-progress, is stated in periodic financial statements should be the total of the lower of cost and net realisable value of the separate items of stock and work-in-progress or of groups of similar items.

(b) *Long-term contract work-in-progress*.

The amount at which long-term contract work-in-progress is stated in periodic financial statements should be cost plus any attributable profit, less any foreseeable losses and progress payments received and receivable. If, however, anticipated losses on individual contracts exceed cost incurred to date less progress payments received and receivable, such excesses should be shown separately as provisions.

Although the two Standard Accounting Statements are virtually the same in other respects, M.9 does not go so far as I.A.S.2, which also allows the use of the lifo or base-stock formula. It states in para. 26:

The lifo or base-stock formulas may be used provided that there is disclosure of the difference between the amount of the inventories as shown in the balance sheet and either
   (a) the lower of the amount arrived at in accordance with the fifo formula or average weighted cost formula and net realisable value or
   (b) the lower or current cost at the balance sheet date and net realisable value.

(c) *Disclosure in financial statements*. In the interests of continuity this section of Statement M.9 is dealt with in conjunction with I.A.S.2, section "Presentation in the Financial Statements", on p. 192.

14. Further practical considerations concerning the statement M.9.

(a) *The allocation of overheads*.

Production overheads are included in cost of conversion, together with direct labour, direct expenses and sub-contracted work. All abnormal conversion costs, however (such as exceptional spoilage, idle capacity and other losses), which are avoidable under normal operating conditions need, for the same reason, to be excluded.

Where firms' sales contracts have been entered into for the provision of goods or services to customer's specification, overheads relating to design, and marketing and selling costs incurred before manufacture may be included in arriving at cost.

The costs of general management, as distinct from functional management, are not directly related to current production and are, therefore, excluded from cost of conversion and hence from the cost of stocks and work-in-progress.

In the case of smaller organisations whose management may be involved in the daily administration of each of the various functions, particular problems may arise in practice in distinguishing these general management overheads. In such organisations, the cost of management may fairly be allocated on suitable bases to the functions of production, marketing, selling and administration.

Problems may also arise in allocating the costs of central service departments, the allocation of which should depend on the function or functions that the department is serving. For example, the accounts department will normally support the following functions:

(a) production—by paying production direct and indirect wages and salaries, by controlling purchases and by preparing periodic accounts for the production units;

(b) marketing and distribution—by analysing sales and by controlling the sales ledger;

(c) general administration—by preparing management and annual accounts and budgets, by controlling cash resources and by planning investments.

Only those costs of the accounts department that can be reasonably allocated to the production function fall to be included in the cost of conversion.

The *allocation of overheads* included in the valuation of stocks and work-in-progress needs to be based on the company's *normal level of activity*, taking one year with another. The governing factor is that the cost of unused capacity should be written off in the current year.

Although temporary changes in the load of activity may be ignored, persistent variation should lead to a revision of the previous norm.

Where management accounts are prepared on a marginal cost basis, it will be necessary to add to the figure of stock so arrived at the appropriate proportion of those production overheads not already included in the marginal cost.

15. Methods of costing.

It is frequently not practicable to relate expenditure to specific units of stocks and work-in-progress. The ascertainment of the nearest approximation to cost gives rise to two problems:

(a) the selection of an appropriate method for relating costs to stocks and work-in-progress (e.g. job costing, batch costing, process costing, standard costing);

(b) the selection of an appropriate method for calculating the related cost where a number of identical items have been purchased or made at different times (e.g. unit cost, average cost or fifo).

In selecting the methods referred to above, management must exercise judgment to ensure that the methods chosen provide the fairest practicable approximation to "actual cost". Furthermore, where standard costs are used they need to be reviewed frequently to ensure that they bear a reasonable relationship to actual costs obtained during the period. Methods such as base stock and lifo do not usually bear such a relationship.

The method of arriving at cost by applying the latest purchase price to the total number of units in stock is unacceptable in principle because it is not necessarily the same as actual cost and, in times of rising prices, will result in the taking of a profit which has not been realised.

One method of arriving at cost, in the absence of a satisfactory costing system, is the use of selling price less an estimated profit margin. This is acceptable only if it can be demonstrated that the method gives a reasonable approximation of the actual cost.

In industries where the cost of minor by-products is not separate from the cost of the principal products, stocks of such by-products may be stated in accounts at their net realisable value. In this case, the costs of the main products are calculated after deducting the net realisable value of the by-products.

(a) *I.A.S.2—cost formulas.* The I.A.S.2 "Valuation and Presentation of Inventories in the Context of the Historical Cost System" also lists the various methods of cost formula used:

Several different formulas with widely different effects are in current use for the purpose of assigning costs, including the following:

(a) First-in, first-out (fifo).
(b) Weighted average cost.
(c) Last-in, first-out (lifo).
(d) Base stock.
(e) Specific identification.
(f) Next-in, first-out (nifo).
(g) Latest purchase price.

The fifo, weighted average cost, lifo, base stock, and specific identification formulas use costs that have been incurred by the enterprise at one time or another. The nifo and latest purchase price methods use costs that have not all been incurred and are therefore not based on historical cost.

Specific identification is a formula that attributes specific costs to identified items of inventory. This is an appropriate treatment for goods that have been bought or manufactured and are segregated for a specific project. It it is used, however, in respect of items of inventory which are ordinarily interchangeable, the selection of items could be made in such a way as to obtain predetermined effects on profit.

EXAMPLE OF FIFO AND LIFO

(1) *Effect on profits*. To illustrate the effect of the systems of fifo (first in, first out) and lifo (last in, first out), the following trading accounts (where only one particular commodity is dealt with) are given. This may clarify the effect on trading profits in conditions where prices are rising.

Fifo
Trading Account

Purchases (in chronological order)				
200 @ £1.00	£200		Sales 360 @ £2.00	£720
200 @ 1.25	250		Closing stock	
200 @ 1.50	300		40 @ £1.25 £ 50	
	— £750		200 @ 1.50 300	
Gross profit	320		—	350
	£1,070			£1,070

Lifo
Trading Account

Purchases				
200 @ £1.00	£200		Sales 360 @ £2.00	£720
200 @ 1.25	250		Closing stock	
200 @ 1.50	300		40 @ £1.25 £ 50	
	— £750		200 @ 1.00 200	
Gross profit	220		—	250
	£970			£970

(2) *Economic effects*. It will be observed that in a time where prices and profits are rising the result of the lifo method of valuation is to have a neutralising effect on profits. In the illustration given, the effect is actually to reduce profits, but the further complication of possible increases in sale prices where inflationary tendencies are in operation cannot be ignored; in this case, the profits would still be lessened, although not to such a marked degree.

As the opposite effect of that shown above would operate

in a period of falling prices, i.e. profits would tend to increase, economists sometimes favour the lifo method of stock valuations since if applied on a national scale a lessening of purchasing power would apply in times of inflation, and conversely, greater profits might be distributed in times when the economy is running down.

(3) *Accountancy standpoint.* Viewed, however, from the accountancy standpoint, the application of the lifo method presents recording and pricing difficulties and is not very practical unless applied to special types of business where purchase orders may be easily allocated to particular contracts.

(*b*) *The determination of net realisable value.* Under this heading, M.9 states:

The initial calculation of provisions to reduce stocks from cost to net realisable value may often be made by the use of formulae based on predetermined criteria. The formulae normally take account of the age, movements during the past, expected future movements and estimated scrap value of the stock, as appropriate. Whilst the use of such formulae establishes a basis for making a provision which can be consistently applied, it is still necessary for the results to be reviewed in the light of any special circumstances which cannot be anticipated in the formulae, such as changes in the state of the order book.

Where a provision is required to reduce the value of finished goods below cost, the stocks of the parts and sub-assemblies held for the purpose of the manufacture of such products, together with stock on order, need to be reviewed to determine if provision is also required against such items.

Where stocks of spares are held for sale, special consideration of the factors will be required in the context of:

(*a*) the number of units sold to which they are applicable;
(*b*) the estimated frequency with which a replacement spare is required;
(*c*) the expected useful life of the unit to which they are applicable.

Events occurring between the balance sheet date and the date of completion of the accounts need to be considered in arriving at the net realisable value of the balance sheet date (e.g. a subsequent reduction in selling prices). However, no reduction falls to be made when the realisable value of material stocks is less than the purchase price, provided the goods into which the materials are to be incorporated can still be sold at a profit after incorporating the materials at cost price.

(c) The application of net realisable value.

The principal situations in which net realisable value is likely to be less than cost are where there has been:

(a) an increase in costs or a fall in selling price;
(b) physical deterioration of stocks;
(c) obsolescence of products;
(d) a decision as part of a company's marketing strategy to manufacture and sell products at a loss;
(e) errors in production or purchasing.

Furthermore, when stocks are held which are unlikely to be sold within the turnover period normal in that company (i.e. excess stocks), the impending delay in realisation increases the risk that the situations outlined in (a) and (b) above may occur before the stocks are sold and needs to be taken into account in assessing net realisable value.

16. Disclosure in financial statements. The standard as laid down in M.9 states:

The accounting policies which have been used in calculating cost, net realisable value, attributable profit and foreseeable losses (as appropriate) should be stated.

Stocks and work-in-progress should be sub-classified in balance sheets or in notes to the financial statements in a manner which is appropriate to the business and so as to indicate the amounts held in each of the main categories.

In relation to the amount at which long-term contracts are stated in the balance sheet there should be stated:

(a) the amount of work-in-progress at cost plus attributable profit, less foreseeable losses;
(b) cash received and receivable at the accounting date as progress payments on account of contracts in progress.

17. The Romalpa case (1976) 1 W.L.R. 676. Aluminium Industrie Vaassen obtained what was previously thought to be unobtainable under English law: the payment of a sum of £35,000 for goods supplied before anything was paid to any preferential or other creditors in the case of a company under liquidation. The point of importance to auditors is that the plaintiffs were able to maintain retention of ownership as sellers until all sums due by the buyers had been paid. This case was supported in the case *Borden (U.K.) Ltd.* v. *Scottish Timber Products* (1978). But more recently the original decision has been limited in the *Monsant* v. *Bond Worth* case, although the latter case may go to appeal. As auditors are concerned to see that the balance sheet shows a true and fair view in particular here with regard to stocks and creditors or sales and debtors, the accountancy bodies have issued U.24 and V.24. Paragraphs (4), (5) and (8) of V.24 are quoted here:

In drawing up the accounts of undertakings trading on terms whereby goods are supplied subject to a reservation of title, it is necessary to decide at what stage they should be treated as sold by the supplier and purchased by the party to whom they are supplied ("the customer"). In reaching this decision, it is considered that the commercial substance of the transaction should take precedence over its legal form where they conflict. The substance of transactions of this nature has to be decided from consideration of all the surrounding circumstances.   (4)

The circumstances surrounding the transaction may indicate that the reservation of title is regarded by the parties as having no practical relevance except in the event of the insolvency of the customer. The goods concerned may be supplied and payment for them may be due in a manner identical with other goods which are not subject to a reservation of title. In such circumstances, where the customer is a going concern, it is considered that the omission of the stock (or, if resold, the debtors) and of the corresponding liabilities from the balance sheet of the customer would prevent it from showing a true and fair view of the state of affairs. Similarly, the accounts of the supplier would also be distorted by the omission of such goods from sales and debtors. Accordingly *it is recommended* that in such circumstances *the goods should be treated as purchases in the accounts of the customer and as sales in the accounts of the supplier*.   (5)

Where the accounts are materially affected by the accounting treatment adopted in relation to sales or purchases subject to reservation of title, the treatment should be disclosed.   (8)

INTERNAL CONTROL QUESTIONNAIRE

STOCKS AND WORK-IN-PROGRESS

(A) *General*

Note that certain aspects of the Internal Control Questionnaire in respect of receipt and issue of stocks are dealt with in sections covering Purchases and Trade Creditors and Sales and Trade Debtors.

1. Has a list of all warehouses and stores been received or prepared and duly certified by a responsible official?

2. Is stock efficiently handled as to storage and packing and properly safeguarded?

3. Is a continuous or annual stock-taking maintained? List centres if partially applied as to which is in operation.

4. Do all goods pass through stores or are some delivered direct to customers or sites?

(*B*) *Documentation*

5. Are goods only released on authorised requisitions?

6. Who has authority to authorise these?

7. Are Returned to Stores dockets completed when stores are returned?

8. Are proper bin cards maintained in respect of all goods?

9. Are the warehouse records maintained in quantity and value?

10. Are stock records maintained by:

(*a*) storekeepers,

(*b*) persons independent of those handling stores?

11. From what sources are entries made in respect of:

(*a*) receipts,

(*b*) issues?

12. Is any system of internal check operated to ensure that only authorised transactions and documents are entered on stock records?

13. Are control accounts maintained in respect of stocks, and are these compared and reconciled with warehouse records?

14. Are the staff who prepare and check control accounts independent of those maintaining stock records?

15. Are all inter-company sales clearly recorded for later identification on valuation?

(*C*) *Work-in-progress*

16. Is an efficient system of costing in operation?

17. Are costing figures reconciled with financial accounts or is a fully integrated system in operation?

18. If reconciliations are made, how regularly is this done?

19. Is it possible to trace the amount of expense involved on jobs at any given time, i.e. direct costs and indirect expenses?

20. By what method are overheads charged to jobs?

21. Are overheads divided into fixed and variable?

22. What system is operated to ensure that charges to works orders are properly allocated?

23. If standard or pre-determined costs are used:

(*a*) At what intervals are variances compiled?

(*b*) How often are standards revised?

(c) How often are variances written off?

(d) Whose responsibility is it to deal with this?

24. What records are compiled when materials and labour are transferred between jobs or between departments?

25. What system is applied to ensure the accuracy of work-in-progress values and existence, e.g. physical verification or otherwise?

(D) *Scrap and by-products*

26. What types of these arise?

27. What control is exercised over these and what documentation arises?

(E) *Stock-taking*

28. Is a responsible official in charge of stock-taking at each centre? (List names and centres.)

29. Are detailed written instructions given to staff as to method, recording, teams, marking off completed bins, etc.

30. Are stock checkers:

(a) independent of those maintaining the stores,

(b) never less than two working together?

31. Are specially printed and numbered stock sheets issued and checked for continuity on return?

32. By what method are stock quantities entered:

(a) By stock checkers, or

(b) Previous to stock-taking from continuous stock records?

33. Is comment called for as to condition or movement of stock?

34. By what method is work-in-progress counted:

(a) As having reached a certain stage in production?

(b) As a complete job less certain parts?

(c) As an assembly of various parts?

35. Are all stock sheets signed by those taking stock and countersigned by the official in charge?

36. What system is in operation to ensure that purchases returns, sales returns, transfers between departments, are recorded in the correct accounting periods?

37. What arrangements have been made to ensure that where liabilities for goods in transit are accepted the goods are included in the stock figures?

38. Are certificates obtained from third parties where goods are held by them, and how often are these obtained?

39. (a) Are stock sheets compared with stock records?

(b) Are the stock records adjusted to agree with physical stock-taking?

(c) Are material differences investigated?

(d) Whose responsibility is it to carry out (c) above?

(F) *Stock valuation*

40. Is stock valued on the basis of the total of the lowest of:

(a) cost, or

(b) net realisable value?

If cost, state method applied, e.g. fifo, lifo, average or standard.

41. Are any stocks consistently valued below cost?

42. Are any stocks valued on an estimated basis below cost, if so, by whom is the estimate made, and for what reason?

43. Work-in-progress—*see* 16–25 above.

44. If profit is taken on uncompleted contracts:

(a) On what basis is this calculated?

(b) Is such profit authenticated by a responsible official?

45. Is provision made against unrealised profit on inter-company sales made on a cost plus basis?

46. On what basis are:

(a) by-products,

(b) scrap,

(c) obsolete stocks valued,

and who is responsible for this?

47. From what sources are prices on stock sheets obtained? Are these independently checked?

48. If forward purchases or sales are made:

(a) What system is operated to ensure that such contracts are recorded in the accounting records?

(b) Are forward profits and/or losses brought in or provided against in the current period. If so, on what basis are stocks valued?

STANDARD AUDIT PROGRAMME

STOCK AND WORK-IN-PROGRESS

(A) *General*

1. Obtain a copy of any instructions to staff as to method of stock-taking and examine as to adequacy.

2. Ensure that issue of stock sheets has been properly controlled—where pre-numbered, test for complete sequence, noting that all have been signed and countersigned.

3. If final stock sheets are supplied, request originals and test these enquiring into any relevant differences.

4. If continuous stock records are maintained, test the stock sheets with the records, noting that the records are adjusted and that the cards have been marked as to the physical check amounts. Enquire into any material differences, and examine authority for writing off differences.

5. If the continuous stock records are used for the year-end figures, ensure that a physical check has been made at least once during the year and that the records have been marked accordingly.

6. Enquire as to method for dealing with work-in-progress, ascertain whether physical inspection takes place. If not, check how the company verifies its existence. Test-check records of some of the larger items.

7. Check that stock in transit is received after closing date.

8. Examine stock sheets to ensure that items other than stock are excluded, e.g. capital items, property of third parties.

9. Ensure that the cut-off procedures are properly operated by testing items of sales, sales returns, purchases and purchases returns, to ensure that items are excluded or included as necessary (*see* p. 177).

(*B*) *Valuation*

10. Test prices shown at cost value with suppliers' invoices or other evidence. Where net realisable value or replacement prices are less than the cost figures shown, ensure that stocks are of normal production requirements and that a profit may still be made on the finished product.

11. Where base stock is valued, ascertain the reason for the application and that the valuation is consistently applied. Ascertain that the fact of such valuation has been notified to the Inland Revenue authorities.

12. Ascertain the method of valuation of any scrap or by-products.

13. The value of work-in-progress should be checked with the costing records (*see* I.C.Q. Section *C*);

(*a*) noting that individual cost records are in agreement with control accounts,

(b) comparing overhead rates with those used in the current period,

(c) examining a number of items to ensure that with estimated future costs a profit may still be made in view of the ultimate sale or contract price.

14. Ensure that any inter-company or inter-branch unrealised profit on stock or work-in-progress is eliminated. (This may be traced back from the type of stock or work-in-progress concerned.)

15. Where contracts are outstanding, ensure that any profit taken is calculated on a consistent basis (see I.C.Q.) and investigate the possibility of losses of retention moneys or penalties arising.

16. Investigate slow-moving or obsolete stocks, ensure that the system will reveal these, and that the method of valuation is satisfactory and duly certified.

17. If standard or pre-determined costs are used, ensure that:

(a) The method of overhead recovery is satisfactory.

(b) The standards applied are in accordance with current conditions.

(c) The variances arising are properly accounted for so far as stock is concerned.

18. Investigate overall stock position as compared with previous year, check with previous gross profit, and if possible, account for any material changes. Check stock to turnover ratio.

19. Obtain a stock certificate from chairman or managing director.

PROGRESS TEST 10

1. What is the governing principle with regard to the auditor's duty concerning the verification and valuation of stock-in-trade? (1)

2. What peculiar difficulties are experienced in the verification and valuation of stock-in-trade? (1)

3. What are cut-off procedures? Why is their efficient operation of importance to the auditor? (3)

4. Enumerate the auditing procedures in verification of stock-in-trade. (4)

5. How may work-in-progress be verified? (6)

6. What overall tests may be applied to ascertain the reliability of the stock records? (7)

7. What audit procedures should be applied regarding finished goods? (7)

8. Is the certificate of an expert valuer sufficient evidence of the existence and value of stock for audit purposes? (8)

9. What, in brief, is the main method of valuation of stock recommended by the Councils of the accounting bodies? (10)

10. What are the deciding factors regarding the inclusion of overheads in stock valuation? (11)

11. Should fixed overheads be excluded from stock values? (14)

12. In what circumstances may special bases of stock valuation be appropriate? (15)

13. Explain the effect of fifo and lifo, and summarise the Standards of the I.S.A. in connection with them. (15)

SPECIMEN QUESTIONS

1. As auditor of Exwy Ltd., a manufacturing company, you are required to state concisely what audit tests you would apply in relation to the ascertainment of the physical quantities and ownership of stock-in-trade, excluding work-in-progress.

You may assume that the company maintains continuous stock records and that all stocks are held at the factory. *I.C.A. (E.W.)*

2. Write an essay on the auditor's duties in relation to the verification (but not the valuation) of stock-in-trade and work-in-progress of a manufacturing company. *I.C.A. (E.W.)*

3. The stock-in-trade of a limited company as on the balance sheet date has been based on a physical count made ten days previously and valued at cost, the total being adjusted for transactions subsequently arising.

State what steps you would take to ascertain that the proper amount has been included in the balance sheet.

You are not required to discuss the basis of valuation.

I.C.A. (E.W.) (Inter.)

4. After completion of the general routine audit of the accounts of Russell Ltd., you find that, although the books appear to be in order, the rate of gross profit on sales appears to be unduly high. You suspect that profits have been deliberately inflated. What steps would you take to satisfy yourself on the matter? *A.C.A.*

5. The accounts of a firm of wholesalers disclose an un-

expected increase in the rate of gross profit on sales. You suspect that the profits may have been overstated.

State the steps you would take to satisfy yourself of the accuracy of the accounts. *I.C.A. (E.W.)*

6. When carrying out an audit of the accounts of a firm of public works contractors:

(*a*) What steps can an auditor take to ascertain whether stock inventories contain any obsolete, old or slow-moving stocks?

(*b*) In what circumstances, and to what extent, can he accept the written-down book value of old stocks being written up during stock-taking?

(*c*) What principles should he apply to determine whether any element of profit may properly be included in the value placed on work-in-progress in the case of a long-term contract?

(*d*) What particular matters will he need to take into account when considering the valuation of an item of work-in-progress, the estimated final cost of which is expected to exceed the contract price? *I.C.A. (E.W.)*

7. (*a*) For what purpose, and in what circumstances would you consider it desirable for the auditor of a limited company to attend at stock-taking?

(*b*) To what extent is the auditor affected by the employment by the company of independent stock takers and valuers?

(*c*) What overall audit tests may be appropriate when assessing the reliability of records of stock-in-trade and work-in-progress?
I.C.A. (E.W.)

8. What enquiries and tests should be made by an auditor to satisfy himself that at the date of the balance sheet:

(*a*) the balances on continuous stock records can be relied upon to prove accurate figures of stock quantities;

(*b*) the cost figures appearing in stock sheets are correct; and

(*c*) the values placed on by-products can be accepted?
I.C.A. (E.W.)

9. Where raw materials, work-in-progress and finished stocks are maintained in the books of a business at standard cost:

(*a*) What particular matters would an auditor normally need to consider when examining the values placed on these items in the annual financial accounts, and

(*b*) to what special points should he have regard:

(*i*) where the accounts relate to the first year's trading of a new factory, and

(ii) where raw materials are subject to continual violent fluctuations in price?

It can be assumed that the auditor has already satisfied himself as to the physical quantities. *I.C.A. (E.W.)*

CHAPTER XI

Retention and Distribution of Profits

NATURE OF PROFITS

The recognised object of any business is that of earning profits, but what constitutes profits is a matter not easily established.

1. Definition of profits. Profits may be defined as "the increase in the net value of the assets of a business over their net value at the commencement of a given period which has arisen other than by capital adjustment".

Whilst this definition has the advantage of brevity, because of the many difficulties which have arisen in practice it is necessary to have a more exact description, and the following is that given by the Court in the case of the *Spanish Prospecting Co., Ltd.* (1911):

> ... If the total assets of the business at the two dates be compared, the increase which they show at the later date as compared with the earlier date (due allowance, of course, being made for any capital introduced into or taken out of the business in the meanwhile) represents in strictness the profits of the business during the period in question. ... The strict meaning of the word "profit" is rarely observed in drawing up the accounts of firms or companies. ... Certain assumptions have become so customary in drawing up balance sheets and profit and loss accounts that it may almost be said to require special circumstances to induce parties to depart therefrom. For instance, it is usual to exclude gains and losses arising from causes not directly connected with the business of the company. ... The value assigned to trade buildings and plant is usually fixed according to an arbitrary rule, by which they are originally taken at their actual cost and are assumed to have depreciated by a certain percentage each year, though it cannot be pretended that any such calculation necessarily gives their true value either in use or exchange. ... It is better to under-rate than to over-rate the profits, since it is impossible for you to see all the risks to which a business may in future be exposed. ... But though there is a wide field for variation of practice in these estimations of profit, this liberty ceases at once when the rights of third parties intervene. ... In the absence of certain stipulations to the contrary, "profits", in cases where the

rights of third parties come in, mean actual profits, and they must be calculated as closely as possible, in accordance with the definition to which I have referred.

It is in the *distribution* of profits, or the charges to be set against them, that most of the difficulties mentioned have arisen, but before proceeding to these matters, the *retention* of profits for various purposes will be considered.

2. Ploughing back of profits. In dealing with the subject of depreciation it has been pointed out that to distribute profits without making adequate provision for the replacement of assets is an unwise policy to pursue. In the case of sole traders and partnerships they are free to pursue any course of action in this respect which they may desire to do, and even with limited companies it is not legally required that fixed assets shall be depreciated. Nevertheless, to ignore depreciation of the fixed assets of a business, save in isolated cases, would tend towards ultimate failure. Furthermore, assets have now often to be replaced at figures higher than cost. Therefore any efficiently-run business will normally "plough back" profits either for specific purposes or for the general strengthening or expansion of the organisation.

When considering the amount of profit available for "ploughing back" purposes, the auditor must first satisfy himself that the sums to be appropriated are available, not only after having provided against all known liabilities but also after having checked that provisions have been made against any liability likely to arise which is uncertain as to amount.

3. Provisions.

(*a*) *Definition.* At this stage it is apposite to consider the relevant definitions of provisions and reserves as given in the Companies Act 1967 (Sch. 2, Part IV):

> For the purpose of this Schedule, unless the context otherwise requires:
>
> (*a*) the expression "provision" shall . . . mean any amount written off or retained by way of providing for depreciation, renewals or diminution in value of assets, or retained by way of providing for any known liability of which the amount cannot be determined with substantial accuracy;
>
> (*b*) the expression "reserve" shall not, subject as aforesaid, include any amount written off or retained by way of providing for depreciation, renewals or diminution in value of assets or

retained by way of providing for any known liability or any sum set aside for the purpose of its being used to prevent undue fluctuations in charges for taxation;

and in this paragraph the expression "liability" shall include all liabilities in respect of expenditure contracted for and all disputed or contingent liabilities.

. . .

Where:

(a) any amount written off or retained by way of providing for depreciation, renewals or diminution in the value of assets. . . .

(b) any amount retained by way of providing for any known liability;

is in excess of that which in the opinion of the directors is reasonably necessary for the purpose, the excess shall be treated . . . as a reserve and not a provision.

The definitions are not so obscure as might at first appear, since, once a provision has been defined, any other amounts provided fall clearly under either of the headings of a reserve—an appropriation, or a liability—a specific amount.

(b) *Auditor's duty.* From the auditor's point of view a provision requires careful attention. As no actual sum constituting the liability exists, which would be indisputable, and since a reserve is an appropriation of ascertainable profit, a provision not being of such a certain nature may cause difficulty in assessment as to whether it is adequate or otherwise.

(c) *Provision for bad debts.* The provision for bad debts has on occasions been the cause of controversy. The debtors shown on a balance sheet form part of the current assets and it is of importance to ensure that they come within the requirement of showing a "true and fair view", therefore if there is the likelihood of bad debts arising, they must be provided against.

(d) *Auditing case law.* There are certain cases having a bearing on the subject of amounts to be provided against bad debts, for example:

(i) *Verner* v. *General and Commercial Investment Trust* (1894). This case has already been mentioned with regard to the depreciation of fixed assets (*see* p. 160) and although book debts are current assets the case is relevant in that the judge stated that:

Floating or circulating capital must be kept up, as otherwise it will enter into and form part of such excess, in which case, to divide such excess without deducting the capital which forms part of it, will be contrary to law. . . . That is, if a profit is shown without provision having been made for the fall in the value of current assets an illegal distribution of capital would ensue.

(*ii*) *Re London and General Bank* (1895). Where the auditor reported to the directors, but not to the shareholders, the unsatisfactory state of the company's book debts which, as the company was a bank, consisted of "Loans to customers and other securities", and he was held liable. (*See also* Chapter XIV.)

(*iii*) *Arthur E. Green & Company* v. *The Central Advance and Discount Corporation Ltd.* (1920). The auditor accepted from the Managing Director and the Board a schedule of the amounts to be written off for bad and doubtful debts each year. The auditor knew of the retention of old debts on the books but accepted the explanation of the Managing Director that such debts would eventually be paid as the debtors would return for further loans.

The auditor here was held to have failed in his duty, not only by not making proper enquiries where these seemed necessary, but also in that he at no time reported the state of affairs to the members.

(*e*) *Summary.* The foregoing cases serve to emphasise the importance of ensuring that book debts are shown at their true value, and if this is not done, and if adequate provision is not made against bad debts, the auditor must report thereon.

4. Provisions for the extinction of goodwill. One further provision which might cause difficulty to the auditor is that made in order to write down the value of goodwill.

As goodwill is considered a fixed asset there is no necessity in normal circumstances to write this off: *Wilmer* v. *McNamara & Co. Ltd.* (1895). (*See* 10(*a*), (*iii*), 3.)

Where, however, goodwill has been lost in such circumstances as, for example, where a business is acquired and retained as a branch which is subsequently closed down, to retain an asset of goodwill would be untrue and not complying with the requirements of the Companies Act 1948, necessitating the showing of a true and fair view of the company's affairs. In this case, the goodwill should be written off.

5. Reserves. Various types of reserves and the distinction between capital and revenue are dealt with in Chapter VII.

DISTRIBUTION OF PROFITS

6. Right to distribute profits. Definitions of profits have been given at the commencement of this chapter and as the object of any business is the earning of these, when any profits arise it would appear that they may be distributed to the proprietors without any question as to their rights to do so.

Such is the case with respect to sole traders and partnerships; the proprietors have subscribed the capital of the business concerned and those who deal with them should act under the principle of *caveat emptor* (literally, "let the buyer beware", but as a principle for creditors and others "let those who deal with them look to their own interests"). In the case, however, of limited companies, where the wider field of the public at large and shareholders is concerned, the courts are prepared to ensure that the rights of the various parties are protected. Creditors and other third parties, as well as minority interests, have sought the aid of the courts quite frequently when they have considered their rights to be infringed by acts concerning the distribution of profits.

7. Governing factors. These are as laid down in decided cases and as specified in the Memorandum and Articles of the companies concerned.

There is some conflict of view as to what may be considered legally distributable and what prudent business policy dictates should be distributed. Profit may legally be distributable, but we have already mentioned that to run down the main assets of a business without making any provision for future trading is unwise. The auditor has the responsibility of seeing that the legal position is complied with.

8. Capital profits. Profits may arise during the course of the life of a business other than those directly concerned with its actual trading, for example, in connection with disposal of its fixed assets. Such profits may be realised or take the form of book figures only created by such matters as revaluation.

(*a*) *Realised capital profits.*

(*i*) *Lubbock* v. *British Bank of South America Ltd.* (1892). This case was brought by a shareholder against the company in order to ascertain the legal position with regard to the proposal to distribute certain capital profits. These had arisen on the sale by the bank of its assets and liabilities in Brazil, agreeing as it did so to discontinue operating there. It subsequently repurchased rights to operate its original branch and a profit arose on the whole transaction of some £205,000. The Articles of the company permitted the carrying of such profits to the profit and loss account and the distribution of dividends subject to passing a necessary resolution.

It was held that the profit was a sum in excess of the capital and not part of the capital itself and as the Articles so permitted it was distributable.

(ii) *Foster* v. *The New Trinidad Lake Asphalt Co. Ltd.* (1901). The company had taken over a debt on its formation, which at the time was deemed to be valueless. Subsequently the debt was paid together with interest which had accrued. The directors proposed to distribute the sum arising as dividends.

The interest arising was not brought into question but the sum received in payment of the original debt was considered by the judge to be a capital profit.

Taking into consideration the decisions of the cases *Lubbock* v. *British Bank of South America*, mentioned above, and the case of *Verner* v. *General and Commercial Investment Trust* (1894), Byrne, J. stated:

> If I rightly appreciate the true effect of the decisions, the question of what profit is available for dividend depends upon the result of the whole accounts fairly taken for the year, capital, as well as profit and loss, and although dividends may be paid out of earned profits, in proper cases, although there has been a depreciation of capital, I do not think that a realised accretion to the estimated value of one item of the capital assets can be deemed to be profit divisible amongst the shareholders without reference to the result of the whole accounts fairly taken.

To summarise from the foregoing cases the position with regard to distributable capital profits, should fulfil the following requirements:

(1) They must be realised.

(2) They must exist after taking into consideration the value of the total assets and liabilities of the business at the same time.

(3) The Memorandum and Articles must permit such a distribution.

(b) *Unrealised capital profits.* When we turn to the subject of unrealised capital profits the difficulty becomes immediately apparent (as we have stated above) that as, *inter alia*, capital profits must be realised before being available for distribution, then the question of distributing unrealised capital profits should not arise.

The summary given above has been accepted as the rules governing the distribution of capital profits, but two more recent cases have caused some doubt as to the restriction of distributions of profits only when realised.

(*i*) *Dimbula Valley* (*Ceylon*) *Tea Co. Ltd.* v. *Laurie* (1961). In this case the preference shareholders raised objections to the capitalisation of unrealised reserves, submitting that the case of *Westburn Sugar* mentioned below was relevant.

(*ii*) *Westburn Sugar Refineries Ltd.* v. *I.R.C.* (1960). In this Scottish Court of Sessions case it was held that an unrealised capital profit was not a "distributable sum". Lord Sorn categorically stating that in his view capital profits were not distributable until they were realised.

However, in the *Dimbula* case this restriction on the right of a company to distribute unrealised profits was rejected by Buckley, J., who stated that:

(*i*) If the reserve fund arising from a revaluation of capital assets could not be distributed, it likewise could not be capitalised, and such a result conflicted with the generally accepted view of the law. As a general rule, only that which could be distributed in dividends can be capitalised, the exception to this general rule being the share premium account or a capital redemption reserve fund which never at any time were distributable, being governed by ss. 56 (1) and (2) and 58 (1) and (2) of the Companies Act 1948.

(*ii*) The fact that the reserve in question, being an unrealised profit, was dependent for its existence upon a valuation should not (provided the valuation was itself not open to criticism) be allowed to prejudice the foregoing conclusion. Since trading concerns having on opening and closing stock relied to a varying extent upon the valuation placed upon such stock in arriving at their profit and loss account, it was a difference of degree rather than of principle to calculate capital profits by comparing their estimated with their book value.

With the frequent revaluation of assets, because of the influence of continued inflation, it is likely that companies will put much weight behind the decision in the *Dimbula* case, but as the position as to the distribution of capital profits, whether realised or unrealised, is now not settled decisively, no doubt some further legislation may be expected on this subject.

9. Profits prior to incorporation. As a company comes into existence on the date of its incorporation, any profits earned by a business taken over are considered to be part of the capital assets taken over and not revenue earned by the new company.

The usual diffidence to distribute profits of a capital nature applies with regard to such revenue, but legally it seems that no objection can be raised, provided that the Memorandum and Articles permit such distributions.

It would appear advisable rather to set off such profit earned against any payment made for goodwill. Likewise, where interest is payable to vendors, the interest may be set off against the profits arising. Conversely, if a loss is sustained between the date of takeover and the incorporation date, this may be added to goodwill.

The auditor should be careful to ascertain that the calculations arising are made up to the date of incorporation of the company and not to the date from which the certificate to commence business operations, as any transactions between the incorporation date and the commencement of business date can always be back-dated.

10. Distributable profits. In the case of sole traders and partnerships, the distribution of sums to the partners, provided it is in accordance with any agreement, may be paid out of capital or revenue.

In the case of limited companies, however, any payment of dividends other than out of profits is illegal and constitutes a breach of s. 66 of the Companies Act 1948. Table A (*see* p. 211) likewise specifies that "no dividend shall be paid otherwise than out of profits", but should the Table A clause be excluded any such distribution would come under the jurisdiction of s. 66.

From the point of view of sound financial policy, losses should always be made good before taking funds from the business in the form of dividends unless there are adequate reserves, but this is not the legal position.

The following principles with regard to the distribution of dividends have been dealt with in the cases shown.

(*a*) *Dividends may be paid before losses sustained on fixed assets are made good.* This is so provided that: (1) there is an excess of current income over current expenditure; (2) the regulations of the company so permit; (3) sufficient assets are retained to meet current liabilities.

Examples of this can be seen in the following cases:

(*i*) *Lee* v. *Neuchatel Asphalte Co. Ltd.* (*see* p. 161).

(*ii*) *Verner* v. *General and Commercial Investment Trust*. These cases have been dealt with earlier in Chapter VIII, regarding depreciation.

(*iii*) *Wilmer* v. *McNamara & Co. Ltd.* (1895) (*see* **4**). Although depreciation had been written off adequately in former years, without writing off any depreciation for the current year, a resolution was passed to distribute the profit shown as a dividend to the preference shareholders. The ordinary shareholders sought the aid of the court to restrain the directors from carrying out the terms of the resolution.

The court refused to grant the injunction desired.

(*b*) *Directors are entitled to place profits to reserve.* They may do this before recommending the payment of preference dividends.

Cases which exemplify this are as follows:

(*i*) *Fisher* v. *Black and White Publishing Co.* (1901), and *Burland* v. *Earle* (1902). In the first of these two cases the court would not interfere where directors were given discretion to determine how much profit should be put to reserve before recommending the payment of a dividend, even though this would obviate the payment of a dividend on founders' shares. In the second case, the court acted similarly and would not compel the distribution of total profits as it was considered right and lawful for a company to carry forward a proportion of current profits.

(*ii*) *Bond* v. *The Barrow Haematite Steel Co. Ltd.* (1902). This case has already been dealt with in detail (*see* p. 163). Here it may be mentioned that the profit shown on the profit and loss account was carried forward, depreciation on assets, which a valuation had revealed to be apparently worth considerably less than shown, not having been written off. After refusing to allow an application for reduction of capital on the grounds that the losses sustained on the assets were not proven, certain preference shareholders sought the court's aid to compel the payment of the dividend on their shares out of the profit and loss account. The court refused to do so in accordance with the principle stated above.

(*c*) *Debit balances.* A debit balance on profit and loss account consisting of accumulated losses of previous years need not be written off prior to the payment of dividends out of current profits.

A case which exemplifies this is *Ammonia Soda Co., Ltd.* v. *Chamberlain* (1918). The company, having sustained losses on revaluation of its land, created a reserve account and wrote off a proportion of its adverse profit and loss account; the remaining proportion was written off subsequently out of current profits.

Preference dividends were paid, but it was contended that in so far as the whole of the debit balance on the profit and loss account had not first been written off out of current profits, there had been a payment of dividends out of capital.

The Court of Appeal rejected this contention, Swinfen, L.J., stating:

> The Companies Acts do not impose any obligation upon a limited company nor does the law require it, that it shall not distribute as dividend the clear net profit of its trading unless its paid-up capital is intact, or until it has made good all losses incurred in previous years.

But the words of Warrington, L.J., are important, as they emphasise the fact that such cases will be judged according to their own particular circumstances:

> The nature of the business and the amount of the loss may be such that no honest and reasonable man of business would think of paying dividends without providing for it. In such a case, I apprehend the court would take the view that a payment which no honest and reasonable man of business would think it right to make could not properly be made by directors.

(*d*) *Goodwill written off in past years*. This may be written back to profit and loss account and a dividend paid from it.

An example of this can be found in the case of *Stapley* v. *Read Bros. Ltd.* (1924). Having written off goodwill against a reserve account created out of profits, the company subsequently sustained losses which caused the profit and loss account to show a debit balance. Thereafter, a profit was made, but it was not sufficient to pay a dividend with arrears to the preference share-holders. The directors proposed to restore the profit and loss account and to utilise the reserve to write off the debit balance on profit and loss account, and to appropriate the sum remaining, plus the profit earned, to pay the preference dividends.

An injunction was sought to restrain the directors, but this was refused, Russell, J., stating:

If they had retained goodwill as an asset in their balance sheet, and if, instead of writing off its value out of profits, they had carried those profits to a goodwill depreciation reserve fund, they would have been at liberty at any time to distribute those profits, at all events to the extent by which the amount of such a reserve fund exceed the amount of the actual depreciation.

11. Table A clauses. Whilst the Companies Act itself lays down no rule as to the distribution of profits in the form of dividends, Table A does contain certain clauses affecting profit distribution. Table A, the first Schedule to the Companies Act 1948, is a model set of rules which are taken to apply as governing the internal matters of a company unless they are excluded in whole or in part, and if completely excluded, a company is required to register its own Articles of Association.

The clauses referring to the payment of dividends are as follows:

Clause 114: The right to declare dividends shall be vested in the members in general meeting, but no dividend may be declared at a rate exceeding that recommended by the directors.

Clause 115: The directors may pay such interim dividends as appear to be justified by the profits.

Clause 116: No dividend shall be paid otherwise than out of profits.

Clause 117: Before recommending any dividend the directors may transfer to reserve such sums as they deem desirable.

The foregoing clauses are in accord with the legal decisions outlined in **10**, and where Table A is modified no Article may be introduced which would alter the overriding legal requirements.

12. No dividends out of capital. No dividend may be paid out of capital, and directors who knowingly pay dividends out of capital are personally liable to make good the amount of such dividends to the company: *Re London and General Bank* (1895). This does not, of course, exclude the payment of dividends out of capital profits, as explained above, but if members receive dividends knowing them to have been paid out of capital, then the directors have a right of indemnity against them: *Moxham* v. *Grant* (1910). From the foregoing it is abundantly clear that the courts will not tolerate any reduction of capital unless it take place under their own supervision.

13. Declaration and payment of dividends. The following matters affect the declaration and payment of specified kinds of dividend:

(*a*) *Scrip dividends*. Unless there is a specific agreement to the contrary, shareholders are entitled to receive these dividends in cash: *Hoole* v. *Great Western Railway Company* (1868). Where, however, there is express agreement, then dividends may be paid in kind, e.g. in the form of shares, debentures or assets.

(*b*) *Preference dividends*. Whether preference dividends are to receive simple or cumulative dividends is a matter to be ascertained from the Articles. Where cumulative dividends are in arrears, it is required (Companies Act 1948, Sch. 8) that:

> There must be shown as a note or in a statement or report annexed to the accounts the amount of any arrears of preference dividends before deduction of income tax, and the period for which the dividends or, if there is more than one class, each class of them, are in arrear. When the dividends are payable free of income tax, the free of tax amount of the arrears will be shown, and this fact stated.

There is an implied power in every company to pay dividends but this is not to state that a company is legally required to do so. Furthermore, if the Articles require the payment of dividends in a particular manner, then profits must be applied only in the manner specified: *Oakbank Oil Co.* v. *Crum* (1883).

The wisdom of clauses of Table A, and of the decisions as mentioned above (*see* **10**) is apparent, for often revenue reserves may indicate the prosperity of a company; but if its resources are tied up in assets not readily realisable, it may not be possible to utilise such reserves for the payment of dividends without putting the company into a difficult position regarding working capital.

It is with this latter point in mind that care has to be exercised with regard to the payment of interim dividends.

14. Interim dividends. Whilst the responsibility for the declaration and payment of interim dividends is not that of the auditor but of the directors, nevertheless he may often be consulted as to the desirability of declaring an interim dividend, in which case the following matters have to be borne in mind:

(*a*) If the Articles permit, the directors may declare interim dividends before the end of the company's financial year; where Table A is in operation, Clause 115 applies.

(*b*) If an interim dividend is declared and the company's accounts subsequently show a loss for the year, there is the possibility of the dividend having been paid out of capital. It is essential, therefore, that adequate interim accounts be prepared in order to give a true position of the company's financial state, from which the justification mentioned in Table A, Clause 115 may be obtained. Where a receipts and payments account was prepared which incorrectly showed a surplus, a bonus issue was deemed to have been improperly declared on the strength of the account, and a director who benefited was ordered to refund the amount received by him. *Rance's case* (1871) stipulates that directors may from time to time pay to the members such interim dividends as appear to the directors to be justified by the profits of the company.

(c) Where shares are quoted, to declare an interim dividend at a certain rate, and then to have to declare a final dividend at a lower rate, would be regarded as a sign of financial weakness, with subsequent effect on share prices. Every care should be taken to estimate carefully the course of the company's trading when deciding upon the rate of an interim dividend, or whether to pay one at all.

(d) The effect on the liquid resources of the company must be taken into consideration. If profits are tied up in assets other than in a liquid state, the drain on immediate resources might cause embarrassment in an otherwise prosperous company.

(e) Unlike a final dividend, which is sanctioned by the shareholders in general meeting, and after declaration becomes a debt due, an interim dividend if declared by the directors does not constitute a debt, and consequently a shareholder cannot claim payment thereof. (*Lagunas Nitrate Co.* v. *Schroeder* (1901)).

PROGRESS TEST 11

1. Give a brief definition of profits. (1)
2. For what reason is it advisable to plough back profits into a business? (2)
3. What is a provision and how does it differ from a reserve and a liability respectively? (3)
4. Why must the auditor pay particular attention to provisions? (3)
5. Have any decided cases had any bearing upon the provision for bad debts? If so, what is the main principle involved? (3)
6. How may the auditor ascertain whether profits are available for distribution or not? (6)
7. Give a summary of the principles maintained in decided cases with regard to the distribution of capital profits. (8)

8. Recently, the governing principle regarding the distribution of capital profits changed. In what way has it changed? **(8)**

9. It is legally possible to distribute pre-acquisition profits. Is it to be advocated, however? **(9)**

10. Enumerate the main principles regarding the distribution of dividends. **(10)**

11. In certain circumstances it is forbidden to distribute profit. What are they? **(11, 12)**

12. What is the principle governed by *Rance's case* (1871)? **(14)**

13. When distributing interim dividends, what factors should be borne in mind? **(14)**

SPECIMEN QUESTIONS

1. (*a*) Define the following terms used in the Companies Act 1967:

(*i*) Capital reserve.

(*ii*) Provision.

(*iii*) Revenue reserve.

(*b*) State, giving your reasons, in which of the above three categories you consider each of the following items should be placed:

(*i*) The surplus arising on a professional revaluation of the company's properties.

(*ii*) The estimated cost of maintaining, for the remaining period of guarantee, machines sold during the year.

(*iii*) An amount, transferred from profit and loss account, equal to the reduction in taxation in respect of initial allowances.

(*iv*) An amount, appropriated from profits, to provide for the increased cost of replacement of fixed assets.

(*v*) A sum, set aside from profits, towards a special publicity campaign which the directors are considering starting in the following year. *I.C.A.* (*E.W.*)

2. Write an essay, of not more than three pages, upon the general principles underlying the availability for distribution to members of the profits of a company limited by shares.

I.C.A. (*E.W.*)

3. A limited company has asked you, as auditor, to advise as to the treatment in the accounts of the following:

(a) Surplus on revaluation of leasehold property, £8,000.

(b) Surplus on sale of freehold property, £5,000.

(c) Excess of valuation over cost of investments, quoted on the Stock Exchange, held in respect of Leasehold Redemption Fund, £7,000.

Write a letter to the Company explaining the principles applicable to the distribution of capital surpluses and advising them on the treatment of the above three items.

I.C.A. (E.W.) (Inter.)

4. Where a limited company has declared and paid a dividend "out of capital profits", bearing in mind case law on the subject, discuss the considerations which an auditor should take into account in deciding whether or not the payment was *intra vires*.

I.C.A.

5. Discuss briefly the factors governing distribution of the profits of a limited company. The directors of a limited company, of which you are the auditor, seek your advice as to the distribution of surplus following a professional revaluation of their shop premises. Draft a report to them and include therein your opinion of the uses to which the surplus might be put.

A.C.A. (Inter.)

6. In ascertaining the profits of a company which are legally available for dividend, consider the following points and state, giving your authority where possible, whether:

(a) Depreciation of fixed and wasting assets must be made good before current income is to be distributed.

(b) Depreciation of current assets must be made good before dividends out of current income.

(c) A debit balance on Profit and Loss Account brought about by losses in past years must be made good before dividends are paid out of current profits.

(d) Goodwill written off in past years may be brought back to the credit of Profit and Loss Account and a dividend paid thereout.

(e) Directors are entitled to place profits to reserve before recommending payment of preference dividends. *A.C.A.*

7. The board of a private limited company, of which you are the auditor, has discovered that one of the boardroom paintings recently bought at a local auction for £10 is in fact an "old master" currently valued at £150,000, and has sought your advice. Set out concisely the accounting alternatives that will be

available to the board when it comes to prepare its next annual accounts and the particular matters that, in your opinion, it should take into account in connection with this discovery when formulating its dividend proposals for the year. *I.C.A. (E.W.)*

8. You are auditor of XY Ltd. The directors produce the following profit and loss account:

	£	£
Trading profit		20,000
Less Depreciation	16,000	
Directors' Remuneration	26,000	
Auditor's Remuneration	2,000	
		44,000
Net loss		24,000
Income Tax Recoverable		8,000
		16,000
Gain on sale of premises	10,000	
Gain on revaluation of other assets	26,000	
Balance brought forward from last year	8,000	
		44,000
		28,000
Dividend		20,000
Balance carried to balance sheet		8,000

The company has no revenue reserves apart from the balance on profit and loss account. Comment on the accounts and the provisions therein. *A.C.A.*

CHAPTER XII

Specialised Audits

1. Varieties of audit. Neither for practical purposes, nor for answering examination questions, is it possible to have had personal experience of every type of audit for which information is required. It is necessary, therefore, in compiling an audit programme to use knowledge and experience gained on similar types of audit, and to augment this with imagination concerning the type of procedures likely to be involved.

(*a*) *Application of experience.* Thus, if a programme for the audit of a cinema is required, then if the box office is brought to mind, the checking of daily takings with ticket numbers of various denominations should be apparent; thereafter, the procedures with regard to daily banking and the proper segregation of takings from disbursements and so forth, should come to mind.

(*b*) *Examination requirements.* It may be mentioned that in answering questions on specialised audits, the routine procedures attaching to all audits need not be listed.

In the following examples, for the sake of brevity, only the main points have been given. If time allows in an examination, additional specialised points might be added from the student's experience.

2. Building Societies. The Building Societies Act 1962 was the culmination of a number of changes affecting Building Societies brought about by the need for a more rigid legal control over their affairs.

(*a*) *Report of auditors.* Auditors now have to report specifically as to:

(*i*) the keeping of records of the valuation of the security on which advances are made: s. 27;

(*ii*) the keeping of proper books of account, the maintenance of a system of control of the books and transactions and the safe custody of deeds and documents of title: s. 76;

(*iii*) the revenue and appropriation account and balance sheet giving a true and fair view . . .: ss. 77 and 78.

In effect, the auditor is now required by statute to carry out such a complete audit as will enable him to report on all the foregoing.

(b) *Form of accounts.* The Chief Registrar of Friendly Societies has, under the Act, prescribed the form the balance sheet and revenue and appropriation account shall take, stating certain matters which must be shown therein (Building Societies (Accounts) Regulations 1962).

Furthermore, the auditors have also to report on the annual return, stating:

(i) whether in their opinion the return is properly drawn up in accordance with the requirements of the Act and regulations made under these requirements;

(ii) whether the return gives a true and fair view of the matters to which it is addressed (other than those with which the auditors are not required to deal);

(iii) whether the return is in agreement with the books of account and records of the society.

(c) *Disclosure of advances to officers.* Regarding (a) above, where advances are made to any director or the manager or secretary, or to companies in which any person is interested, these must be disclosed: s. 89. The importance of this requirement to the auditor is obvious.

3. Suggested audit procedures for Building Societies. In order to offer guidance regarding the new phase in the audits of building societies, the Institute of Chartered Accountants have issued in separate booklet form, *Audits of Building Societies,* from which the following quotations on matters of outstanding importance are taken:

Testing the System of Internal Control

The auditors should compile and maintain an up-to-date record of the system of internal control, obtaining copies of rules, standard forms, internal instructions and any publications showing terms of business. This record should cover each aspect of the society's activities (such as advances, shares deposits, custody of assets, handling of cash) . . . (Para. 27).

Mortgage Advances

The auditors will have to decide upon the nature and extent of the tests which they should apply to the new advances on mortgage, including such tests "in depth" as may be appropriate. Some may find it expedient to do this work during the year of account, concurrently with the transactions. The auditors' procedures will be governed by their assessment of the system in the light of the considerations referred to in the following paragraphs (Para. 34).

The proper control of advances on mortgage is of fundamental importance in the operations of a building society. A sound and effective system of internal control is vital. The system must take into account the provisions of the Act relating to "special advances"; these are defined in s. 21 and s. 22(1) provides specifically that a society "shall so conduct its business as to secure that special advances are not made by it except as authorised by this section". When the Act of 1962 came into force an essential step for every building society was to identify existing advances which fell within the definition of "special advances" (Para. 35).

Safe Custody of Deeds

The directors must, in order to comply with sub-sections (3) and (4) of s. 76, establish and maintain a system to ensure the safe custody of all documents of title belonging to the building society and of the deeds relating to property mortgaged to the building society. Sub-section (4) provides specifically that a society shall not be taken to have established a proper system unless, under the system, on each occasion on which any such document of title or deed is released from the custody of the officers of the society, the consent is obtained of the board of directors of the society, or of a person authorised by the board to give such consent (Para. 43).

The auditors have a statutory duty (s. 87(4)) to carry out such investigations as will enable them to form an opinion whether the foregoing requirement has been complied with (Para. 44).

Prior to the Act of 1962 the auditors of a building society were required by law to examine all deeds relating to each property in mortgage to the society at the balance sheet date. This obligation has now been superseded by the more important obligation to form an opinion on the system of control throughout the year and on the view of the state of the society's affairs as presented in the annual accounts. The number of deeds to be examined is a matter for the judgment of the auditors of each society in the process of examining the soundness and effectiveness of the system. Deeds which are not available for inspection will call for special enquiries, to be pursued until the auditors are satisfied with the explanation (Para. 45).

Cash

The handling of cash is always accompanied by possibilities of error and misappropriation, concealed by "teeming and lading", manipulation of dormant accounts and other devices. This problem is of special importance to auditors of building societies because of the large extent of the cash transactions, but it does not involve audit considerations which differ in principle from those encountered in many other businesses. In assessing the system and testing its effectiveness the auditors will need to apply rigorously their professional techniques. Discrepancies revealed by surprise cash counts or by searching tests "in depth" will call for exhaustive investigation (Para. 59).

Interest and Other Amounts Paid by Borrowers

The prescribed form of revenue and appropriation account requires separate disclosure of "interest on mortgages" and "other amounts paid by borrowers as consideration for advances". The auditors will therefore need to satisfy themselves that the records are maintained in such a way that this important distinction is properly made in the revenue and appropriation account (Para. 61).

Provision for Mortgage Losses

The provision for anticipated losses on mortgages is required to be stated separately in the balance sheet as a deduction from the total amount outstanding on mortgages. The auditors will need to be satisfied that where repayments are in arrear a realistic provision is made if the security is not adequate; and even if the account is dormant, interest should be accrued and the provision for mortgage losses augmented accordingly. Where arrears have been satisfied by the granting of additional advances the soundness of the debts will need special examination, including a review of transactions with those borrowers subsequent to the balance sheet date (Para. 66).

"Window Dressing"

Auditors should examine transactions which have the effect of showing as on the balance sheet date a state of affairs (particularly the society's liquidity) which is materially better than it was during the year and shortly after. Items requiring particular attention are:

(a) large deposits received shortly before the year end and repaid shortly after;

(b) large mortgage repayments received shortly before the year end and readvanced on the same property shortly after;

(c) unusual delay until after the year end in making payments in accordance with applications received before the year end for withdrawals of shares or deposits;

(d) an abnormal year-end accumulation of commitments for advances followed by the making of the advances shortly after the year end;

(e) the significance of the items in bank reconciliation statements (Para. 70).

Auditor's report

Where the auditors have no reservations to make in respect of any of the matters specified in s. 87 a suitable form of report would be:

Report of the auditors to the members of the . . . Building Society

The foregoing balance sheet and revenue and appropriation account are properly drawn up in accordance with the requirements of the Building Societies Act 1962 and the regulations made thereunder. In our opinion they give respectively a true and fair view of the state of the society's affairs as on . . . . and of its income and expenditure for the financial year ended on that date (Para. 73).

4. Banks.

(*a*) The efficient working of a system of internal control is vital here, and this should be investigated thoroughly on commencement and checked in part regularly thereafter.

(*b*) Ascertain that the system of internal check is not only reduced to writing, but continually applied. Such matters as the changing of machine operators, cashiers not having access to customers' ledgers, etc., should be carefully checked.

(*c*) Verify balances with other banks and the Bank of England.

(*d*) Examine investments and bills, care being taken to obviate the possibility of substitution.

(*e*) Check the market value of securities, ascertaining that provision is made against any material losses.

(*f*) Verify the existence and adequacy of securities given for loans and overdrafts.

(*g*) Ensure that true valuation is placed upon all assets held, especially in view of the abolition of the former provision to allow secret reserves under the Companies Act 1948.

5. Clubs.

(*a*) The regulations of the club should be studied, noting the extent of activities and requirements as to accounting matters.

(*b*) Entrance fees and members' subscriptions should be checked with minutes of meetings in which applications for membership are passed and resignations noted, and also with lists of members.

(*c*) The receipt of cash for membership fees should be checked with counterfoil receipts.

(*d*) Where the club's activities include the running of a hotel or restaurant, the audit will follow that as stated in that of a hotel (*see* 8).

(e) The auditor should ensure that any honorarium paid to any officer is properly voted and minuted.

(f) Petty cash balances held by any club officers should be checked as well as careful vouching of their petty cash books.

6. Contractors.

(a) Normally, it is necessary for such businesses to prepare accounts in respect of each contract or of each section of certain contracts undertaken. This necessitates the maintenance of records which will facilitate the efficient allocation of expenses. The system of cost accounting should be carefully examined, as the auditor may have to make considerable use of such records.

(b) The internal check system governing the payment and allocation of wages should be examined.

(c) Wages sheets should be tested exhaustively with employees' records, time cards, etc., through the payment of wages on sites and the frequent turnover of certain staff, the system may leave itself open to easy abuse.

(d) The system governing the recording of stores issues, and transfer of plant to various sites, should be checked.

(e) Control accounts should be carefully checked, or if not kept, should be compiled in order to verify the allocation of the total wages and stores issued to various contracts.

(f) Liabilities to sub-contractors at the close of the period should be carefully checked.

(g) Receipts on account of contracts should be vouched with architects' or engineers' certificates, retention moneys being ascertained.

(h) Stocks of raw materials should be verified carefully as well as value placed upon work-in-progress. The value placed upon the latter should be considered in conjunction with architects' or engineers' certificates, the possibility of losses arising being provided against.

(i) Where credit is taken for profit on uncompleted contracts, the auditor should satisfy himself that this is justified and calculated on a conservative basis (methods of bringing in such profits are outlined in costing textbooks). (*See also* p. 185.)

(j) Frequently, work of a capital nature is undertaken by the company's own staff. The allocation of such work to capital as opposed to revenue expenditure should be checked.

7. Executors' and trustees' accounts.

(*a*) *Executors' accounts.*

(*i*) The will should be examined, noting points of interest as to disposition of property, creation of trusts, investment of estate funds, distribution of residue, etc.

(*ii*) To ensure all the estate is brought in, access should be obtained to private books of account, tax returns, etc., checking the information obtained with the estate duty account.

(*iii*) Dealings in estate property should be verified by auditing in normal manner, including the disposal of property in form of investments or otherwise.

(*iv*) All interest, rents, or other regular payments should be checked to ensure their due receipt. Apportionments should be checked in accordance with the Apportionments Act 1870.

(*v*) Receipts for payment of estate duty and legacies should be vouched.

(*vi*) Where the estate is not fully distributed, the auditor should verify the actual holding of the assets.

(*b*) *Trustees' accounts.* This type of audit is similar to that in respect of executors' accounts. The trust deed should be examined, notes being taken of the instructions contained in it. The payments made should be checked to see that they are in accordance with the deed, and where the trust is in respect of an infant, the auditor should ensure that payments are properly authorised and appear reasonable in the light of the provisions contained in the deed.

8. Hotels.

(*a*) It is essential in this type of business that a sound system of internal check be operated. This should be examined in particular with regard to:

(*i*) receipt of cash and accounting for it by waiters;

(*ii*) the requisitioning for wines and spirits and the maintenance of adequate stock records, and the checking of stocks on hand with balances shown.

(*b*) The visitors' ledger should be examined, care being taken to ensure that all charges against visitors are duly entered against them. The daily totals should be checked to the summary, and from thence to the ledger account.

(c) The depreciation rates applied to fixtures, furniture and fittings should be checked.

(d) The internal check system with regard to restaurant services should be checked, especially with regard to the full accountability in respect of bills issued to residents and outside customers for meals. All bills should be serially numbered and accounted for.

(e) The method of valuation applied to expendable assets, such as crockery, should be examined.

(f) The payment of wages to outside staff and casual workers should be carefully checked.

9. Insurance Companies.

(a) Insurance companies are governed by the Companies Acts, the Insurance Companies Act 1974 and the Insurance Companies (Accounts and Forms) Acts 1964, 1978. Such companies (which include life assurance companies) must prepare a revenue account and a balance sheet and, save where only one type of business is carried on, a profit and loss account, annually. The form of such accounts is prescribed by the Insurance Companies (Forms) Regulations 1958.

(b) The internal control and check systems should be examined in depth, as this type of business is highly specialised. The systems prevailing regarding post opening and the recording of cash and maintenance of ledger accounts should be thoroughly checked.

(c) Premium income should be vouched with new policy books, renewals register and lapsed policies.

(d) Commission paid and due to agents should be compared with agents' receipts and with their returns and accounts.

(e) Where policies are surrendered those should be checked with receipts and the endorsed policies.

(f) Claims paid should be tested with documents and correspondence arising. Claims made but not settled should be examined to ascertain that adequate provision is made against these.

(g) Re-insurance and recoveries on re-insurance and provision for all amounts outstanding should be checked.

(h) The premium reserve carried forward should be checked to ensure its adequacy.

(i) It should be ascertained that, where separate funds are kept, no part of any such fund has been applied directly or indirectly for any purpose other than the class of business to which it is applicable. The auditor is required to certify this fact.

10. Publishers.

(a) *Book publishers*. The following points must be noted:

(*i*) Ascertain system of accounting regarding publications. This would normally involve debiting to a separate account the expenses involved for each book published.

(*ii*) Check values of stocks of publications on hand which should be at cost of publishing divided by the number produced.

(*iii*) Note whether stocks have been held over a protracted period with little or no movement, for writing-down of value or otherwise.

(*iv*) Ensure that books sent on "sale or return" are properly shown as stock at a figure not in excess of cost.

(*v*) Check system maintained whereby the volume of sales is recorded in order to credit authors with royalties due. Ascertain that all those due have been properly credited within the period. Vouch a number of authors' contracts noting rates payable.

(*vi*) If it is desired to carry forward certain costs of publication on books of a popular nature, ascertain that such costs are those which would be saved on subsequent editions.

(b) *Journal publishers*. Where weekly or monthly journals are published, the outstanding matters to be dealt with are as follows:

(*i*) Ascertain that an advertising journal is properly maintained, showing advertising bookings over each edition.

(*ii*) Ascertain that where advertisements are to appear over a number of editions, that the advertising revenue in advance is properly carried forward to the next period.

(*iii*) Vouch a number of the advertisements with the journals published.

(*iv*) Check the advertising journal with the advertisers' accounts.

(*v*) Ensure that all outstanding amounts due to contributors are brought into account.

(*vi*) Vouch a number of contributions in the publication with the contributors' journal.

11. Share transfer audit. As the accounts of the company are not affected by share transfers it is not part of normal audit procedure and, if to safeguard itself against losses arising through fraudulent transfers or otherwise, the company requests that such an audit be carried out, the auditor may charge an additional fee for such work.

The programme should be on the following lines:

(a) Examine the Articles for relevant clauses.

(b) Each transferor should have been notified of the lodgment, and it should be seen that no objections have been received. Where any calls due have not been paid, the transfer should have been refused if the Articles so require.

(c) Check that the transfer is properly stamped, that the distinctive numbers (if any) of the shares are shown and that the consideration is stated.

(d) Note whether the consideration appears adequate. If not, enquiry should be made unless the document has already been stamped by the Revenue Stamp Office.

(e) Check the particulars on the old certificates to the transfer deeds and see that the old certificates are cancelled.

(f) Vouch the transfer deeds with particulars in the transfer register.

(g) Check the transfer ledger postings to the share ledger.

(h) See that work done by registration clerks is duly initialled.

(i) Vouch receipt of transfer fees.

(j) See that the directors' minute is passed in respect of the transfers.

12. Solicitors. Whilst a normal audit may be carried out, special rules have to be observed by solicitors as required under the Solicitors' Accounts Rules, the Solicitors' Trust Accounts Rules, the Accountant's Report Rules and the Solicitors' Accounts (Deposit Interest) Rules, all of which were issued in 1975. The object is to ensure adequate book-keeping and recording systems, a particular concern being to avoid any confusion of clients' monies with those of the solicitor.

With so many relevant Acts and Rules, the position might appear complex, but the Law Society publish a handbook outlining clearly the necessary requirements (*see also* Recommendation V.15).

The general effect of the legislation concerned is to:

(a) require the keeping of books of accounts and separate bank accounts for solicitors' and clients' monies respectively;

(b) require the solicitor to state annually when applying for his practising certificate whether or not the Solicitors' Account Rules apply to him; and

(c) provide for the compulsory examination each year of the solicitor's accounts by a duly qualified accountant for the delivery to the Law Society of an Accountant's Report as to his compliance with the Solicitors' Account Rules.

With regard to actual examination and report by the accountant, the following are points of outstanding interest:

(a) The Accountant's Report refers to an individual solicitor whether he is a member of a firm of solicitors or not. So if there are a number of partners in a firm of solicitors a Report is necessary for each.

(b) Save in exceptional circumstances, the place of examination should be at the office of the solicitor and not of the accountant.

(c) Any partner of a firm of accountants may sign the Report, but whoever signs is deemed by the Council of the Law Society to accept responsibility for the accuracy of the Report.

The rules are quite specific as to the work that shall be carried out by the accountant in order to enable him to give the Report:

(a) Examination of the book-keeping systems in each office of the solicitor's office to ensure that separate ledger accounts are maintained for each client with distinction being kept between clients' or other monies.

(b) The test-checking of postings and castings of clients' ledger accounts.

(c) Comparison of lodgments and payments from clients' accounts as shown on the bank statements with the solicitors' records.

It is also required that the accountant shall not extend his enquiries beyond the information contained in the relevant documents relating to clients' matters supplemented by the information and explanations given by the solicitor. He need not enquire into securities or documents of clients held by the solicitor.

A discretion is allowed to the accountant, however, that when he has carried out the examination as specified in the rules, he may carry out such further examination as he deems necessary to complete his report with or without qualification.

13. Statutory report.

(a) Examine the Prospectus and Articles as to terms of the issue, etc., and see that these have been complied with.

(b) Vouch the application and allotments sheets with application forms and check cash received *per* the application and allotment sheets with the Bank pass book; usually a special one is maintained.

(c) Check the "numbers of shares allotted" with the directors' minutes of allotment. Ascertain that provisions as to minimum subscription have been complied with, and that the allotments do not exceed the amount of the authorised capital, or the amount offered for subscription.

(d) Check the "amount payable on application and allotment" column and "balance due on allotment" column on the application and allotment sheets, check cash received on allotment with the pass book and vouch any amounts returned as excess applications with receipts, or returned paid cheques, and counterfoils of "letters of regret"; these are sent where applications are refused and application moneys are refunded; check the amounts returned with pass book.

(e) Check particulars of members, the numbers of shares allotted, and balances payable and unpaid on shares, from application and allotment sheets to the register of members and share ledger.

(f) Ascertain that return of allotments has been filed with Registrar of Companies within one month.

(g) Test counterfoils of share certificate books with the share ledger and the application and allotment sheets. See that receipts for certificates have been duly returned to the company.

(h) Check casts of application and allotment sheets, seeing columns agree in total (i.e. shares allotted agree with cash columns). Check postings of totals of cash to main and cash book, vouch journal entries for the issue of capital and agree the balances on share ledgers with the balance on share capital account in nominal ledger. Similar work will be necessary in regard to instalments paid or calls made before the date of the statutory report.

(i) If there are various classes of shares, they should be dealt with separately, i.e. with separate pass sheets, etc.

(j) Check the main cash book with bank pass sheets and reconciliation statement and obtain bank certificate.

(*k*) Vouch any capital expenditure and check to the ledger accounts concerned.

(*l*) Check entries with the statutory report.

PROGRESS TEST 12

1. Under the Building Societies Act 1962, what is the auditor required to report upon? (2)

2. In what form should a building society's accounts be prepared? (2)

3. What important aspect regarding building societies' advances is of concern to the auditor? (2)

4. With what particular aspects of building society activities should the auditor concern himself? (3)

5. What is an essential feature necessary in the audit of a bank? (4)

6. What aspect of a contracting business is particularly liable to manipulation? (6)

7. What is the first matter to which the auditor should pay attention when acting as auditor in respect of executors' or trustees' accounts? (7)

8. To what should the auditor pay particular attention in hotel audits? (8)

9. Why is the system of internal control of vital importance in the audit of insurance companies? (9)

10. Is it essential that the auditor should carry out a share transfer audit on the occasion of each annual audit? (11)

11. Mention the particular statutory requirements affecting the audit of solicitors' accounts. (12)

12. What aspect of the audit of solicitors' accounts requires special attention? (12)

13. Enumerate the procedures necessary for the conduct of the audit of a statutory report. (13)

SPECIMEN QUESTIONS

1. Indicate the special points to which your attention would be directed in verifying the income of a sports and social club.

I.C.A. (*E.W.*)

2. As auditor of a licensed non-residential Country Club, owning its own Golf Course and Squash and Tennis Courts, outline the steps which you would take to verify its income. *I.C.A.*

3. In auditing the accounts of a large company of Public Works Contractors state the uses which you would make of the costing records and the extent to which you would consider yourself entitled to rely upon the figures appearing therein. *I.C.A.*

4. Outline a programme for the audit of estate accounts for the first two years from the date of death when there is a life interest. The assets include leasehold properties and shareholdings in private companies and quoted public companies. *I.C.A.* (*E.W.*)

5. Outline the audit procedure you would adopt to verify the amounts included in the balance sheet of a builder and contractor for work-in-progress and materials on sites. *I.C.A.* (*E.W.*)

6. Draft your programme for a Share Transfer Audit. State the objects of such an audit. *I.C.A.*

7. What are the principal matters to which the auditor of a building society should have regard when examining the deeds of properties in mortgage to the society? *I.C.A.* (*E.W.*)

8. The directors of a building society are required by law to maintain a system to ensure the safe custody of all documents of title belonging to it, and of the deeds relating to property mortgaged to it.

What is the statutory duty of a society's auditor with regard to the above requirement, and what in your opinion are the principal matters on which he should satisfy himself when reviewing such a system and when examining the deeds?

I.C.A. (*E.W.*)

9. (*a*) State the underlying objects of the *Solicitors' Accounts Rules* and describe in outline the requirements.

(*b*) What work is the accountant required by the *Accountants' Certificate Rules* to do with a view to signing the certificate?

I.C.A. (*E.W.*)

CHAPTER XIII

Investigations

INVESTIGATIONS AND REPORTS

1. Definition of an investigation. An investigation may be defined as an examination of the accounts and balance sheet of an organisation and the supporting documents for the specific purpose of obtaining information to be submitted to an interested party. An audit is a form of investigation, but the term is more usually applied to all work of an interrogatory nature other than that of an audit.

2. Events necessitating an investigation. Such work may be undertaken on request of interested parties for such matters as:

(a) the purchase of a business;

(b) admission of a partner into a business;

(c) investing money in a concern by way of loan or otherwise;

(d) ascertaining the extent of a known fraud or negligence, or investigating whether one has taken place;

(e) reporting on profit forecasts for take-over or merger purposes.

3. Statutory investigations. Investigations may be necessary to satisfy some legal requirement under statutory authority:

(a) The report required by a company's promoters for prospectus purposes.

(b) An investigation by inspectors appointed by the Department of Trade in accordance with the provisions of ss. 164 and 165 of the Companies Acts 1948 and s. 38 of the Companies Act 1967 (*see* p. 240).

(c) An investigation under the Public Trustee Act 1906 on application of a trustee or beneficiary.

(d) An investigation by the liquidator of a company where directors are suspected of fraud or misfeasance regarding the affairs of the company.

(e) An investigation by a trustee in bankruptcy where the bankrupt is suspected of having acted fraudulently in the past.

4. Liability of investigating accountant. In conducting an investigation and submitting his report on it, the accountant is exercising a professional skill and expressing his opinion as an expert. It is necessary, therefore, to exercise particular care in the conduct of such work and to be guarded in the expression of any opinions in his report. He may be generally liable to anyone who, having employed him to do such work, puts money into a business and subsequently suffers loss due to the negligence of the accountant in not discovering the true state of affairs.

In *Short and Compton* v. *Brackett* (1904), it was held that the investigating accountants were entitled to assume that the figures appearing in the defendants' books were correct, when in fact an employee had defrauded the company by defalcation of the wages sheets, so there was no negligence on this part.

On the other hand, where a loss was suffered due to the negligence of the investigating accountants, despite extenuating circumstances, which were taken into consideration in the damages awarded, the accountants were held liable (*Colmer* v. *Merrett, Son and Street* (1914)).

In a later case, *R.* v. *Wake and Stone* (1954), where it was admitted that stock and work-in-progress had been valued at a figure considered to be false, deceptive and misleading, having accepted an explanation by the managing director of various alterations in stock sheets without making any independent investigations, the auditor was convicted in respect of his having signed the report recklessly and was fined £200 (with the alternative of six months' imprisonment).

It behoves the accountant, therefore, in undertaking any investigation work to obtain explicit instructions, and to exercise great care both in his method of working and in his report.

5. The purchase of a business.

(*a*) *Accounting aspects.*

(*i*) Obtain details of nature of business and of current trend of trade generally.

(*ii*) Ascertain whether book-keeping is satisfactory and properly audited and examine auditors' reports for any reservations.

(*iii*) Ascertain whether adequate stock records are maintained.

(*iv*) Set out accounts in columnar form for comparative

purposes, showing percentages to turnover, as relevant. Investigate material differences.

(v) Pay particular attention to gross profit ratio. This may tend to rise in latest years as stocks may be inflated to increase profits.

(vi) Examine sales figures, note that no goods on sale or return are included and that sales cover only periods referred to. In particular, check last period to note whether sudden fall in sales occurs after last balance sheet date.

(vii) Obtain analysis of customers, if possible, noting any proportionately large buyers and ascertaining whether any fall in sales recently occurred.

(viii) Examine purchases records. Check with stock records. Note whether any very slow-moving stocks are still maintained at cost.

(ix) Examine the columnar analysis of profit and loss accounts. Note any material changes. Adjust profit figures for exceptional items either of income or expenditure. If income shown on assets is not to be taken over, e.g. investments, this should be eliminated.

(x) Examine variations in assets held and note adequacy or otherwise of depreciation. Note any exceptional profits or losses arising on disposal of assets. Losses may signify inefficient management.

(xi) Prepare percentage balance sheets and note any material changes. Accounting ratios, in particular, with regard to liquid position, should be noted.

(xii) Make enquiries as to any outstanding contracts likely to affect the business.

(b) *Profits available.*

(i) Using the adjusted profits as mentioned in (a) (ix) above, note the percentage return on capital employed.

(ii) Calculate any super-profits arising as compared with similar business. From this figure capitalised at the percentage rate of return on similar businesses, a figure for goodwill may be obtained to be added to a net tangible assets figure. This may then be compared with the price demanded.

(iii) Consider the effect of retirement of any partner or of the sole proprietor. Ascertain whether any agreement to be given as to non-competition within a stated area.

(iv) Ascertain whether any important professional or

technical staff are likely to be leaving in the near future. Examine service agreements, if any.

6. Admission of a partner into a business. An investigation may arise, either on behalf of a person intending to bring in capital and to become a partner, or for the existing proprietors who intend to take in a partner.

These investigations would be somewhat similar as in the case of the purchase of a business, but with the additional requirements to ascertain the rights and responsibilities which will arise under the agreement. Here the investigating accountant would have to examine the proposed agreement to ensure that nothing detrimental would arise in respect of his client.

7. Investigation in the event of fraud or negligence. The nature of the work to be carried out in the event of either fraud or negligence, or in order to ascertain whether these have taken place, will depend on the type of fraud or negligence, and on the instructions received by the accountant.

If the fraud should concern only a section of the work, such as the entry of dummy workmen on a wages sheet by one clerk, then the extent of the investigation would be restricted. On the other hand, a fraud of the nature mentioned in X, 1, involving collusion between responsible officials, would necessitate work of an extensive nature.

Whilst the normal audit procedure would still apply, the following matters should receive particular attention:

(*a*) *Misappropriation of cash.* All cash received would have to be checked in detail, and this would involve the following steps:

(*i*) The rough cash book should be checked with the cash book and bank paying-in slips obtained from the bank.

(*ii*) Where receipts are issued, the copies of these should be checked with the cash book.

(*iii*) Statements should be sent to debtors who have paid amounts asking for notification if they do not agree with any details shown on them.

(*iv*) Payments should be vouched with returned cheques and original documents, checking authorisation for payment signatures on the documents concerned. If vouchers are missing, copies should be requested.

(*v*) Payments to directors or partners should be confirmed.

(*vi*) Petty cash should be vouched and any IOUs outstanding checked with those who have received them.

(*vii*) All balances should be counted—production of them being at one and the same time—and all other balances confirmed direct with banks and duly reconciled after checking the pass sheet entries.

(*b*) *Wages defalcations.*

(*i*) The internal check system should be investigated and any loopholes noted.

(*ii*) The original documents from which the wages sheets are compiled should be checked. This would include such matters as changes in wage rates, as well as original notifications of staff taken on.

(*iii*) Every care should be taken to ensure that all those shown as employees are actually in the employ of the business, or have been so (dates of cessation of employment are very important in the latter case).

(*iv*) Payments out in respect of deductions should be checked, such as those in respect of National Insurance stamps.

(*v*) Casts and cross-casts should be checked and wages control accounts compiled where these have not been kept.

(*vi*) The system operated with regard to unclaimed wages should be checked.

(*c*) *Manipulation of stock figures.* Matter affecting stocks and work-in-progress have been dealt with in detail (*see* X). It is emphasised that the original stock sheets should be obtained and checked, and items shown in the sales and purchases day books at the end of financial periods should be checked with the goods outwards and inwards books respectively.

Again, fraud (*see* p. 176) reveals the need to investigate stocks held at outlying branches, and personal inspection may be necessary.

Quite recently the over-valuation of stocks has been discovered despite the checking of stock records by the company's auditors. This involved the pricing of various lots of steel by a director. The difficulty in checking such stocks of a specialised nature is emphasised, and the investigating accountant should do all within his power to obtain confirmation of prices from outside sources, such as market reports or trade associations.

(*d*) *Defalcation of sales and purchases.* The defalcation of sales is not so likely to be met as this requires the creation of fictitious debtors. If this arose, the details regarding the debtors on checking by direct statements would reveal these, or by noting long-standing debts. The more likely fraud to increase profit figures would be to increase stock figures.

Although concerned with misappropriation of cash, the entering of credit notes in accounts where such misappropriations have taken place may be mentioned. Credit notes, therefore, should be carefully checked, ascertaining that they are properly authorised and initialled.

Fictitious purchases, on the other hand, are more likely than fictitious sales; this might facilitate paying out sums of money and also reducing profits for taxation purposes.

Invoices have been printed (*see* p. 176), and employees have sometimes also submitted invoices received in respect of purchases made in their own private businesses, for payment by their employing organisations.

Such manipulations as these should be revealed by careful vouching in full of documents and also by comparison with the goods inwards book and stock records.

8. Investigations for accountants' reports for prospectuses and similar documents. In accordance with the requirements of the Companies Act 1948, any prospectus issued by a company, or in respect of one to be formed, must contain the reports specified in Part Two of the Fourth Schedule.

Such reports involve heavy responsibilities for the reporting accountant (*see* p. 232), *R.* v. *Wake and Stone* (1954). The Institute of Chartered Accountants has issued its Recommendations N.13 and N.16 regarding such reports, from which the following quotations are taken:

*Accountants' Reports for Prospectuses:
Adjustments and Other Matters*

1. ADJUSTMENTS GENERALLY.

   In the preparation of accountants' reports for the purpose of inclusion in prospectuses (which, where appropriate, should be read as including offers for sale and similar documents) it may be necessary to make various adjustments, in addition to giving consideration to the special matters dealt with in Recommendations s. 13 and s. 18 on *Accountants' Reports for Prospectuses and Similar Documents: Fixed Assets and Depreciation and Absence of Detailed Stock Records.*

The reports required under the Third, Fourth and Fifth Schedules to the Companies Act 1948 must either indicate by way of note any adjustment as respects the figures of profits or losses or assets and liabilities dealt with by the report which appear necessary to the persons making the report, or must make those adjustments and indicate that adjustments have been made. There is no statutory guidance as to the nature of the adjustments to be made; the accountants making the report must form their own judgment. Where required by s. 41(1) of the Act, a signed statement, setting out the adjustments and giving the reasons therefor, must be attached to or endorsed on the copy of the prospectus delivered to the Registrar of Companies.

The accountant's report is necessarily confined to past results and does not purport to deal with future prospects. The intending investor is concerned with the future and he will regard the accountants' report, showing the trend of past results, as being submitted to assist him in forming his own assessment of the prospects. It may therefore be necessary, in order that the trend of past profits may be fairly presented having regard to the purposes of the prospectus, either to make appropriate comments thereon or to adjust the figures.

The circumstances in which adjustments to the figures of profits or losses are usually required fall generally under the following headings:

(a) where there are material facts which should have been taken into account in preparing the profits and loss accounts for the various years covered by the report if those facts had been known at the time when the accounts were prepared;

(b) where there have been material sources of revenue or categories of expenditure which are expected not to recur;

(c) where during the period covered by the report there has been a material change in the accounting principles applied or where accepted accounting principles have not been applied.

In considering whether an adjustment is required it is essential to bear in mind that the accountants' duty is to report on past profits or losses and not to attempt to forecast results in future conditions.

Adjustments or comments may also be necessary in relation to the statement of assets and liabilities shown in the accountants' report. In particular it will be necessary to consider to what extent it is relevant to include notes which appeared on the last balance sheet and to consider the appropriate treatment of matters such as the market value of investments, the accumulated amount of profits tax non-distribution relief, and reserves for future income tax. The accountants' report deals with the assets and liabilities as on the last balance sheet date, but the reporting accountants may have knowledge of events subsequent to that date which may have a material bearing on the conclusions which the intending investor may draw from the prospectus, and in such cases the accountants will need to consider their report in the light of that knowledge.

2. PERIOD COVERED BY THE REPORT.

Apart from the question of adjustments, the period to be covered by the report requires consideration, having regard to the importance of presenting a fair view of the trend of results. At present the Stock Exchange requires the report on profits or losses to cover a period of at least ten years, instead of the statutory minimum of five years specified in the Companies Act 1948. A period of ten years ending in 1954 or earlier will include part of the 1939–45 war period, when conditions were exceptional.

Not only has the reporting accountant to consider the statutory requirements of the Companies Act 1948, but also the regulations of the Stock Exchange, regarding which the Recommendations (s. 17, Para. 18, *et seq.*) are relevant, and to which reference should be made.

It is with respect to the "adjustments" to the profit figures that the accountant must exercise care, as stated in Recommendation No.16: *Profits or losses.*

Presentation. The figures relating to profits or losses should be set out in the report in columnar form, accompanied by appropriate definition of the bases on which the figures have been computed. A figure of "average profits" should not be stated.

Adjustments generally. The reporting accountants should make such adjustments to the profits or losses as shown by the accounts as they consider appropriate and the report should state that this has been done. If the amount involved in any adjustment is of special importance in relation to the results disclosed, the nature of the adjustment should be stated. The accountants should consider whether the amount involved in any such adjustment should also be stated.

Adjustments regarding capital expenditure may be properly written back where it has been charged against profits, and as promoters will have every incentive to show profits to be as large as possible, the auditor should be careful in the making of such adjustments as stated in N.16.

Capital expenditure. Where an item which has been charged in the accounts has been disallowed for taxation purposes as being capital expenditure, it should not necessarily be adjusted. Moreover no adjustment should be made to write back, as being capital, expenditure which has been charged in the accounts and allowed for taxation purposes, even though some items may be of a kind which might have been regarded as of a capital nature if a different accounting practice had been followed. Where an adjustment is made, it is necessary to consider whether it has a significant effect on the provisions for depreciation.

Where a business is to be acquired, it may be necessary to obtain two certificates, for if the proceeds of the issue, or any part thereof, are or is to be applied in the purchase of any business, a report must be included, made by named accountants, in respect of (a) the profits of the business for each of the five financial years immediately preceding the issue of the Prospectus, (b) the assets and liabilities of the business at the last date to which the accounts of the business were made up. (Companies Act 1948, Sch. 4.)

The two certificates supplied are, one by the accountants of the vendor company, and the other by the accounts of the purchasing company as required.

3. ABSENCE OF DETAILED STOCK RECORDS (s.18). Whether for prospectuses or similar documents, it will be necessary for accountants to satisfy themselves as to whether the stock and work-in-progress have been properly and consistently ascertained and valued during the period, while Stock Exchange requirements must also be complied with.

Where such a report covers ten years, records may not be available. Despite this, it is still possible for the reporting accountants to satisfy themselves without repeating all the detailed audit procedures; but the procedures which they should apply will include:

  reviewing the system of controls and stock-taking procedures applying during the period;

  examining stock summaries and such other supporting records as are available;

  reviewing the auditors' working papers and discussing with them the work carried out year by year;

  comparing the detailed profit and loss accounts and obtaining satisfactory explanations for unusual variations;

  considering various key ratios such as gross profit/sales and stock/cost of sales;

  ensuring that any apparent discrepancies arising during the period have been properly investigated and explained.

If, as a result of the above procedures and any others appropriate, reporting accountants are satisfied that the adjusted profits to be set out in the report are fairly stated, no reservation should be expressed concerning the lack of certain stock records, but if they cannot satisfy themselves and consider that the amounts involved are material, the reservations should appear in the paragraph which introduces the table of profits and not among the notes which usually follow that table. Wherever possible, the extent and materiality of such a reservation should be indicated.

It may be felt that the deficiencies are sufficiently serious as to preclude the issue of a report. In reaching such a decision, weight should be given to the number and incidence of the years. The more recent the years the more acute the problem becomes. While specific guidance cannot be given, the Recommendations do give an example requiring requisite action on a serious deficiency of information in the last three years to be covered where the trend of the profit might be materially distorted.

Where auditors have been appointed during the period covered, they cannot decline to report, as the Companies Act 1948 requires them to do so. In such a case, their qualification should give appropriate emphasis to the reasons for it and may even include a disclaimer of opinion.

9. Investigations by inspectors appointed by the Department of Trade. The Companies Act 1948, as amended by the Companies Act 1967, specifies as follows:

The Department of Trade (DT) (before October 1971, the Board of Trade) may appoint one or more competent inspectors to investigate the affairs of a company and to report thereon in such manner as the Department directs:

(*a*) in the case of a company having a share capital, on the application either of not less than 200 members or of members holding not less than one-tenth of the shares issue;

(*b*) in the case of a company not having a share capital, on the application of not less than one-fifth of the persons on the company's register of members.

The application shall be supported by such evidence as the DT may require for the purpose of showing that the applicants have good reason for requiring the investigation, and the Department may, before appointing an inspector, require the applicants to give security, to an amount not exceeding one hundred pounds, for payment of the costs of the investigation (s. 164).

Without prejudice to their powers under the last foregoing section, the Department:

(a) Shall appoint one or more competent inspectors to investigate the affairs of a company and to report thereon in such manner as the Department directs, if:

(i) the company by special resolution; or

(ii) the court by order:

declares that its affairs ought to be investigated by an inspector appointed by the Board; and

(b) May do so if it appears to the Board that there are circumstances suggesting:

(i) That its business is being conducted with intent to defraud its creditors or the creditors of any other person or otherwise for a fraudulent or unlawful purpose or in a manner oppressive of any part of its members or that it was formed for any fraudulent or unlawful purpose; or

(ii) that persons concerned with its formation or the management of its affairs have in connection therewith been guilty of fraud, misfeasance or other misconduct towards it or towards its members; or

(iii) that its members have not been given all the information with respect to its affairs which they might reasonably expect.

Section 38, Companies Act 1967, amends this in stating after the words "is being" in (b) (i) above shall read as if the words "or has been" were inserted and the Board's powers shall be exercised in the case of a body corporate notwithstanding that it is in the course of being wound-up.

Section 166 empowers such inspectors to investigate the affairs of any other body corporate which has been or is its holding company or subsidiary. The following sections give the inspectors wide powers to examine on oath officers and agents of the company, and where he has no such power, he may apply to the court.

Section 167 of the original Act is also amended by s. 39 of the 1967 Act to give even wider powers to inspectors whereby attendance before the inspectors may be required as well as production of books and documents.

Such investigations would leave the method of working to the discretion of the inspector and would, no doubt, include work such as is included in a detailed audit, as well as the exercise of powers exceeding those of a statutory auditor.

10. Reports on investigations. The report submitted in respect of *any* investigation should cover the following points:

(a) Reference to instructions given and summary thereof.

(b) Reference to basic documents covering information obtained. Copies attached if necessary.

(c) General outline of work done.

(d) Summary of information obtained.

(e) Recommendations in accordance with information obtained. In dealing with matters affecting investigations, the reporting accountant should be most careful to avoid making unwarranted assumptions or giving forecasts, e.g. of prospective profits.

ACCOUNTANTS' REPORTS
ON PROFIT FORECASTS

11. I.C.A. Recommendations. The Council of the Institute of Chartered Accountants has proffered its guidance for auditors and consultant accountants with reference to any independent accountants' review of profit forecasts, having particular regard to the City Code on take-overs and mergers (s. 15).

The Council has pointed out that, although normally for internal use, such forecasts may be disclosed to outsiders. Owing to inherent uncertainties both numerous and substantial, profit forecasts are not capable of verification by reporting accountants and cannot be audited in any sense, even though the reporting accountants may also be the company's auditors. It is important, therefore, that reporting accountants should make this clear when they accept instructions to review profit forecasts, and in the wording of their report they should take care to avoid giving any impression that they are in any way confirming, underwriting, guaranteeing or otherwise accepting responsibility for the ultimate accuracy and realisation of forecasts. They can, however, within limits (*see* below), properly undertake a critical and objective review of the assumptions on which profit forecasts are based, and can verify that the forecasts have been properly computed, on a basis consistent with the company's previous accounting principles, from the underlying assumptions and data.

In guidance as to preliminary consideration, the Council point out the following:

(a) The time allowed for the compilation of the report should not be such as to make it impossible for the accountants properly to exercise their professional judgment.

(b) That the accountants' instructions and responsibility under the Code should be concerned with accounting bases as opposed to commercial matters.

(*c*) The forecast should cover normally only the current accounting period or the next following year.

(*d*) Although the accountants may give some reassurance by the nature of their review, they cannot relieve the directors of their responsibilities.

The main points to be considered, briefly stated, are as follows:

(*a*) The nature and background of the company's business.

(*b*) The accounting practices normally followed by the company, i.e. such matters as the methods of dealing with overheads in stock valuation, profit on long-term contracts, depreciation, etc.

(*c*) The assumptions on which the forecasts are based. If a circular includes profit forecasts, Rule 15 of the Code requires the assumptions, including the commercial assumptions, upon which the directors have based their profit forecasts, to be stated. It is fundamental that the reporting accountants should report whether or not the forecasts are consistent with the given assumptions, economic, commercial, marketing and financial, which underlie them.

(*d*) In carrying out their review of the accounting bases and calculations for forecasts, and the procedures followed by the company for preparing them, the main points which the reporting accountants will wish to consider include the following:

(*i*) Whether the profit forecasts under review are based on forecasts regularly prepared for the purpose of management, or whether they have been separately and specially prepared for the immediate purpose.

(*ii*) Where profit forecasts are regularly prepared for management purposes, the degree of accuracy and reliability previously achieved, and the frequency and thoroughness with which estimates are revised.

(*iii*) Whether the forecasts under review represent the management's best estimate of results which they reasonably believe can and will be achieved, as distinct from targets which the management has set as desirable.

(*iv*) The extent to which forecast results for expired periods are supported by reliable interim accounts.

(*v*) The extent to which the forecasts are built up from

detailed forecasts in respect of the main divisions or lines of activity of the business, distinguishing where possible between those which may be regarded as showing a proved and consistent trend and those of a more irregular, volatile or unproved nature.

(*vi*) How the forecasts take account of any material exceptional items, their nature, and how they are presented.

(*vii*) Whether adequate provision is made for foreseeable losses and contingencies.

(*viii*) Whether working capital appears adequate for requirements as shown by properly prepared cash flow forecasts; and, where short-term finance is to be relied on, whether the necessary arrangements have been made and confirmed.

(*ix*) Whether the forecasts have been prepared and presented on acceptable bases consistent with the accounting principles and practices adopted by the company in previous years, and, if not, whether the fact and effects of any material change of basis are made clear.

Under the heading *The main matters to be stated in the accountants' report* (Para. 14), it is stated:

The accountants' report under the Code will be addressed to the directors and will normally include statements dealing with the following matters, so far as appropriate:

(*a*) The fact that the reporting accountants have carried out a review of the accounting bases and calculations on which the profit forecasts have been based.

(*b*) Specific identification of the forecasts and documents to which the report refers.

(*c*) If, as will usually be the case, the reporting accountants have not carried out an audit of estimated results for expired periods, a statement to that effect.

(*d*) Whether in the opinion of the reporting accountants the forecasts have been properly compiled on the basis of the assumptions made by the board of directors, as set out in the circular, and are presented on a basis consistent with the accounting practices normally adopted by the company.

Again, it is emphasised that if the reporting accountants have not been able properly to exercise their professional judgment they should qualify their report.

12. City Code on Take-overs and Mergers. The following extracts are from the Rules as contained in *The City Code on Take-overs and Mergers* (1969) issued by the City Working Party. Paragraphs

14 and 15 are quoted in full as they are of particular interest to reporting accountants.

13. Any document or advertisement addressed to shareholders under these headings must be treated with the same standards of care with regard to the statements made therein as if it were a prospectus within the meaning of the Companies Act 1948. This applies whether the document or advertisement is issued by the company direct or by an adviser on its behalf. . . .

14. Shareholders must be put into possession of all the facts necessary for the formation of an informed judgment as to the merits or demerits of an offer. Such facts must be accurately and fairly presented and be available to the shareholder early enough to enable him to make a decision in good time. The obligation of the offeror company in these respects towards the shareholders of the offeree company is no less than its obligation towards its own shareholders.

15. Without in any way detracting from the imperative necessity of maintaining the highest standards of accuracy and fair presentation in all communications to shareholders in a take-over or merger transaction, attention is particularly drawn in this connection to profit forecasts and asset valuations.

Notwithstanding the obvious hazard attached to the forecasting of profits, profit forecasts must be compiled with the greatest possible care by the Directors, whose sole responsibility they are.

When profit forecasts appear in any document addressed to shareholders in connection with an offer, the assumptions, including the commercial assumptions, upon which the Directors have based their profit forecasts, must be stated in the document.

The accounting bases and calculations for the forecasts must be examined and reported on by the auditors or consultant accountants.

Any Merchant Bank or other adviser mentioned in the document must also report on the forecasts. The accountants' report and, if there is an adviser, his report, must be contained in such document and be accompanied by a statement that the accountants and, where relevant, the adviser, have given and not withdrawn their consent to publication.

Wherever profit forecasts appear in relation to a period in which trading has already commenced, the latest unaudited profit figures which are available in respect of the expired portion of that trading period together with comparable figures for the preceding year must be stated. Alternatively, if no figures are available, that fact must be stated.

When revaluations of assets are given in connection with an offer the Board should be supported by the opinion of independent professional experts and the basis of valuation clearly stated.

PROGRESS TEST 13

1. For what reasons are investigations conducted? **(1, 2)**

2. How do investigations differ from normal audits? **(1)**

3. Under what statutory provisions may investigations take place? **(3)**

4. Why should the investigating accountant take every care when conducting an investigation? **(4)**

5. Enumerate the matters to receive attention when conducting an investigation regarding the purchase of a business. **(5)**

6. Enumerate the procedures to be adopted when investigating the affairs of a business, when fraud has taken place or is suspected. **(7)**

7. When conducting an investigation (as in 6 above) is it necessary completely to investigate the affairs of the business on all occasions? **(7)**

8. When making an investigation for the accountant's report to be included in a prospectus, what matters should be attended to and what should be avoided? **(8)**

9. Under what conditions will the DT appoint inspectors to investigate the affairs of a company? **(9)**

10. Specify the general matters to be included in an investigating accountant's report. **(10)**

SPECIMEN QUESTIONS

1. A client of yours is contemplating the purchase of an interest in a partnership and requests you to make an investigation of the firm's accounts. There are three partners in the firm, one is full-time and has intimated that he intends retiring in two years, the other two are part-time. Outline the procedure you would follow, illustrating your answer with assumed figures where desired. *A.C.A.*

2. Outline the points to which you would give attention when carrying out an investigation on behalf of a client who is considering the purchase of a retail business. You may assume that the books have been properly kept and that the accounts have been audited. *I.C.A. (E.W.)*

3. You are asked by the secretary of an incorporated trade association to investigate an apparent cash deficiency. The cashier's duties included the payment of wages to the weekly-paid employees.

List, in tabular form, the steps which you would take to determine the extent of the deficiency. *I.C.A. (E.W.)*

4. A client is considering the purchase of a retail drapery store and has requested you, as his accountant, to carry out an investigation. In particular, he is concerned about the considerable variation in the ratio of gross profit to turnover disclosed by the accounts of the business for the past five years.

Outline the procedure you would follow and suggest possible reasons for the variation in gross profit ratios. *A.C.A.*

5. When conducting the audit of a manufacturing company, you suspect that fraud has been committed in connection with wages.

(*a*) Outline the investigation you would carry out.

(*b*) Indicate three different ways in which fraud might have occurred. *I.C.A. (E.W.)*

6. Mr Rich proposes to invest a substantial sum in a private company by acquiring a holding of ordinary shares which will not give him control. He asks you to carry out an investigation and to advise him whether the price to be paid for the shares is reasonable.

Set out the matters to which you would direct your enquiries.

I.C.A. (E.W.)

7. The *City Code on Take-overs and Mergers* requires, *inter alia*, that the calculations and the bases for any profit forecasts must be examined and reported on by the auditors or consultant accountants. Answer either (*a*) or (*b*).

(*a*) What are the main points to be considered in the reporting accountant's review?

(*b*) What are the main matters to be stated in the Accountant's Report? *A.C.A.*

8. Your client advises you that he has recently dismissed his cashier as a result of discovering that money received by him from debtors has been misappropriated. He feels that other sums may have also been misappropriated.

(*a*) What steps would you take to determine the extent of the defalcations?

(*b*) What changes would you recommend to avoid a repetition of the misappropriations? (You may make any assumptions you consider appropriate.) *A.C.A.*

9. The partners of a trading firm have suffered a heavy loss

due to defalcations carried out by their chief clerk over a long period, and are considering claiming against their auditors for the recovery of the amount involved.

You are asked to state (*a*) the legal grounds on which an action may be brought, and (*b*) the principal factors that are likely to affect the outcome of such an action. *I.C.A. (E.W.)*

10. The Articles of Association of Undertakers Limited, a Private Limited Company, provide that the Shares in the company must be offered to other members, *inter alia*, on the death of a member, at a valuation to be made by the auditor. The recent death of a member has rendered such a valuation necessary. Briefly describe the factors which you would take into account when determining the basis of your valuation. You should restrict your answer to the basic principles which underlie all share valuations and should not attempt to deal with the detailed points which might arise in any particular case. *A.C.A.*

11. A manufacturing company has the opportunity of acquiring the shares of another company in the same industry and has instructed you to carry out an investigation of that company on its behalf. You are required:

(*a*) To draw up a preliminary outline plan for the report to be made to your client, showing the main and subsidiary headings that you are likely to need, and giving a brief indication of the probable scope of the matters to be covered under each head.

(*b*) To state the chief matters on which you would normally expect to concentrate when making your initial visit to the company under investigation. *I.C.A. (E.W.)*

NOTE. Fully to cover the field required by the last two questions, the reader is referred to Chapter XVI, *Principles and Practice of Management Accountancy*, Brown & Howard, third edition, 1975, Macdonald & Evans Ltd.

CHAPTER XIV

The Auditor

TERMS OF OFFICE

1. Audits generally.

(a) *Engagement letters.* Under this title, the I.C.A. has issued its Statement V.16 which, although included here, also affects certain additional accountancy work. It is in the interests of both client and accountant that the scope of work undertaken should be defined in writing.

Certain general points are applicable to all cases and V.16 gives advice to practising accountants as well as supplying specimen letters of engagement for a company client as well as for a sole trader, partnership or incorporated associations.

It points out that two main matters should be set out clearly:

(*i*) that the functions of an auditor are distinct from the provision of accountancy and other services;

(*ii*) that it is not the main purpose of an audit to discover defalcations and irregularities, and that an audit should therefore not be relied on for that purpose.

Further matters to be dealt with in such letters are to point out to the client the occasions when it may be necessary to qualify the report, while care must be taken to ensure that the impression is not given (regarding defalcations and irregularities) that the auditor assumes no responsibility. The directors' responsibilities in respect of the maintenance of adequate accounting records and the portrayal of a true and fair view in annual accounts, with the maintenance of proper systems of internal control—the best method of preventing irregularities—should also be mentioned.

Regarding the scope of engagement, the letter should stress two points in connection with the scope of the work to be done:

(*i*) that an essential feature of an audit is a critical review of the client's system of internal control;

(*ii*) that the audit tests and enquiries made:

(1) will be those that the auditor thinks necessary, which will be influenced by the effectiveness of the system of internal control;

(2) may cover all aspects of the business, not only the financial records.

Mention could also be made of any particular audit procedures such as attendance to observe the client's stock-taking procedures. Auditors should bring to the attention of the directors, preferably in writing, material weaknesses in the system of internal control which come to their notice. In the case of a larger company client, it may be preferable to bring to the attention of that client the fact that it will be practicable for the auditors to review only a proportion of the internal control system each year.

Other services which the accountant is asked to provide should be defined as clearly as possible, and it is appropriate to use such phraseology as "You require us to assist you with certain accounting services, namely:" or "you have authorised us to act on your behalf in the preparation of tax computations". When recording an engagement to assist a client to deal with taxation affairs, the phraseology adopted should be consistent with the fact that in these affairs the accountant is acting as the agent of the client.

The letter should include a note of any limitations as to time or otherwise imposed by the client, and of any assumptions upon which he has required the work to be based. Where such limitations may affect the quality of the work to be done, this should be pointed out in the letter.

Regarding fees, accountants may consider it appropriate in a letter of engagement to mention fees and the general basis on which fees are normally computed. It is also desirable that fees should be charged separately for each main class of work carried out for the client (e.g. auditing, accounting, taxation services and other services), and that the client should be so informed.

(b) *Notification to retiring auditor.* The necessary notification to the retiring auditor, where there is one, has already been mentioned (*see* pp. 15 and 16), and terms affecting notice of termination of agreement by either the client or the auditor should be settled.

2. Statutory audits. Where the auditor is appointed under statute he should ascertain that his client complies with any statutory requirements before he officially takes office. This is most important, and the auditor may have to advise his client of the procedures involved. We should now consider the matters affecting the terms of office of the auditor under the following statutes:

(a) The Companies Acts 1948, 1967 and 1976.

(b) The Building Societies Act 1962.

(c) The Friendly and Industrial and Provident Societies Act 1968, and the Friendly Societies Act 1974.

(d) The Public Trustee Act 1906, and Trustee Act 1925.

3. The Companies Acts 1948, 1967 and 1976. Under the Acts the following matters are relevant. The actual wording of the Acts has been slightly condensed for the sake of brevity.

(a) *Appointment of auditors.* Section 13, 1976 Act: No person shall be qualified for appointment as auditor of a company unless he is a member of a body of accountants recognised by the Secretary of State. These include the three chartered bodies and the Association of Certified Accountants. (This is subject to an exception regarding persons with overseas qualifications.)

Section 14, 1976 Act: Where at any general meeting of a company no auditors are appointed or reappointed, the Secretary of State may appoint a person to fill the vacancy; and the company shall, within one week of the Secretary of State's power under this subsection becoming exercisable, give the Secretary of State notice of that fact.

The first auditors of a company may be appointed by the directors at any time before the first general meeting of the company and auditors so appointed shall hold office until the conclusion of that meeting.

If the directors fail to exercise their powers under the above-mentioned paragraph, those powers may be exercised by the company in general meeting.

The directors, or the company in general meeting, may fill any casual vacancy in the office of auditor, but while any such vacancy continues, the surviving or continuing auditor or auditors, if any, may act.

A company may by ordinary resolution remove an auditor before the expiration of his term of office, notwithstanding anything in any agreement between it and him; and where a resolution removing an auditor is passed at a general meeting of a company, the company shall within fourteen days give notice of that fact in the prescribed form to the Registrar of Companies.

(b) *Remuneration of auditors*. The remuneration of the auditor of a company (which includes expenses):

(i) in the case of an auditor appointed by the directors or by the Secretary of State, may be fixed by the directors or by the Secretary of State, as the case may be;

(ii) subject to paragraph (i) above, shall be fixed by the company in general meeting or in such manner as the company in general meeting may determine.

(c) *Resolutions concerning appointment and removal of auditors*. Section 15, 1976 Act:

(i) Special notice shall be required for a resolution at a general meeting of a company:

(1) appointing as auditor a person other than a retiring auditor; or

(2) filling a casual vacancy in the office of auditor; or

(3) reappointing as auditor a retiring auditor who was appointed by the directors to fill a casual vacancy; or

(4) removing an auditor before the expiration of his term of office.

(ii) On receipt of notice of such an intended resolution as aforesaid the company shall forthwith send a copy thereof:

(1) to the person proposed to be appointed or removed, as the case may be;

(2) in a case within (i)(1) above, to the retiring auditor; and

(3) where, in a case within (i)(2) or (3) above, the casual vacancy was caused by the resignation of an auditor, to the auditor who resigned.

(iii) Where notice is given of such a resolution and the retiring auditor, or as the case may be, the auditor proposed to be removed, makes with respect to the intended resolution representations in writing to the company (not exceeding a reasonable length) and requests their notification to members of the company, the company shall (unless the representations are received by it too late for it to do so):

(1) in any notice of the resolution given to members of the company state the fact of the representations having been made; and

(2) send a copy of the representations to every member of the company to whom notice of the meeting is or has been sent.

(*iv*) If a copy of any such representations is not sent out as required becaused received too late or because of the company's default, the auditor may (without prejudice to his right to be heard orally) require that the representations shall be read out at the meeting.

(*v*) Copies of the representations need not be sent out and the representations need not be read out at the meeting if, on the application either of the company or of any other person who claims to be aggrieved, the court is satisfied that the rights conferred by this section are being abused to secure needless publicity for defamatory matter; and the court may order the company's costs on an application under this subsection to be paid in whole or in part by the auditor, notwithstanding that he is not a party to the application.

(*vi*) An auditor of a company who has been removed shall be entitled to attend:

(1) the general meeting at which his term of office would otherwise have expired;

(2) any general meeting at which it is proposed to fill the vacancy caused by his removal; and

(3) to receive all notices of, and other communications relating to, any such meeting which any member of the company is entitled to receive, and to be heard at any such meeting which he attends on any part of the business of the meeting which concerns him as former auditor of the company.

(*d*) *Disqualifications for appointment as auditor.* Section 161, 1948 Act: None of the following persons shall be qualified for appointment as auditor of a company:

(*i*) An officer or servant of the company.

(*ii*) A person who is a partner of or in the employment of an officer or servant of the company.

(*iii*) A body corporate.

Section 13, 1976 Act: No person shall act as auditor of a company at a time when he knows that he is disqualified for appointment to that office; and if an auditor of a company to his knowledge becomes so disqualified during his term of office he shall thereupon vacate his office and give notice in writing to the company that he has vacated it by reason of such dis-qualification.

(e) *Resignation of Auditors.* The 1976 Act has extended the protection to both the auditor and shareholders on the resignation of the auditor. No reasons should be concealed which may adversely affect the rights of either of the parties.

Section 16 requires that the auditor must deposit a notice of his resignation at the company's registered office. The notice will bring his office to an end on the date on which it is deposited or on such later date as may be specified therein.

The notice must contain either a statement to the effect that there are no circumstances connected with his resignation which he considers should be brought to the notice of the members or creditors or, alternatively, a statement of any such circumstances.

The company is required within fourteen days to send a copy of the auditor's notice to the Registrar of Companies and, if it contains a statement to be brought to the notice of members, etc., or to every person entitled to be sent a copy of the company's accounts, etc., this need not be sent if, on the application of the company or of any other person who claims to be aggrieved, the court is satisfied that the auditor has used the notice to secure needless publicity for defamatory matter.

When, in consequence of such an application, copies of notice of the auditor's resignation are not sent to persons entitled to the company's accounts, the company is required to send them, within fourteen days of the court's decision, a statement of that decision or, if the court does not make an order, a copy of the auditor's representation.

Section 17 lays down the procedures to be followed when an auditor's notice of resignation contains a statement of any circumstances that he considers should be brought to the notice of members of creditors, and are as follows:

(i) The auditor may deposit with the notice a signed requisition calling on the directors to call an extraordinary general meeting for the purpose of receiving and considering such explanation of the circumstances connected with his resignation as he may wish to place before the meeting. He may also request the company to circulate to its members, either before the annual general meeting at which his term of office would otherwise have expired or before any extraordinary general meeting at which it is proposed to fill the vacancy, or convened on his requisition, a statement in writing (not exceeding a reasonable length) or the circumstances connected with his resignation.

(*ii*) The company must (unless the statement is received too late) in any notice of the meeting given to members state the fact of the statement having been made and send a copy to every member to whom notice of the meeting is sent.

(*iii*) If a copy of the auditor's statement is not sent out as required by the section because it has been received too late or because of the company's default, the auditor may (without prejudice to his right to be heard orally) require that the statement be read out at the meeting. Directors are liable to a fine of up to £400 if they do not within twenty-one days of the deposit of an auditor's requisition convene a meeting for a day not more than twenty-eight days after the date of the notice.

Copies of a statement need not be sent out and the statement need not be read out at the meeting if, either on application of the company or of any other person who claims to be aggrieved, the court is satisfied that the rights conferred by the section are being used to secure needless publicity for defamatory matter.

An auditor who has resigned is entitled to attend any meeting at which his statement is presented and to receive all notices of, and other communications relating to, any such meeting, and to be heard at any such meeting on any part of the business which concerns him as former auditor of the company.

4. The Building Societies Act 1962. The terms of office of the auditor are covered by ss. 84, 85 and 86.

The appointment and removal of auditors under ss. 84 and 85 are similar to those under the Companies Act 1967.

Regarding eligibility, however, the provisions covering qualifications and independence are more stringent. Under s. 86 a person is not eligible for appointment as auditor if he is:

(*a*) an officer or servant of the building society;

(*b*) a partner of, or in, the employment of, *or if he employs,* an officer or servant of the building society.

It is the section in italics above which narrows the requirement as compared with the Companies Act 1948 provision.

5. The Friendly and Industrial and Provident Societies Act 1968.

(*a*) *I.C.A. Recommendations U.13 and U.26* deal in detail with this specialised area of the auditor's work, to which reference is advocated. Briefly, it may be stated that any "society" as registered under the former separate Acts is now required to keep proper books of account, to prepare a revenue account and balance sheet and to appoint a qualified auditor or auditors (ss. 1, 3 and 4).

Under s. 4 a qualified auditor is such as is recognised for appointment under the Companies Acts; an "exempt" society need not comply with this provision, but may appoint two or more persons who are not qualified, though the Registrar has power to require the appointment of a qualified auditor. An "exempt" society is a society which is not a collecting society (i.e. a friendly society which carries on industrial assurance business) and in respect of which all three of the following conditions are satisfied:

(*i*) The aggregate of receipts and payments in respect of the preceding year did not exceed £5,000.

(*ii*) The number of members at the end of that year did not exceed 500.

(*iii*) The aggregate value of the assets at the end of that year did not exceed £5,000.

On the same conditions a registered branch can be "exempt". In the case of a registered branch condition (*iii*) above is treated as fulfilled if at the end of the preceding year of account the branch had transferred at least 75 per cent of its assets for investment either to its parent society or to another registered branch of the society which has appointed qualified auditors and the value of the assets not so transferred did not exceed £5,000.

Section 9 requires the auditors to report to the society on the accounts and the revenue account and balance sheet examined by them. The necessity is laid upon the auditor to state that a true and fair view is shown and where the auditor's report is silent it is accounted as a positive report that the auditors are satisfied as to the maintenance of proper books of account by the society, that a satisfactory control has been exercised over its transactions, and that its revenue account(s) and balance sheet are in agreement with the books of account.

(*b*) *Form of report*. The provisions of the 1968 Act and of the other relevant registration Acts relating to accounts, audit and annual returns are to the effect that, while it is open to a society to prepare its annual accounts and balance sheet in any form provided that they give a true and fair view of the matters specified in s. 3, societies remain under an obligation to send to the Chief Registrar annual returns in such form and containing such particulars as he prescribes.

If societies find it convenient to prepare their annual accounts in the form required for the annual return, one form of auditors' report, suitably worded, will cover both the annual accounts required by s. 3 and the annual return.

If, however, a society prepares the accounts and balance sheet required by s. 3 in a form which differs from that required for the annual return, the auditors will have to report on both documents in similar terms, even if they write two separate reports.

6. The Friendly Societies Act 1974. This Act reflects the great progress in more recent years in protecting those who invest in such friendly societies.

The requirements of the Act cover fully those safeguards considered necessary for ensuring the proper recording of transactions, their subsequent presentation in accounts and balance sheet form and their proper and complete audit by those qualified to act as auditors.

Sections 31 to 40 inclusive, which are of particular interest to the auditor, are self explanatory and to which reference should be made directly as to the Act itself when undertaking such work.

The Sections include such headings as: s. 31 "Obligation to appoint auditors"; s. 32 "Audit of exempt societies and branches"; s. 33 "Reappointment and removal of auditors"; s. 34 "Notice of resolutions relating to appointment and removal of auditors"; s. 35 "Proceedings subsequent to receipt of notice under s. 34"; s. 36 "Qualified auditors"; s. 37 "Restrictions on appointment of auditors"; s. 38 "Auditors' report"; s. 39 "Auditors' right of access to books and to attend and be heard at meetings"; s. 40 "Remuneration of qualified auditors".

7. The Public Trustee Act 1906 and Trustee Act 1925. On application in prescribed manner by any trustee or beneficiary, the condition and accounts of any trust shall be investigated and audited by a solicitor or public accountant as agreed between the applicant and trustees or in default of agreement, by the Public Trustee.

The remuneration and expenses are determined by the Public Trustee.

Under the Trustee Act 1925, trustees at their absolute discretion may employ an independent accountant to audit the accounts—but not more than once in three years—unless for special reasons it is desirable more frequently.

RIGHTS AND RESPONSIBILITIES

8. Rights generally. In the case of private audits, the auditor's rights will be accorded him in agreement with the contract drawn up, covering such matters as his method of remuneration, notice to be given on either side, etc. In addition to such contractual rights, one important matter covering all work done in connection with audits, whether private or under statute, is that of the right of lien.

9. Right of lien on client's books and papers.

(a) *Contractual variation.* Whilst the right of lien may be varied contractively or by necessary implication, the accountant may exercise a right of lien over the books and documents of his client for the due payment of his fees.

(b) *Relationship with client.* The Institute of Chartered Accountants has dealt with this matter in Recommendation V.5. Briefly, it may be stated that the accountant may exercise such a lien in respect of audit and accountancy work where the relationship is that of professional man and his client (*re Hill Ex parte Southall* (1848)), but that where he acts in the capacity of an agent, as in the case settling a client's income tax liability with the Inland Revenue, then the documents arising are the property of his principal: *Leicestershire County Council* v. *Michael Faraday and Partners Ltd.* (1941).

(c) *Registered companies.* A doubt arose as to the exercise of such a right in respect of the books of a registered company, but provided the necessary right of access is allowed in accordance with s. 14(5) of the Companies Act 1967, the right still exists.

The I.C.A. has pointed out in Recommendation V.5 that where an accountant acts on behalf of the company's directors while at the same time being the auditor of the company, no right of lien exists over the books or papers of the company in relation to any dispute arising about his having acted for a director in his private capacity. This is a quite obvious recognition of the principle that a company is a separate legal entity.

(d) *Liquidations.* On a summons by the liquidator of a company, the Registrar ordered that the auditor should produce the books and papers of the company in his possession without prejudice to his lien, and that the liquidator should pay fees due to the auditor for all work done before the liquidation, prior to his own remuneration, but after all creditors ranking above the liquidator: *D. M. Carr and Company Ltd.* (1961).

10. Rights under the Companies Acts 1948, 1967 and 1976.

(*a*) *On appointment.* The appointment of the auditor has already been mentioned above (3), and regarding such appointment, important rights exist whcre it is proposed to appoint a person other than the retiring auditor.

(*b*) *Access to all material information.* The auditor is entitled under s. 14, Companies Act 1967, to access at all times to the books, accounts and vouchers of the company. It will be observed that while this gives complete access to the records of the company, not only of double entry accounting records, at the same time it confers an added responsibility in that, if material information is available other than under the normal double entry system, the auditor would be expected to have made proper use of it in the event of any dispute affecting the auditor. This would include such matters as minute books, costing records and internal audit records.

(*c*) *Explanations from officers.* Likewise, under s. 14, the auditors have the right to require from the officers of the company such information and explanations as they think necessary for the performance of their duties.

(*d*) *Attendance at general meetings.* The auditor is also entitled to attend any general meetings and to receive all notices and other communications relating to any general meetings and to be heard on any part of the business which concerns him as auditor: s. 14, Companies Act 1967.

11. Duties of the auditor.

(*a*) *Report to members.* Whilst every facility is afforded to the auditor by statute to enable him to carry out his duties properly, under contract he should ascertain that his rights in this respect are preserved. Nevertheless, as a professional person, a number of onerous responsibilities are laid upon him both under Common Law and under Statute.

Dealing in the first instance with his duties under the Companies Acts 1948, 1967 and 1976, we shall thereafter consider the broader aspects of his responsibilities.

Under the Companies Act 1967, s. 14:

(1) The auditors of a company shall make a report to the members on the accounts examined by them, and on every balance sheet, every profit and loss account and all group accounts laid before the company in general meeting during their tenure of office.

(2) The auditors' report shall be read before the company in general meeting and shall be open to inspection by any member.

Subsection (3) requires (briefly) that the report must state whether in the auditors' opinion the company's balance sheet and profit and loss account and (if it is a holding company submitting group accounts) the group accounts have been properly prepared in accordance with the provisions of the Companies Acts 1948, 1967 and 1976.

The report must also state whether in their opinion a true and fair view is given:

(a) in the case of the balance sheet, of the state of the company's affairs as at the end of its financial year;

(b) in the case of the profit and loss account (if it be not framed as a consolidated profit and loss account) of the company's profit or loss for its financial year;

(c) in the case of group accounts submitted by a holding company, of the state of affairs and profit or loss of the company and its subsidiaries dealt with thereby, so far as concerns members of the company.

Subsection (4) states that:

It shall be the duty of the auditors . . . in preparing their report . . . to carry out such investigations as will enable them to form an opinion on the following matters . . .

(a) whether proper books of account have been kept by the company and proper returns adequate for their audit have been received from branches not visited by them; and

(b) whether the company's balance sheet and (unless it is framed as a consolidated profit and loss account) profit and loss account are in agreement with the books of account and returns.

The 1967 Act simplified the form of the auditors' report in that it requires a positive statement on matters (a), (b) and (c) in subsection (3) above, unless they are unable to report in the affirmative as to (a) and (b) in subsection (4).

A further duty to report to members is laid upon the auditor under s. 6 of the Companies Act 1967, regarding the disclosure of directors' and certain other employees' emoluments, but in this case the necessity to report only applies if the particulars required by the Acts are not disclosed in the accounts. These details are specified in the Companies Acts 1948, s. 196, and 1967, s. 6. For group reports under the 1976 Act, *see* note (3) on p. 262 below.

(*b*) *Nature of report.* In the absence of any qualifications the I.C.A. Council have recommended the following form of reports:

(*i*) *Companies not submitting group accounts.*

AUDITORS' REPORT TO THE MEMBERS OF . . .

(*See* note (1) below.) In our opinion, the accounts set out on pages . . . to . . . (*see* note (2)) give a true and fair view of the state of the company's affairs at . . . and of its profit (or loss) (*see* note (3)) for the year ended on that date and comply with the Companies Acts 1948, 1967 and 1976.

(*ii*) *Companies submitting group accounts* (*see note* (3) *below*).

AUDITORS' REPORT TO THE MEMBERS OF . . .

(*See* note (1).) In our opinion, the accounts set out on pages . . . to . . . (*see* note (2)) together give, so far as concerns members of the holding company, a true and fair view of the state of affairs at . . . and of the profit (or loss) (*see* note (3)) for the year ended on that date and comply with the Companies Acts 1948, 1967 and 1976.

(*iii*) *Banking, discount, insurance and shipping companies.* In the case of a company which is entitled to avail itself and has availed itself of any of the provisions of Part III of Schedule 2 to the Companies Act 1967, the auditors are not required to report whether, in their opinion, the accounts give a true and fair view. This dispensation, however, applies only to the consequences of the exemptions from disclosures which are permitted by Part III and does not extend to other matters (for example, the over-statement of assets or the omission of liabilities) which, in the auditors' opinion, prevent the disclosure of a true and fair view in the generally accepted sense. In the absence of qualifications the following form of auditors' report is considered appropriate by the Council:

AUDITORS' REPORT TO THE MEMBERS OF THE . . . BANK
(OR THE . . . INSURANCE CO., ETC.)

(*See* note (1).) In our opinion, the accounts set out on pages . . . to . . . (*see* note (2)) comply with the provisions of the Companies Acts 1948, 1967 and 1976, applicable to (banking or insurance, etc.) companies.

NOTES OF VARIATIONS TO SUIT PARTICULAR CIRCUMSTANCES

The following are the notes referred to in the forms of audit report set out in paragraphs (*i*)–(*iii*) above:

(1) If it is desired to refer to the auditors' examination, each of the forms of auditors' report may appropriately commence as follows:

> We have examined the accounts set out in pages . . . to . . . and report that, in our opinion, they. . . .

(2) The documents to which the auditors' report relates should be clearly identified by reference to the page numbers, or if the pages are not numbered, the word "accounts" should be replaced by a description, e.g. "the annexed balance sheet, profit and loss account and notes". If it is necessary for the auditors to make reference to information included in the directors' report (for example, if the directors have taken advantage of the proviso to s. 163 of the Companies Act 1948 to include in their report certain matters which the Act requires to be included in the accounts), the auditors' report should clearly specify the paragraphs of the directors' report which fall within its scope.

(3) *Group Accounts—Reliance on Other Auditors.* Difficulties have arisen in practice due to auditors issuing their reports on holding companies where they have not fully acquainted themselves regarding information shown on accounts of subsidiary and associated companies. They may have understandably considered they might rely completely on the information duly accepted by other auditors. However, it is essential that the information given in group accounts should be unmistakably clear.

The councils of the accountancy bodies have facilitated the work of auditors in their Statement U.21, *Group Accounts— Reliance on Other Auditors.*

Since publishing their Statement, the Companies Act 1976, s. 18, had added statutory rights to the holding companies auditors by stating "it shall be the duty of the subsidiary and its auditors to give to the auditors of the holding company such information and explanation as those auditors may reasonably require" and if the subsidiary is abroad and required by its auditors it shall be its duty to take all such steps as are reasonably open to it to obtain from the subsidiary such information and explanations as required.

Returning to the council's Statement, it clearly puts the onus of the group-reporting auditors to accept full responsibility for the information upon which they issue their report.

The following summarises the Statement to which reference should be made.

1. Statutory requirements and councils' recommendation. Sections 150 to 152 of the Companies Act 1948 provide that where a company has subsidiaries at the end of its financial year, group or consolidated accounts covering the company and its subsidiaries shall be dealt with as a whole as far as concerns the members of the company. At the same time, S.S.A.P. 1, *Accounting for the Results of Associated Companies*, requires the investing group or company, except in certain circumstances, to incorporate in its accounts its share of the profits, less losses of the associated company.

Where a company acts as a member of a partnership or joint venture, the relevant figures of its interests of such consortium activities will normally be included in the accounts of the company itself.

2. Duties of auditors. The statement is unequivocable in placing the responsibility for the disclosing of a true and fair view wholly on the "primary" (holding company) auditors. They may rely to what extent they feel justified on the secondary (subsidiary or associated companies) auditors. Nevertheless, they should conduct any further enquiries as they feel necessary.

3. Primary auditors' responsiblities. The responsibilities of primary auditors are shown under four headings:

(*a*) *Accounting policies.* Directors may not require other companies to adopt their own accounting policies. In these circumstances, the primary auditors should check that the directors have obtained information which will enable them to make the necessary adjustments and that the differing policies are fully explained in the group accounts.

(*b*) *Availability of information.* The directors should be able to exercise sufficient control over subsidiary companies as will enable them to obtain sufficient information from them. In the case of associated companies, their control may be less complete. Nevertheless, they should be able to obtain adequate information from the primary auditors. Where associated companies are listed on recognised stock exchanges, only published financial information should be used (*see* S.S.A.P. 1, paras. 11 and 13).

If the primary auditors find that the directors of the primary lack information about the accounting policies, items for disclosure, or consolidation adjustments relating to the accounts of other group companies, they must ask for the omission to be made good. It may also be necessary to seek permission to obtain the additional information direct from the other companies or from their auditors.

(*c*) *Scope of the work of secondary auditors.* In arriving at their opinion on accounts audited by secondary auditors, the primary auditors will need to consider at least the following matters:

(*i*) Have all the material aspects of the underlying accounts been subject to an audit examination? If so—

(*ii*) Are they, as primary auditors, aware of any reasons why they should not rely on the work and reports of the secondary auditors?

The answer to (*ii*) above will depend on the following questions:

(*i*) What is the primary auditors' knowledge of the standard of work of the secondary auditors?

(*ii*) What auditing "standards" govern the work of the secondary auditors?

(*iii*) What are the auditing requirements in the country in which the secondary auditors work?

(*iv*) Who appointed the secondary auditors, and to whom do they report?

(*v*) Has any limitation been placed on the work of the secondary auditors, or are they free to decide the scope and levels of their audit tests?

(*vi*) Are the secondary auditors independent in all respects?

(*vii*) Is the nature and extent of the secondary auditors' examination adequate and reasonable in the judgment of the primary auditors to provide a sound basis on which the primary auditors can form their opinion?

Before drafting their report, the primary auditors will also need to consider:

(*i*) whether the secondary auditors' reports contain any

qualifications which should be incorporated in the primary auditors' report; and

(*ii*) whether any answers to the above questions require the primary auditors to qualify their report.

(*d*) *Materiality.* In deciding how extensive their enquiries ought to be, the primary auditors must always bear in mind the materiality of the amounts involved (*see* Recommendation V.10).

4. Consultations with the auditors. In all material cases, after having received authority from respective boards, the primary auditors will need to consult with auditors of companies within the group in order to familiarise themselves with the procedures and standards applied.

In conducting such consultations, the primary auditors may request written explanations of the secondary auditors' procedures and findings, the secondary companies' accounting policies supplemented if necessary by oral explanations, and examination of audit files, working papers, and any relevant management letters.

The use of audit questionnaires is not unreservedly advocated unless specifically designed and discussed in advance with the secondary auditors.

If not satisfied with their first enquiries, the primary auditors may require independent confirmation, additional information or additional audit tests.

5. Reference to other auditors. In order not to give the impression that responsibility is avoided by stating in their report that the primary auditors have not audited the accounts of certain companies within the group, an indication may be given, say, in the schedule of the principal subsidiary and associated companies or in the directors' report or in the notes to the accounts, which of those companies are audited by other auditors. It is desirable to indicate the significance to the group of the companies that have been so audited by reference to the amount of their assets, sales or profits or losses before tax.

6. Absence of an audit. The fact that the accounts of a subsidiary company are not subject to regular audit, for example, in a country where such may not be legally required, does not absolve the directors of the primary company to prepare ac-

counts which show a true and fair view. If the amounts involved
are material, the primary auditors may request the directors
to arrange for an audit to be carried out.

7. *Branches.* In the case of branches, it may be necessary for
the primary auditors to arrange for local auditors to act on
their behalf, and for such work they must take full responsibility.

8. *Auditors' reports.*

(a) *Where satisfactory information is not available.* Where
the primary auditors are not satisfied in relation to secondary
companies that they themselves have not audited, they
should qualify their report, clearly indicating their reasons
and identifying the material items affected.

(b) *Where material unaudited amounts are incorporated in
group accounts.* In this case the primary auditors should
express a reservation in their report. The primary auditors
cannot be so satisfied as to the true and fair view presented
by the unaudited accounts as if they had been audited.

(c) *Information about companies audited by other auditors.*
Where information as recommended in 5 of the statement
above is not disclosed about material group companies that
have been audited by other auditors, the primary auditors
should consider whether to refer to this fact in their report.
It is important, however, to ensure that the additional information is not placed so as to mislead the reader into think-
ing that the scope of the audit opinion is therebyl imited.

(d) *The effect of statements of standard accounting practice
on auditors' reports.* The I.C.A. has issued its Statement on
Auditing U.17 in association with the Councils of the
Scottish and Irish Institutes, which is to be read in conjunction with U.10 on auditors' reports.

The Statements describe methods of accounting approved
by the I.C.A. for application to all financial accounts. As
these can be referred to directly, we are concerned here only
with U.17, which points out that:

All significant departures from accounting standards made by the
directors in preparing the accounts should be referred to in the
auditors' report, whether or not they are disclosed in the notes to the
accounts. The extent of the detailed description in the auditors'
report will depend upon whether the departure is fully explained in
the notes to the accounts. If it is, the auditors need make only a brief

reference to the circumstances in their report, but if it is not, a more detailed reference will be necessary.

If the auditors consider that a departure is not justified and that the true and fair view shown by the accounts is thereby impaired, they should, in addition to referring to the notes and disclosing the necessary information in their report (in accordance with the preceding paragraph), express a qualified opinion and quantify the financial effect of the departure, unless this is impracticable. If it is considered impracticable to give this quantification, the reasons should be stated.

If, in exceptional circumstances, the auditors consider that the directors, in preparing the accounts, have necessarily departed from an accounting standard in order to show a true and fair view, the auditors should nevertheless refer to the departure in their report and state that they concur. In these circumstances, the auditors should not express a qualified opinion or quantify the financial effect of the departure on the accounts.

There may be rare circumstances in which adherence to an accounting standard does not, in the auditors' view, produce a true and fair view. In such circumstances, the auditors should express a qualified opinion and quantify the financial effect on the accounts, unless this is impracticable.

Two examples are given "for illustrative purposes only", under the heading "*Departure from an accounting standard impairing the true and fair view*":

(*i*) *When full disclosure is made in the accounts.*

As indicated in Note . . . to the accounts, the group profit for the year and the amount of the investment in the associated company are stated before deducting £ . . ., the group's share of the loss incurred in the year by the associated company, and are therefore not in accordance with Statement of Standard Accounting Practice No. 1 (*Accounting for the results of associated companies*).

With this exception, the accounts set out on pages . . . to . . . in our opinion give a true and fair view . . . (followed by an appropriate form of wording).

(*ii*) *Where there is no disclosure, or inadequate disclosure, in the accounts.*

The company follows the policy of including in the accounts only the dividends received from X Limited, its associated company. This is not in accordance with Statement of Standard Accounting Practice No. 1 (*Accounting for the results of associated companies*). If the company had recorded its share of the increase in the net assets of X Limited, in accordance with that accounting standard, the profit after tax shown in the profit and loss account would have been increased by £ . . . and its group's interest in X Limited, as shown in the consolidated balance sheet, would have been increased by £. . . .

With this exception, the accounts set out on pages . . . to . . . in our opinion give a true and fair view . . . (followed by an appropriate form of wording).

12. Qualified report. Where the auditor is not satisfied as to any particular matter of importance and feels that the shareholders or others should be made aware of the fact, he may find it necessary to mention the matter in his report. The inclusion of such a statement serves to create what is called a qualified report. The I.C.A. have issued U.10 *Auditors' Reports: Forms and Qualifications*, on this subject in which they mention particularly that any matter requiring qualification should be of "material" importance. The report required under the 1967 Act necessitates qualification where the auditor is not satisfied as to various general matters (*see* p. 250), but there are a number of other matters which may justify qualification. These are listed in Recommendation U.10 and may justify qualification where in the opinion of the auditors the accounts, though otherwise complying with the requirements of Sch. 2 of the Companies Act 1967, fail to disclose a true and fair view, for example:

(*a*) because in the auditors' opinion they do not conform to accounting principles appropriate to the circumstances and nature of the business;

(*b*) because they are prepared on principles inconsistent with those previously adopted and without adequate explanation and disclosure of the effects of the change;

(*c*) because the auditors are unable to agree with the amount at which an asset or liability is stated;

(*d*) because the auditors are unable to agree with this amount at which income or expenditure or profit is stated;

(*e*) because the accounts do not disclose information which, though not specifically detailed in the Acts, is necessary for the presentation of a true and fair view;

(*f*) because additional information given in a note, or in the directors' report, materially alters the view otherwise given by the accounts.

In some instances more than one of the foregoing matters may be applicable—for example, where the internal control is such as to cast doubt upon the reliability of the records so that the auditors cannot satisfy themselves that a true and fair view has been shown by the balance sheet and profit and loss account.

Normally, points of disagreement or other matters causing dissatisfaction on the part of the auditor may be settled with the management, but, where the auditor is still not satisfied, the Council of the I.C.A. point out that the auditor's duty is inescapable. Where any qualifying statement is found necessary then it should:

(a) be as concise as is consistent with clarity;

(b) be specific as to the items and facts and as far as possible the amounts involved;

(c) within the limits of the information available to the auditors, make clear its effects on the accounts; and

(d) express the auditors' opinions without possibility of misinterpretation.

The Council have given examples of various types of qualified reports which should be taken to serve only as a guide, the specific circumstances applicable being the overriding factor. The following have been selected:

Some of the detailed stock-taking sheets relating to stocks held at the balance sheet date have been destroyed. In their absence we have been unable to substantiate the basis of computation of stock amounting to £ . . . out of the total of £ . . . at which stock is shown in the balance sheet.

Subject to the foregoing reservation the accounts set out on pages . . . to . . . in our opinion give a true and fair view . . . (followed by an appropriate form of wording).

In the absence of adequate analyses of factory wages we are unable to verify the charge for labour and overhead amounting to £ . . . included in the additions of £ . . . to plant and machinery during the year.

Subject to the foregoing reservation the accounts set out on pages . . . to . . . in our opinion give a true and fair view . . . (followed by an appropriate form of wording).

Group profits are overstated by £ . . . by the inclusion of unrealised profits on products transferred at selling price between members of the group and remaining in stock at the date of the balance sheet. With this exception the accounts set out in pages . . . to . . . in our opinion give a true and fair view . . . (followed by an appropriate form of wording).

The International Standard I.A.S.1 is also relevant as qualification may be required in the event of wrong or inappropriate treatment of items in balance sheet or accounts even though disclosure may be made in notes or otherwise (*see* p. 4).

A qualified report is also required where a statement of source and application of funds is not supplied with audited accounts of companies other than those with a turnover gross income of less than £25,000.

13. Statements of source and application of funds. "Although not required by Statute, for a fuller understanding of a company's affairs it is necessary also to identify the movements in assets, liabilities and capital which have taken place during the year and the resultant effect on net liquid funds. This information is not specifically disclosed by a profit and loss account and balance sheet but can be made available in the form of a statement of source and application of funds (a 'funds statement')." This quotation is taken from S.S.A.P. 10.

This standard applies to all financial accounts intended to give a true and fair view of the financial position and profit or loss other than those of enterprises with turnover or gross income of less than £25,000 per annum. It requires that all audited accounts subject to the exception mentioned should include a statement of source and application of funds both for the period under review and for the corresponding previous period. The statement should show the profit or loss for the period together with the adjustments required for items which did not use (or provide) funds in the period. The following other sources and applications of funds should, where material, also be shown:

(*a*) Dividends paid.

(*b*) Acquisitions and disposals of fixed and other non-current assets.

(*c*) Funds raised by increasing, or expended in repaying or redeeming, medium or long-term loans or the issued capital of the company.

(*d*) Increase or decrease in working capital sub-divided into its components, and movements in net liquid funds.

Where the accounts are those of a group, the Statement of source and application of funds should be so framed as to reflect the operations of the group.

S.S.A.P. 10 gives examples of the Statement which should be consulted. Statement on Auditing U.23, issued by the councils of the accountancy bodies refers to S.S.A.P. 10 and states that reference to the statement of source and application of funds should be made in the opening paragraph of the auditor's report.

Where a company is subject to the requirements of the Standard and fails to provide a funds statement, the auditor will need to qualify his report to this effect, that the Standard has not been complied with. Paragraph 3 of Statement on Auditing, U.17, *The Effect of Statements of Standard Accounting Practice on Auditors' Reports*, should not be interpreted as requiring the auditor to make good this deficiency by including a funds statement as part of his audit report.

14. The interpretation of "material" in relation to accounts. The necessity to qualify reports leads naturally to the consideration of the circumstances where such definitive action is required. The word "material" signifies "of relative importance", and in this sense it devolves on the auditor to decide when a matter is of such outstanding importance as to justify his qualifying his report. In V.10 the illustration is given that £100 in a small firm might be material, whereas £1 million may not be significant in classifying expenditure in a very large undertaking, especially as much elaboration might obscure the true and fair view.

The nature of the item concerned may determine the importance attaching to any variation. Shareholders are most concerned with such matters as directors' emoluments, auditors' fees and investment income, whereas depreciation, which might be based upon an arbitrary assessment, may cause no concern. The following constitutes a brief extract from V.10 of items likely to affect the auditors' decision as to whether an item should be considered of material importance or otherwise.

Degree of approximation. The degree of estimation or approximation which is unavoidably inherent in arriving at the amount of an item may be a factor in deciding on materiality. Examples include contingency provisions, stock and work-in-progress, and taxation provisions.

Losses or low profits. The use of the profit figure as a point of comparison tends to be vitiated when the profits are abnormally low or where there is a loss; when judging the materiality of individual items in the profit and loss account in such cases, the more normal dimensions of the business have to be considered.

Critical points. The view given by accounts may sometimes be affected by the trend of profit, or turnover, and of various expense items. An inaccuracy which might not otherwise be judged to be material could have the effect of reversing a trend, or turning a profit into a loss, or creating or eliminating a margin of solvency in a balance sheet. When an item affects such a critical point in accounts, then its materiality has to be viewed in that narrower context.

Disproportionate significance. An item of small amount may, nevertheless, be of material significance in the context of a company's particular circumstances, especially if the context would lead the reader to expect the item to be of substantial amount.

15. Liabilities. The liability of an auditor may arise under civil law, or he may be held criminally liable. Where an action is brought against him under civil law, he will be required to make good any loss suffered by his client due to his negligence; on the other hand if he has been negligent, but his client has suffered no loss, he will not be liable for damages.

Briefly, an auditor may be held liable in any of the following circumstances:

(a) *In civil actions.*

(i) *Under common law (negligence).* As a professional person employed as an agent, a high standard of care, skill and diligence may be expected of him. If it is considered that he has not brought this to bear on his work, he may be held liable for any loss arising to his client.

(ii) *Under statute (misfeasance).* Under s. 333 of the Companies Act 1948, as an officer of the company, if he has been guilty of misfeasance, he may be required, on the winding-up of the company, to contribute a sum to the assets of the company by way of compensation (*see* 17).

(b) *In criminal prosecutions.*

(i) *Under the Companies Act* 1948, *s.* 438. Under this section he may be liable if he wilfully makes a statement false in any material particular, knowing it to be false.

(ii) *Under the Theft Act* 1968, for publishing or concurring in publishing a written statement or account, which to his knowledge is, or may be, misleading, false or deceptive in a material particular. . . .

(iii) *Under the Prevention of Frauds (Investment) Act* 1958, for making any statement, promise or forecast which he knows to be misleading . . . to induce another person to enter into any agreement . . . to invest.

(c) *Liability to third parties in tort* (*see* **18**).

16. Cases of auditors' liabilities: negligence. A number of legal decisions affecting the auditor have been dealt with (*see* XI) concerning distribution of profits, and (*see* X) regarding stock-in-trade. The following decisions concern the auditor's liability in respect of negligence.

(*a*) *Wilde & Others* v. *Cape & Dalgleish* (1897). The defendants in this case did not discover defalcations which it was contended could have been discovered had the auditors examined the bank pass books. The defence submitted that it was not part of the original arrangement that the pass books should be examined, but this was not sustained and it was held an auditor is liable for losses arising due to his negligence.

(*b*) *Smith* v. *Sheard* (1906). Here the defendants maintained that no agreement had been made by them to conduct an audit and they, in fact, gave no certificate. Nevertheless they were held liable for loss arising through their negligence in not discovering certain defalcations.

This case is of importance since the matter of the auditor's report is mentioned, the principle being applied that, despite the weight given to the existence of an audit report, it is not the governing factor as to liability for losses arising due to negligence.

(*c*) *Fox & Son* v. *Morris Grant & Co.* (1918). In a case somewhat similar to (*a*) above, the accountants were employed to check books and prepare accounts. They maintained that accuracy could be arrived at without reference to the pass book, and that as no audit was conducted, it was not necessary to refer to this. The court held, however, that as the balance sheet contained the item "Cash at Bank", the accountants should have verified its existence, and so were held liable.

(*d*) *Irish Woollen Company* v. *Tyson and Others* (1900). Various inaccuracies arose in the accounts of the company regarding its stock, book debts and trade liabilities, due to falsification. The work carried out by the auditor's staff was inadequate, and although the auditor was not held liable in respect of the matters affecting the stock and book debts, nevertheless it was considered it would have been possible to detect the under-statement of liabilities had adequate tests been carried out. The fact that he did not carry out the work himself was no defence. He was entitled to employ a deputy but he must still be held responsible for ensuring that reasonable care, skill and diligence be exercised.

(*e*) *London Oil Storage Co. Ltd.* v. *Seear Hasluck & Co.* (1904).

The secretary of the company had misappropriated petty cash over a number of years. The auditor did not check the petty cash balance, which should have been in the sum of £796 of which, in fact, only £30 was on hand.

Although the case was brought against the auditors for negligence, contributory negligence on the part of the directors was held to have been the main factor in causing the loss arising, since they should not have allowed such a large sum to remain in the hands of the petty cashier. The auditors were found liable only in the nominal sum of five guineas, but it was pointed out that it was the duty of the auditor to verify the items on the balance sheet and in this they had been negligent.

(*f*) *Arthur E. Green and Co.* v. *The Central Advance and Discount Corporation Ltd.* (1920). In seeking to recover fees due to them as auditors, the plaintiffs were met with a counter-claim in respect of the fact that the auditors had been negligent in their duty.

The auditors had relied upon the word of the managing director (who was remunerated according to a commission on profits), when they queried the veracity of a schedule of debtors which, in fact, contained various statute-barred and bad debts. It was maintained that they should have brought their dissatisfaction to the notice of the directors, and if still dissatisfied, to the notice of the members.

(*g*) *Armitage* v. *Brewer and Knott* (1932). The defendants were specifically employed to conduct an audit in such a way as would obviate the plaintiff from being the subject of petty frauds. The auditors gave their assurance to this effect and were allowed to conduct the audit in any way they deemed necessary. It transpired that the audit necessitated a considerable amount of detailed checking work, there being in effect no internal check.

The defendants submitted that the frauds, which had been perpetrated by an employee, could not have been discovered by the exercise of reasonable care, but the Judge pointed out that though the work involved in detecting such a fraud might necessitate the minute examination of a large number of documents, this was exactly what the auditors had undertaken to do. The auditors were found to be liable for damages to the extent of £1,200.

17. Cases of misfeasance. Misfeasance may be described as the "wrongful performance of a fiduciary duty"; damages will only be awarded against the tortfeasor, however, if actual loss has been suffered arising out of the breach.

The auditor is an officer of the company for the purpose of s. 333 of the Companies Act 1948, and in that capacity may be held liable in damages in the event of winding-up provided his misfeasance has been the cause of damage arising to the company.

(a) *In re London and General Bank* (1895). The auditor in this case had reported to the directors the serious position of the company because loans had been made on insufficient security and also his opinion as to their being doubtful.

The directors refused to take any action so the auditor qualified his report by stating that "the value of the assets is dependent upon their realisation".

Although the wording of the report was such that it might have led to further enquiry on the shareholders' part, nevertheless the auditor was held to have been negligent, for to give shareholders such information as may induce them to ask for more is not discharging his duty.

The following statements by the Judge are reproduced as they constitute fundamental principles covering the duty of the auditor.

He (the auditor) must be honest—that is he must not certify what he does not believe to be true and he must take reasonable care and skill before he believes that what he certifies is true . . . His business is to ascertain and state the true financial position of the company at the time of the audit, and his duty is confined to that. But then comes the question: How is he to ascertain such position? The answer is: By examining the books of the company. But he does not discharge his duty by doing this without enquiry and without taking any trouble to see that the books of the company themselves show the company's true position. He must take reasonable care to ascertain that they do.

(b) *In re Kingston Cotton Mill Company* (1896). This case has already been mentioned (*see* p. 176) in particular reference to stock-in-trade. By over-valuation of stocks for a number of years, profits had been inflated by a manager who received a commission on them.

The famous phrase referring to the "watch dog and blood-hound" are referred to in the following extract from the words of Lopas, L.J. in the course of his judgment; however, the important point to observe is the principle laid down that the auditor should apply reasonable care and skill and that he should not undertake his work with suspicion and the foregone conclusion that something is wrong:

It is the duty of an auditor to bring to bear on the work he has to perform that skill, care and caution which a reasonably competent, careful and cautious auditor would use. What is reasonable skill, care and caution must depend on the particular circumstances of each case. An auditor is not bound to be a detective, or, as was said, to approach his work with suspicion or with a foregone conclusion that there is something wrong. He is a watch dog, but not a bloodhound. He is justified in believing tried servants of the company in whom confidence is placed by the company. He is entitled to assume that they are honest, and to rely upon their representations, provided he takes reasonable care. If there is anything calculated to excite suspicion he should probe it to the bottom, but in the absence of anything of that kind, he is only bound to be reasonably cautious and careful.

(c) *In re City Equitable Fire Insurance Co. Ltd.* (1925). The auditors in this case were held to be guilty of misfeasance, but, due to a protecting clause in the company's Articles that directors and officers should not be answerable for any loss occurring in the execution of their offices or trusts or in relation thereto, the auditors were able to escape any damages against them. Such clauses are now no longer effective as laid down in the Companies Act 1948, nevertheless the case is important as it reveals the auditor's negligence in accepting a certificate from the company's stockbrokers in respect of securities purporting to be held by them for safe custody which did not exist, or if they did, that had been pledged by them. Such a certificate should be accepted at the auditor's discretion only from a person who deals with, and holds, securities in the normal course of business, and who he considers is a trustworthy person to give such a certificate.

(d) *In re Westminster Road Construction and Engineering Co. Ltd.* (1932). The liquidator brought this action against the directors and auditors of the company in order to recover a dividend which had been paid when the profits for the year were stated to have been £3,458 while they were, in fact, £297. The profit figure had been arrived at by under-stating liabilities and over-valuing the company's work-in-progress. The directors were not held liable as they believed the balance sheet on which the auditors had reported. The auditors, however, were held to be guilty of misfeasance on two counts:

(*i*) They had failed to detect the omission of liabilities which normal enquiries during the course of an audit would have revealed.

(*ii*) They had failed to ascertain the true valuation of the work-in-progress when there was ample evidence from which they might have ascertained it.

18. Liability to third parties for negligence. The liability of an auditor to his *client* has been considered already (*see* **16**); a newer form of liability should now be examined: liability *to persons other than clients* for negligent mis-statements. (This form of liability did not exist until the ruling of the House of Lords in *Hedley Byrne & Co. Ltd.* v. *Heller & Partners Ltd.* (1963).) The House of Lords ruled in this case that liability can now be imposed in tort for negligent mis-statements. So the position is that *if a person supplies information or advice to the plaintiff, knowing that it may be relied on, he owes a duty of care to the plaintiff and is liable in negligence for any breach of such, if the breach of duty occasions actual loss.*

In *Hedley Byrne & Co. Ltd.* v. *Heller and Partners Ltd.* (1963), before entering into a transaction with X, the plaintiffs sought a reference as to X's standing from X's bankers. The bankers provided the reference (but stated therein that they accepted no responsibility for its accuracy). The reference proved to be misleading, and the bankers had been negligent. The plaintiffs suffered loss and sued the bankers for damages for negligence.

The House of Lords held (*i*) that the bankers could be held liable for negligence contained in a reference, but (*ii*) that the disclaimer of liability in the reference exonerated them from liability on the particular facts of the case.

The case is therefore important since it lays down a general head of liability for negligent mis-statements by professional advisers of all sorts, and in particular means that an auditor could now be liable for negligence to persons who are not members of a company which employs him and not, as formerly held in *Candler* v. *Crane, Christmas & Co.* (1951), that no claim in tort for negligence could arise as the law did not recognise tortious liability for negligent mis-statements.

19. I.C.A. recommendations. The Institute of Chartered Accountants have now taken legal advice in the light of the foregoing case and have issued their Statement V.8:

(*a*) *Accountants liability to third parties—The Hedley Byrne decision.* The reader is referred to the full text but we quote the following paragraphs under the heading "Counsel's advice".

Counsel has advised that the *Hedley Byrne* decision is much more restricted in its effect than may first appear, and has drawn attention to the development of the law in this sphere overseas, referring particularly to the cases of *Ultramares Corporation* v. *Touche* (255 N.Y. 170) in the United States, and *Herschel* v. *Mrupi* (1954 S.A. 464) in South Africa. In this connection the *Ultramares* case is of particular interest. There the Court decided that auditors were not liable for negligence to a plaintiff who lent money on the strength of accounts on which the auditors had reported but which they did not know were required for the purpose of obtaining financial assistance or would be shown to the plaintiff. In so deciding the Court recognised that it would be quite wrong to expose the auditors to a potential liability "in an indeterminate amount for an indefinite time to an indeterminate class".

In Counsel's view third parties entitled to recover damages under the *Hedley Byrne* principle will be limited to those who by reason of accountants' negligence in preparing reports, accounts or financial statements on which the third parties place reliance suffer financial loss in circumstances where the accountants knew or ought to have known that the reports, accounts or financial statements in question were being prepared for the specific purpose or transaction which gave rise to the loss and that they would be shown to and relied on by third parties in that particular connection. There is no general principle that accountants may be liable for damages if a report or statement which proves to have been prepared negligently by them is shown casually or in the course of business to third parties who suffer loss through reliance on the report or statement.

The practical applications of the decision have also been dealt with, which cover such matters as:

(*i*) The position of clients' creditors, where clients seek financial assistance—here proof of negligence and knowledge of use for the purpose would be needed.

(*ii*) Shareholders and their judgment of the company's affairs by the use of annual accounts—no action would lie by an individual shareholder but if the company collectively suffered loss due to reliance on accounts negligently prepared the auditors could be liable. The auditors could also be held liable if the accounts were used as an effective part of a document of offer and the auditors knew of or should have known that they were intended to be so used. On the other hand, where an individual shareholder might use them for investment decisions, then the auditors would not be liable as the accounts are not normally prepared for such a purpose.

(*iii*) Where taxation is concerned, although the accountant might know that the accounts would be used for assessment purposes, no action would lie in the case of reliance upon accounts negligently prepared "since in fact any ultimate loss suffered by the Revenue through failure to recover tax lost must be attributed to the death, decamping or insolvency of the tax-payer, not to the negligence of his accountant".

The law relating to principal and client would operate to the exclusion of the *Hedley Byrne* principle where an accountant is instructed to agree his client's liability with the Inland Revenue: "The Counsel of the Institute emphasises that it is recognised best practice . . . in the interests of all concerned, the extent to which the accountant accepts responsibility should be made clear beyond possibility of misunderstanding."

To conclude we quote again from Statement V.8.

> . . . Counsel has further advised that where an accountant specifically restricts the scope of his report or expresses appropriate reservations in a note attached to or referred to in the financial statements he has prepared or the report which he has made thereon, this can constitute a disclaimer which will be effective against any action for negligence brought against him by third parties.

(*b*) *Professional liability of accountants and auditors.*

(*i*) *Liability to clients.* Statement V.18 is concerned only with liability for professional negligence which a member may incur because of an act or default by him or by one of his employees or associates which results in financial loss to a person to whom a duty of care is owed. Negligence implies some act or omission which occurs because the person concerned has failed to exercise that degree of professional care and skill appropriate to the circumstances of the case. Opinions expressed or advice given will not necessarily give rise to claims for negligence merely because, in the light of later events, they prove to have been mistaken.

Actions for negligence can broadly be divided into the following classes:

(1) in contract, by persons to whom the accountant owes a contractual duty of care;

(2) in tort, by persons with whom the accountant is not in a

contractual relationship but to whom the accountant owes a duty in accordance with the *Hedley Byrne* decision.

It would be a defence to an action for negligence to show either that there has been no negligence or, in the case of actions in tort, that no duty of care is owed to the plaintiff. In a case where no financial loss has been suffered by the plaintiff, a claim in tort for negligence could not succeed and a claim in contract for nominal damages is highly unlikely.

Often cases have arisen because of misunderstanding as to the degree of responsibility which the accountant was expected to take in giving advice or expressing an opinion. A clear distinction must be made between (*a*) disputes arising from misunderstandings regarding the duties assumed and (*b*) negligence in carrying out agreed terms. The usefulness of engagement letters cannot be over-emphasised here (*see* p. 249).

Section 205 of the Companies Act 1948 makes void any attempt to exempt the auditor, or indemnify him against liability for negligence, default, breach of duty or trust. And despite the relief the Act may give under s. 448, these powers have been seldom exercised. To exclude or limit liability, therefore, the auditor should ensure that this is dealt with in a letter of engagement.

Where other types of work are involved, e.g. investigation or management consultancy assignments, the auditor should make clear the extent of the responsibility he agrees to undertake. The Statement warns against the danger of giving "snap" answers to complicated problems and advises an oral and subsequently a written statement pointing out the limited time available for consideration and that the opinion may be altered in the light of further consideration.

(*ii*) *Liability to third parties.* Such liability is signified where no direct contractual liability exists. The Statement gives examples of occasions when the accountant may incur liability to third parties under the *Hedley Byrne* doctrine, including:

(1) preparing financial statements or reports for a client when it is known or ought reasonably to be expected that they are intended to be shown to and relied upon by a third party (even if the actual identity of the third party is not disclosed at the relevant time to the accountant);

(2) giving references regarding a client's creditworthiness, or an assurance as to his capacity to carry out the terms of

contracts (e.g. leases), or giving any other type of reference on behalf of the client.

Counsel has advised that where an accountant specifically restricts the scope of his report or expresses appropriate reservations in a note, as shown below, attached to and referred to in the financial statements or in his report thereon, this can constitute a disclaimer which will be effective against any action for negligence brought against him by third parties.

This report (statement) has been prepared for the private use of X (the client) only. No responsibility to any third party is accepted.

However, such a disclaimer should be introduced only where the circumstances warrant it, as, in Counsel's view, an indiscriminate use of disclaimers would tend to impair the status of practising accountants by indicating a lack of confidence in the professional work they carry out.

When giving references or assurances regarding credit-worthiness or other matters, the accountant should adopt the normal commercial practice of stating that although the reference or assurance is given in good faith, he accepts no financial responsibility for the opinion he expresses.

Care should also be exercised to ensure that before his name is used, prior permission should be obtained. Likewise, care should be taken to obtain specialist advice where the report may have to include opinions of a nature outside the field of the auditor's professional work.

20. Unlawful acts or defaults by clients (V.12). This is quite a lengthy Recommendation, and understandably so, as by its nature it has to be precise and should be consulted for fuller treatment. The following are various points to be borne in mind by the auditor regarding his client's unlawful acts or defaults.

Except in cases of treason, a member who acquires knowledge of the commission of a criminal offence (or of a default which is a civil wrong only) is under no legal obligation to disclose what he knows to a proper authority, and it is an implied term of a member's contract with his client that the member will not, as a general rule, disclose to other persons information about his client's affairs which he has obtained by virtue of his professional relationship with his client. There are, however, circumstances in which, while not obliged to do so, a member is contractually free to make a disclosure of his client's affairs if he so wishes in such circumstances as:

(i) where disclosure is authorised by the client either expressly or by implication;

(*ii*) where the disclosure is compelled by process of law;

(*iii*) where the member's interests require disclosure;

(*iv*) where the circumstances are such as to give rise to a public duty to disclose.

If an auditor discovers that accounts he has reported on and submitted to the Inland Revenue are wrong because the client deceived him, he should advise the client to disclose the position to the Inland Revenue. If this is not done, he should inform the client that he can no longer act for him, and write to the Revenue authorities informing them that he has ceased to act, that the accounts are inaccurate but not disclosing details of the inaccuracies.

In the case of a new client, if the auditor finds that reports submitted to the Inland Revenue in previous years were defective, the accounts must be adjusted if possible to make up the defect or his report must be qualified. If no adjustment is possible and the client refuses to approach the Revenue authorities, the auditor has no duty in the matter but may prefer to terminate the association.

If an auditor learns of misdemeanours committed by a client, he should consider:

(*a*) that he must not assist a client to commit a criminal offence;

(*b*) does the offence affect the true and fair view shown in the accounts and should the report be qualified?

(*c*) is it proper for him to continue to act for this client?

Where the client is a limited company, the auditor has a more positive duty to indicate clearly in his report the matters on which he is unable to satisfy himself, even though this may disclose the fact that an offence has been committed.

PROGRESS TEST 14

1. List the statutes under which an auditor may be appointed. (2)

2. What are the rules governing the actual appointment of the auditor under the Companies Acts 1948 and 1967? (3)

3. In what ways may a company's auditor's remuneration be fixed? Are expenses for these purposes considered as "remuneration"? (3)

4. Specify who may and may not be an auditor of a public company. (3)

5. Does it make any difference with regard to above if the company is a private company?

6. In what way does the requirement regarding the qualifications of an auditor differ under the Building Societies Act 1962, from that of under Companies Act 1948? (4)

7. What is an "exempt" society under the Friendly and Industrial and Provident Societies Act 1968?

8. How may an auditor be appointed under the Public Trustee Act 1906 and the Trustee Act 1925? (7)

9. In what way are auditors' rights established in the case of private audits? (8, 9)

10. May a right of lien be exercised at all times? (9)

11. How is the auditor's right of lien varied in the event of liquidation? (9)

12. If it is decided by the directors to appoint someone other than the retiring auditor, what rights has the present auditor? (10)

13. "The auditor is only entitled to concern himself with the books of account of and documents relevant to a business." Do you agree with this statement? (11)

14. Draft an auditor's report to include the matters that are required to be dealt with under the Companies Act 1967. (11)

15. What is signified by a "qualified" report? Give an example of such a qualification. (12)

16. Specify the ways in which an auditor may be held liable at law: (a) Civilly. (b) Criminally. (15)

17. What is meant by the term "misfeasance"? If misfeasance can be proved, will damages always be awarded? (17)

18. If the auditor does not give a certificate, will he be free from any charge of negligence? (16)

19. What important principle regarding the auditor's duty was mentioned in the case of *London Oil Storage Co. Ltd.* v. *Seear, Hasluck & Co.* (1904)? (16)

20. Why did the House of Lords in the case of *Hedley Byrne & Co. Ltd.* v. *Heller and Partners Ltd.* state that the decision in the *Candler* v. *Crane, Christmas* case was wrong? (18)

21. Will the auditor now always be liable to third parties when he knows that they may in any way be affected by a statement made by him? (19)

22. Is an auditor always bound to disclose to proper authorities

any unlawful acts or defaults which he discovers that his client has made? (20)

SPECIMEN QUESTIONS

1. In what manner does the Companies Act 1948 afford protection to an auditor whom the directors seek to remove from office? *I.C.A.* (*E.W.*) (*Inter.*)

2. State, giving your reasons, whether or not the auditor of a public company would be disqualified from acting in the following circumstances:

(*a*) On the appointment of the firm, in which he is a partner, as Registrars of the company.

(*b*) On the appointment of an employee of the firm as secretary of the company.

(*c*) On the appointment of one of his partners as financial adviser to the company. *I.C.A.* (*E.W.*)

3. Discuss the question whether an accountant has the right to retain various types of records with particular reference to:

(*a*) working papers;

(*b*) correspondence with clients;

(*c*) communications with third parties.

You are not required to deal with lien. *I.C.A.* (*E.W.*)

4. Discuss the liability of an auditor of a public company incorporated under the Companies Acts in the following circumstances:

(*a*) Failure to detect omission of liabilities by suppression of several invoices for goods supplied during the last month of company's financial year.

(*b*) Omission to verify balance of petty cash where the books showed that during the last two years this had increased from £80 to £700.

(*c*) Non-detection of serious over-valuation of work-in-progress leading to the declaration of a dividend in excess of the true profits of the company. *A.C.A.*

5. What are the requirements of the Companies Act 1948, in respect of the appointment and removal of the auditor?

What is an auditor's status under the Acts and has he a lien on the company's books for unpaid audit fees? *A.C.A.*

6. As auditor of a holding company with subsidiaries in various

countries, you are examining the group accounts and ascertain that:

(*a*) The directors are of the opinion that the group accounts need not deal with a number of the subsidiaries.

(*b*) The accounts submitted for one of the foreign subsidiaries are unaudited.

Discuss your position in each of these circumstances.

I.C.A. (E.W.)

7. Discuss the extent of the liability for negligence of the auditor of a private company, assuming that he has not qualified his report in any way. *I.C.A.*

8. What do you understand by the concept of materiality in relation to an audit? *A.C.A.*

9. During the course of his professional duties, an auditor may acquire knowledge of unlawful acts committed by his client, such as frauds on the Inland Revenue.

What is the liability of the auditor in such cases, and what line of professional conduct should he follow?

APPENDIX

Examination Technique

In examinations, two main types of questions are likely to arise, those covering auditing techniques and, to a lesser extent, those inviting discussion of a subject, such as matters affecting depreciation.

In this very practical subject a wide experience in auditing would be a distinct asset in dealing with examination problems. Unfortunately, however, it is not always possible to have gained this by the time it is necessary to sit for examinations. It is essential, therefore, for the student to *apply his imagination to augment the experience he has already received.*

Examiners are not unreasonable, and it is not expected that a student should have had personal experience of every type of audit, but in attempting a question it is essential to show that he is capable of using sound reasoning in approaching a problem. To facilitate this the student should endeavour to follow through the principles behind the general audit work he undertakes during the course of his training. This can prove invaluable as a background to audit technique questions and obviates the necessity of committing a great deal of procedural work to memory.

Internal Control and its concomitant, *Internal Check*, are of great importance in modern auditing and as there have been clear and practical *Recommendations* issued by the Institute of Chartered Accountants, questions may be expected on this subject. This type of work requires a knowledge of the flow of work through a business and the proper allocation of duties and responsibilities; *the student should therefore endeavour to see each aspect of the audit work he undertakes as a part, fitting into the whole movement of work through the system.* If this is done conscientiously a valuable background knowledge should be available when dealing with examination problems.

Questions of the essay type on matters arising in the financial sphere and others affected by economic theories, such as inflation and revaluation of assets, and methods of stock valuation, should be dealt with as essays and the student should bring to play his knowledge gained in other studies. On the other hand, *questions of work procedure* covering pure auditing, *should be answered in a logical manner using succinct phrasing,* and wherever possible, *dividing paragraphs into numbered sub-divisions.*

Inevitably, certain *Statutory requirements and legal decisions will have to be committed to memory,* and if when studying kindred subjects, such as Company Law and Mercantile Law, their effect on the auditor and his work, are borne in mind, the study of related subjects may prove very useful.

In the examination room, the following guiding principles should be applied:

(*a*) Read all the questions over briefly.

(*b*) Roughly allocate time according to the marks to be awarded.

(*c*) Attempt the easiest question first.

(*d*) For the second time read the question to be answered carefully.

(*e*) List in brief the matters to be dealt with as they come to mind.

(*f*) Deal with the points listed in a logical order, ticking them off as they are dealt with.

(*g*) Make answers complete in themselves, e.g.: "Is it part of the auditor's duty to check the actual stock-in-trade of the organisation he is auditing?" should not be answered: "No, as it has been stated . . .", but rather: "It is not part of the auditor's duty to check stock-in-trade as . . .".

(*h*) If an essay is requested then this should be submitted, but in other cases be succinct, sub-divide paragraphs and list points wherever this is justified.

(*i*) Headings, or sub-headings, may be underlined but not words and phrases within the body of the answer. The examiner does not need such unnecessary over-emphasis.

Index

Accountant, auditor as distinguished from, 2
Accountants' reports on profit forecasts, 242–5
Accounting Practice, Standard, 2–6, 266–8
Accruals, S.A.P., 69
Appointment of auditor, 15–16, 249–50
  Building Societies Act 1962, 255
  Companies Acts, 251–5
  Friendly *and* Industrial Acts, 255–7
  Public Trustee Acts, 257–8
  Secretary of State, 251
Approved auditor, 251
Assets
  depreciation and appreciation, 154 *et seq.*
  valuation, 166 *et seq.*
  verification, 122 *et seq.*
Audit
  balance sheet, 11–12
  classification, 6–12
  Companies Acts, provisions as to, 251–5
  continuous, 9–10
  definition, 1
  final or completed, 8
  interim, 8–9
  limited company—on taking up, 15–16
  management, 10–11
  objects, 1, 2
  private, 6–7
  procedural, 10
  small company, 39–41
  statutory, 7, 250–1
  working papers, 17–18
Audit, internal, 7, 31, 41–3, 46
  and independant auditor, 41
  recommendations of Institute of Chartered Accountants on, 41–3
Audit file, 17–18
Auditing in depth, 28, 69
Audit note-book, 19
Auditor
  appointment of, 15–16, 251–6
  lien of, 258–9
  primary, 262–6
  qualifications required under:
    Building Societies Act 1962, 255
    Companies Acts, 251–4
  removal of, 252–3
  report of, 259 *et seq.*
  resignation of, 254–5
  retirement of, 250–2
  rights and duties of, 258 *et seq.*
  secondary, 262–6
Auditor's report
  balance sheet, on, 259–60
  Building Societies Act 1962, 217–18
  Companies Acts, 259 *et seq.*
  general meeting, must be read at, 260
  group accounts, 261, 262 *et seq.*
  prospectus, on, 236
  qualification of, 268–70
  reliance on secondary auditors, 262–6
  Solicitors Acts, under, 226–7

Audit programme, 17, 19, 22–3
  balance sheet audit, 11–12
  general specimen of, 19–22
  specialised—*see* Audits, special-
    ised
Audits, specialised, 217 *et seq.*
  balance sheet audit, 11–12
  banks, 221
  building societies, 218–21
  clubs, 221–2
  contractors, 222
  executors and trustees, 223
  hotels, 223–4
  insurance companies, 224–5
  publishers, 225
  share transfer audit, 225–6
  solicitors, 226–7
  statutory report, 228–9

Bad and doubtful debts
  auditor's duty in connection
    with, 203
  provision for, 203
Balance sheet
  audit, 11–12
  auditor's report on, 259–60
  contents, 259–60
Bank
  audit, 221
  reconciliation of balance with
    cash book, 55. 138
  verification of balance, 138
Bearer securities, 134–5
Bonded warehouses, 139
Book debts, verification of, 73, 86,
    129–30
Books of account—Companies
    Acts, 259
Bought day book, 63, 66
  bought ledger, posting to, 66
  invoices, vouching, 64
Bought ledger
  audit, 66, 69
  verification of balances, 66
Building societies
  accounts, audit, 218–21
  auditor, qualifications of, 255

Building Societies Act 1962, 255
  investments in, 135
Buildings, verification of, 124–5

Capital expenditure
  allocation of, 222
  vouching, 78
Capital profits, distribution of,
    205–7
Capital reserve
  appreciation of assets, 156
  definition, 141
  pre-incorporation profits, 208
"Carry-over fraud", 48, 219–20
Cash
  and cheque receipts, I.C.Q. and
    S.A.P., 50–1, 51–2
  payments, 52 *et seq.*
  petty, 59 *et seq.*
  receipts, 46 *et seq.*
  sales, 47
  verification of cash balances,
    137–8
Cash sales, 47
Chartered Accountants, The In-
    stitute of, recommendations
    —*see* Preface
Cheques Act 1957, 47, 52 *et seq.*
Cheques, I.C.Q., and S.A.P., 53–
    54, 54–5
Cheques, unendorsed, as vou-
    chers, 52
City Code on Take-overs and
    Mergers, 244–5
Clubs, audit, 221–2
Computer-based accounting sys-
    tem, audit of, 105 *et seq.*
  audit trail, 107–8
  changes in procedural controls,
    106–7
  internal control, 106
  test packs, 109–11
  tests, 108
  timing, 105–6
  verification, 109
Computers—*see* Electronic data
    processing

Consignment, goods on, 71
Continuous audit, 9–10
Contractors, audit, 222
Control accounts, 66, 70, 73
Copyrights, 123–4
Costing methods, 187–91
Creditors, audit of bought ledger, 53
Credit sales, audit, 47–8
Customs duty, 138–9
Cut-off procedures, 177–8

Debentures
  definition of, 146–7
  discount on issue, 147
  issue of, 147
  redemption of, 143–4
  registration of, 147
Debtors
  bad and doubtful debts, 73, 76–77, 203
  verification of balances, 73, 86, 129–30
Defalcations—see Fraud
Depreciation
  accounting treatment, 158
  amortisation, 159
  definition, 154, 156
  freeholds, 157–8
  land and buildings, 157–8
  provision for, 158
  residual value, 157
Depreciation accounting, 156–60
Directors
  loans to, 131
Discount
  allowable and receivable, 34, 37, 49
  debentures on, 147
Distribution of profits, 205 et seq.
Dividends
  arrears of, 212
  capital profits, when available for, 205 et seq.
  cumulative preference, 212
  interim, 212–13
  paid out of capital, 211

payment of and declaration, 211–12
  preference, 212
  reserve for equalisation, 146
  scrip, 212

Electronic Data Processing (E.D.P.), 91 et seq.
  control section, 92
  error correcting, 97–8
  file control, 98–9
  fire precautions, 99
  input controls, 101–2
  internal control, 98 et seq.
  log book, 92
  master files, 93–4, 103, 104
  operator control, 98
  output controls, 103–4
  print outs, 95–7
  procedural controls, 91–4, 100–104
  processing controls, 93, 102–3
  programme checks, 95
  random tests, 97
  safeguards, 98–9
  service bureaux, 94, 104–5
  stand-by procedures, 94, 99
  systems development controls, 99–100
  test packs, 96
Engagement, letters of, 40, 249–50
Executors, audit of accounts, 223

Fixed assets, I.C.Q., 127–8, S.A.P., 128–9
Fixtures and fittings, vouching, 126–7, 170–1
Formation expenses, 174
Forward purchases, 65
Forward sales, 72
Fraud
  auditor's liability on failing to discover, 272 et seq.
  cash, 234–5
  investigation in case of, 234–6
  purchases, 235–6
  sales, 235–6

Fraud (*contd.*)
  stock-in-trade, 235
  teeming and lading, 48, 219–20
  wages, 235
Freehold properties
  valuation, 169–70
  verification, 124–5
  vouching, 124–5
Friendly societies, 15, 251, 255–7
Funds statement, 270–1
Furniture and fittings, verification, 126–7

Goods inward book, 35, 37, 64, 178, 235
Goods on consignment, 71
Goodwill, 123, 174, 204, 210–11
Gross profit, 233
Ground rents, verification, 125
Group accounts, 261, 262 *et seq.*, 270

Hotel, audit, 223–4

Imprest system, petty cash, 33, 60
Independent stocktakers, 180
Inflation accounting, 167–8
Inscribed stocks, 134
Insurance
  life policies as security for loans, 133
Insurance companies, audit, 224–5
Internal audit, 7, 31, 41–3, 46
Internal auditor and statutory auditor, 41–3
Internal check, 26, 46
Internal control, 26 *et seq.*
  and the auditor, 27–8, 40–1
  definition, 26
  divisions of, 29–30
  letters, 27, 41
Internal control questionnaires
  cheque (payments), 53–4
  cheques and cash receipts, 50–1
  computer-based accounting, 111 *et seq.*

  administrative controls, 111–13
  procedural controls, 115–19
  systems development controls, 113–15
  credit notes, 75–6
  fixed assets, 127–8
  investments and income, 136–7
  petty cash and postage, 61–2
  purchases and purchases returns, 66–7
  purchases ledger, 67–8
  sales and sales returns, 73 *et seq.*
  sales ledger, 76
  stocks and work-in-progress, 192–5
  wages and salaries, 56–8
Inventory letters, 180–1
Investigations, 231 *et seq.*
  admission of partners, 234
  by D.T. inspectors, 240–1
  fraud or negligence, 234–6
  liability of accountant on, 232
  prospectus, for purposes of, 236
  purchase of a business, 232–4
  statutory, 231
Investments, 133 *et seq.*, 171–3
  I.C.Q., 136–7, S.A.P., 137
  income from, 49–50
  internal control, 38
  in respect of reserve funds, 143–4
  sale of, 134
  valuation, 171–2
  verification, 133 *et seq.*
Invoices
  fraud, by omission of, 64
  internal control, 35, 36
  post-dated, 64–5
  reference to goods received book, 64–5
  vouching, 64
I.O.U.s, 60, 62, 63

Journal, vouching of, 78–9

Land and buildings verification, 124–5

Land Registry Certificate for verification, 124

Leasehold property, 125

Letters
engagement, 16, 249–50
internal control, 27, 41
representation, 41

Liabilities, outstanding, 148–9

Liability of auditor, 272 et seq.
assets, for omission to verify, 273 et seq.
bad and doubtful debts, 203, 274
common law, under, 272
criminal, 272
frauds, for non-detection of, 273 et seq.
legal decisions, affecting, 176, 203–4, 272 et seq.
misfeasance, for, 272, 274–7
negligence, for, 272, 277 et seq.
professional, 279–81
stock-in-trade, as to, 176

Lien, auditor's, 258–9

Loans, 130 et seq., 151–2

Loose plant and tools, 126

Machinery and plant, 125–6, 170

"Material" in relation to accounts, 271–2

Mechanised accounting, 83 et seq.
accounting terms, misuse of, 87
code numbers, 85–6
fraudulent manipulation, 84–5
ledger balances, composition of, 86
primary records, absence of, 85
punched card accounting, 87–8
Report of I.C.A. on, 85
specific audit difficulties, 85–7

Minute books, 16, 259

Mortgages, verification, 132

Nominal ledger, 79

Obsolescence and depreciation arising from, 154, 156–7, 159

Obsolete and slow-moving stocks, 178–9

Office furniture, vouching of, 126–7, 170–1

Overheads, production, 185

Patents, 123

Petty cash, 33 et seq., 47, 137–8
auditor's liability for omission to verify, 273–4
imprest system for, 33, 60
internal check, 60–1
and postage, I.C.Q., 61–2, S.A.P., 64–5
vouching, 61

Plant and machinery, 125–6, 170

Preliminary expenses, 174

Primary auditor, 262–6

Profit forecasts, 242–5

Profits
capital, 205–7
distributable, 205 et seq.
prior to incorporation, 208

Property valuation, 168 et seq.

Prospectus, investigation for report, 236

Provisions
bad debts, 203
definition, 202–3

Publishers, audit, 225

Punched card systems of accounting, 87–8

Purchases, 35, 63 et seq.

Purchases and purchases returns, I.C.Q., 66–7, S.A.P., 68

Purchases ledger, I.C.Q., 67–8, S.A.P., 78

Receipts
internal control, 32
issue of, by travellers, 49
vouching, 48–9

Records, absence of, 239–40

Redeemable preference shares, 140, 142

Remuneration of employees, 34–5

Rent receivable, 49

Report
auditors', 259 *et seq.*
on profit forecasts, 242–5
qualified, 268–70
statutory, 228–9

Representation, letters of, 41

Reserves and reserve funds
capital redemption reserve fund, 142–3
disclosures of, 141
dividends, equalisation of, 146
redemption funds for debentures, 143–4
reserve, definition of, 141, 202–3
secret, 169–70, 221

Returned cheques used as vouchers, 53

Returns
purchases, 65–6
sales, 36

Revaluation of assets, 155, 169–70

Royalties, 225

Salaries, vouching, 55–6

Sale or return, goods on, 71

Sales
cash, 47, 69
credit, 36, 69–70
day book, 69
forward sales, 72
goods on consignment, 71
hire purchase, 71–2
I.C.Q., 73–4, S.A.P., 77
ledger, I.C.Q., 76, S.A.P., 78
vouching invoices, 69

Sales ledger, 69–70, 72–3

Sales returns, 36

Sampling, statistical, 79

Scrip dividends, 212

Secondary auditor, 262–6

Securities, verification, 134–5

Share premium account, 142

Shares
bonuses and rights issues, 134
discount, issued at, 140–1
examination of certificates, 134
issue of, 140–1
preference, redeemable, 140, 142
premium, issued at, 142
sale of rights, 134
subsidiary company, in, 172–3
valuation, 173
verification, 134, 139–40

Share transfer audit, 225–6

Sinking funds, 143–4

Solicitors, accounts, audit, 226–7

Standard Accounting Practice, 2–6, 266–8

Standard audit programmes
accruals, 69
cash receipts, 51–2
cheque payments, 54–5
fixed assets, 128–9
investments and investments income, 137
petty cash and postage, 64–5
purchases and purchases returns, 68
sales and sales returns, 77
stocks and work-in-progress, 195–7
trade creditors, 68–9
trade debtors, 78
wages and salaries, 58–9

Statements of source and application of funds, 270–1

Statutory report, 228–9

Stock-in-trade, 176 *et seq.*
auditor's duty in relation to, 176
computing cost, 187–91
cut-off procedures, 177–8
disclosure in accounts, 181–2, 191–2
I.C.Q., 192–5, S.A.P., 195–7
valuation
cost, 187–91
disclosure of, 184, 191–2

fifo and lifo, 188–9
long-term contracts, 181, 183
net realisable value, 183, 185,
   190–1
replacement price, 183
Sandilands report, 181, 192
verification, 77 *et seq.*

Taxation, 144–6, 148
Tax Reserve Certificates, 135
Teeming and lading, 47, 48, 219–
   220
Trade discount, 35, 36
Trade marks, 123
Transfer of shares, audit, 225–6
Travellers, debt collection by, 49
Treasury bills, 135
Trust account, audit, 223

Valuation of assets, 166 *et seq.*
   current, 173
   fixed, 168–71
   freehold property, 169–70
   furniture and fittings, 170–1
   investments, 171–2
   loose plant and tools, 126
   office machinery, 171
   patents, 123
   plant and machinery, 170
   publisher's stock-in-trade, 225
   returnable containers, 72
   shares, 173
   stock-in-trade, 176 *et seq.*
   wasting assets, 161–2
VAT, 70
Verification of assets, 123 *et seq.*
   balance at bank, 138
   bearer securities, 134–5
   book debts, 71, 86, 129–30
   cash in hand, 137–8
   copyrights, 123–4
   debtor balances, 129–30

deposits, 138–9
freehold property, 124–5
furniture, 126–7
goodwill, 123
inscribed stock, 134
insurance policies, 133
investments, 133
leasehold property, 125
loans, 130 *et seq.*
loose tools, 126
motor vehicles, 127
patents, 123
petty cash, 137–8
plant and machinery, 125–6
registered land, 124–5
share capital, 139–41
stock-in-trade, 176 *et seq.*
tax reserve certificates, 135
trade marks, 123
treasury bills, 135
Vouchers, examining, 64

Wages
   auditor's duty, 55–6
   capital expenditure, 170
   defalcations—investigation, 235
   internal control, 34–5
   payment of, 34–5
   piece-work employees, 56
   and salaries, I.C.Q., 56–8,
      S.A.P., 58–9
   time-rate employees, 56
Wasting assets, 161–2
"Window dressing", 220
Working papers, 17–18
Work-in-progress
   auditor's liability, 272
   contractor's accounts in, 222
   disclosure of value of, 186
   long-term contract, 185, 186
   valuation, 181 *et seq.*
   verification, 179–80

Details of some other M&E Handbooks on
related subjects can be found on the following
pages.

For a full list of titles and prices write for the
FREE Macdonald & Evans Business Studies
catalogue and/or complete M&E Handbook
list, available from Department BP1,
Macdonald & Evans Ltd., Estover Road,
Plymouth PL6 7PZ

Bankruptcy Law
P.W.D. REDMOND

The latest edition of this detailed HANDBOOK on the complexities of bankruptcy law expands and brings up to date the text of the previous edition. The nature of bankruptcy is outlined, and the relevant legislation considered. Discharge, trustees, and property provisions are covered in detail, and the problems of partnership bankruptcies and deeds of arrangement cosidered.

Business Administration
L. HALL

This HANDBOOK, specially written for students preparing for A.C.A., I.C.M.A. and I.C.S.A. examinations in business administration and office management, describes the general principles of management, including the most up-to-date techniques, and sets out the organisation and control of office procedure in some detail. Personnel management, channels of communication, marketing and sales are also covered.

Business and Financial Management
B.K.R. WATTS

This HANDBOOK is intended primarily for students preparing for I.C.A. and A.C.A. examinations or for any other intermediate or final professional examinations where a knowledge of industrial structure, investment and financial management is required. "This book is a most competent and concise summary on a wide range of financial matters. If you do not know much about — let us say — the sources of export finance, this book will tell you where to start." *The Director*
The Director

Business Mathematics
L.W.T. STAFFORD

A popular HANDBOOK designed for the business student taking the examinations of the professional bodies, universities and technical colleges, which increasingly require a knowledge of mathematics. Also for those already in business who feel they have an insufficient grasp of the newer mathematical techniques and their applications in the fields of finance, operational research and mathematical statistics.

Capital Gains Tax
VERA DI PALMA

The amount of capital gains tax legislation is substantial and makes great demands on the student already heavily committed in other subjects. This HANDBOOK, written by the taxation correspondent of *The Times*, is intended for such students; every area of the subject in which they are likely to be examined is included and an Appendix contains sample questions from past papers of the relevant professional bodies. For the latest edition the text has been fully revised and brought up to date.

Capital Transfer Tax
R.C. IND

This HANDBOOK covers the syllabuses of the qualifying examinations for the I.C.A., A.C.A., I.o.T. and the Law Society. The whole ambit of the tax is described in concise but clear terms with copious illustrations to show how the tax operates. A section on transfer tax mitigation will furnish the practitioner with useful ideas and the student with a helpful summary of the taxing provisions.

Cases in Company Law
M.C. OLIVER

This CASEBOOK, which is regularly revised and updated, can be used either alone or to accompany the author's popular HANDBOOK on Company Law. In preference to including a great number of cases in abbreviated form, it has been thought desirable to present a smaller selection as fully as possible, chosen for their significance, and set down chronologically without comment, encouraging the reader to draw his own deductions from the facts.

Cases in Contract Law
W.T. MAJOR

Full details of over eighty cases are included in this CASEBOOK which will be a useful companion to any textbook on the law of contract. It gives special emphasis to the leading cases of which students preparing for examinations require a knowledge, and will be particularly valuable to students in colleges of further education lacking ready access to the published law reports.

Case Studies in Auditing
J. SANTOCKI

This HANDBOOK provides an interesting set of case studies for students seeking an understanding of auditing. The material, based on British and foreign case law and on the I.C.A. recommendations, closely reproduces actual audit situations. This book is intended for those taking intermediate examinations in auditing, but it will also be useful for those preparing for final examinations for degrees in accountancy and business studies. Cases on the uses of computers in auditing are included.

Commercial and Industrial Law
A. R. RUFF
This HANDBOOK aims to take account of the considerable body of industrial and commercial legislation, especially that enacted in recent years. In addition, more detail is given to the law of contract than is usually possible in a book of this nature. This book will be invaluable to students, personnel officers, and to others concerned with the administration of factories and offices.

Company Accounts
J. O. MAGEE
The primary purpose of this HANDBOOK is to show the student the basic principles underlying accountancy for limited companies. Each example is broken down into a number of stages, showing the gradual build-up of an account, entry by entry.

Company Law
M. C. OLIVER
This HANDBOOK is by an eminent lecturer and it provides in full for examination requirements, while rendering this important subject interesting and easily assimilable. In the latest edition the author has made several amendments to the text, and the recent judicial decisions of importance have been included.

Company Secretarial Practice
L. HALL

This HANDBOOK is designed for students requiring a knowledge of company secretarial practice for the final examinations of the I.C.S.A. This latest edition takes account of recent legislation.

Corporate Planning and Control
R. G. ANDERSON

The prime purpose of this HANDBOOK is to provide a framework for systematically planning and controlling the operations of a business. The interrelationships of related functions and systems are studied in detail, as are the uses of management information in providing a firm foundation on which to build an effective business structure. It has proved invaluable to students taking the various professional examinations in the subject.

Corporation Tax
B. S. TOPPLE

This HANDBOOK assumes no prior knowledge of taxation on the reader's part. It provides a basic introduction to the principles of company taxation: there are chapters covering capital allowances and losses, the treatment of income tax and close companies. The author provides typical examples of firms' accounts in the text to illustrate each point. The latest edition has been prepared to take account of recent relevant legislation.

Data Processing and Management Information Systems
R. G. ANDERSON

This HANDBOOK, winner of the Annual Textbook Award of the S.C.C.A., provides a comprehensive study of the field of data processing, embracing manual, electro-mechanical and electronic systems and covering such topics as data transmission, systems analysis and computer programming. It is designed to fulfil the needs of students preparing for examinations in data processing and computer applications and ". . . will also be valuable to those no longer concerned with examinations who require an understanding of the methods and techniques available for the processing of data for management." *The Commercial Accountant Illustrated*

Economics for Professional Studies
HENRY TOCH

This HANDBOOK draws on the author's experience over fifteen years of teaching economics to professional students, and uses topical situations and examples to illustrate a detailed survey of economic theory and practice. For the latest edition the statistics have been exhaustively updated. *Illustrated*

General Principles of English Law
P. W. D. REDMOND

Originally designed for those preparing for intermediate professional examinations, this HANDBOOK has also proved itself immensely popular with "A" Level and university students. The latest edition includes the facts of appropriate recent cases and several important new topics.

Income Tax
HENRY TOCH

Intended for students in accountancy, law, secretarial practice and business studies, this HANDBOOK explains in concise form the basic principles of income-tax law and practice. The latest edition incorporates recent changes in the law.

Intermediate Accounts
L. W. J. OWLER

This HANDBOOK offers a lucid and compact coverage of the subject, progressing from first principles by clear and logical steps to the standard required for intermediate examinations. Each new topic is followed by a typical examination question and a fully worked-out answer.

The Law of Contract
W. T. MAJOR

This HANDBOOK, by an experienced lecturer and examiner, reduces a difficult subject to its essentials and will be of particular value to those studying contract for university or professional examinations. The Misrepresentation Act 1967 and the Supply of Goods (Implied Terms) Act 1973 are dealt with, together with some of the more important contract law decisions of 1972-73.

Law of Trusts
L. B. CURZON

This HANDBOOK has been written to provide lucid study notes for those studying the subject for the first time or preparing intensive revision prior to first professional examinations in the subject. A large number of case references are given to guide the student to a closer examination of the development of the concept of the trust.

Mathematics for Economists
L. W. T. STAFFORD

The aim of this HANDBOOK is to help students of economics to handle the mathematical side of their work and to relate their mathematics to essential ideas of economic theory. Topics discussed include differential calculus, vectors and matrices, economic dynamics, and the techniques of regression analysis, and the latest edition includes material on such relatively recent topics as search theory, utility theory and economic decision making. Worked answers to most of the test questions in the book are given in a special appendix. *Illustrated*

Mercantile Law
P. W. D. REDMOND

This HANDBOOK is intended for those studying commercial law for professional examinations. The latest edition takes account of recent changes in the legal framework.

Modern Commercial Knowledge
L. W. T. STAFFORD

Intended for students taking commerce at the commencement of professional studies, this HAND-BOOK provides a comprehensive modern survey of the subject. The latest edition includes, among other matters, the passing of legislation on industrial relations, greater emphasis on consumer protection and changes in the field of inland transport. *Illustrated*

Partnership Accounts
J. O. MAGEE

This HANDBOOK covers the entire field of partnership accounting. The method employed is to explain in simple language the various matters which are peculiar to the accountancy problems relating to partnerships and then by graded examples, to illustrate the type of problems involved.

Partnership Law
P. W. D. REDMOND

This HANDBOOK gives a detailed summary of partnership law, together with specimen articles of partnership and the complete text of the Partnership Act. References to recent cases and up-to-date statutes have been included in the latest edition. Although this book is intended primarily for accountancy and other students taking examinations in partnership law, it has also proved popular with businessmen and lawyers.

Principles of Accounts
E. F. CASTLE & N. P. OWENS
This HANDBOOK is a useful aid to those who, about to begin a study of accounts, need a grounding in the basic principles of the subject. Students taking company secretarial or other professional courses will find it particularly valuable.

Sale of Goods
W. T. MAJOR
This lucid and compact HANDBOOK should be invaluable for students of any branch of commercial law, and also for businessmen as a work of reference. For the latest edition the text has been revised extensively to consider in detail important recent legislation.

Secretarial and Administrative Practice
L. HALL
Students preparing for the final examination of the I.C.S.A. will find this HANDBOOK invaluable. It provides a concise and comprehensive course of study with a built-in method of self-checking.

Statistics
W. M. HARPER
Assuming no previous knowledge on the part of the reader, this clearly-written HANDBOOK sets out to enable the student to take intermediate professional examinations in this subject with success.
Illustrated